DEBT AND SLAVERY IN THE MEDITERRANEAN AND ATLANTIC WORLDS

FINANCIAL HISTORY

Forthcoming Titles

DEBT AND SLAVERY IN THE MEDITERRANEAN AND ATLANTIC WORLDS

EDITED BY

Gwyn Campbell and Alessandro Stanziani

Routledge
Taylor & Francis Group

LONDON AND NEW YORK

First published 2013 by Pickering & Chatto (Publishers) Limited

Published 2016 by Routledge
2 Park Square, Milton Park, Abingdon, Oxfordshire OX14 4RN
711 Third Avenue, New York, NY 10017, USA

First issued in paperback 2015

Routledge is an imprint of the Taylor & Francis Group, an informa business

BRITISH LIBRARY CATALOGUING IN PUBLICATION DATA

Debt and slavery in the Mediterranean and Atlantic worlds. – (Financial history)
1. Peonage – Mediterranean Region – History. 2. Peonage – Atlantic Ocean
Region – History.
I. Series II. Campbell, Gwyn, 1952– III. Stanziani, Alessandro.
306.3'63'091821-dc23

ISBN-13: 978-1-138-66214-8 (pbk)
ISBN-13: 978-1-8489-3374-3 (hbk)

Typeset by Pickering & Chatto (Publishers) Limited

CONTENTS

ACKNOWLEDGEMENTS

This research was supported by the Social Sciences and Humanities Research Council of Canada, the *Fonds de recherché du Québec – Société et culture* and the *Agence nationale de la recherché*, France. Many thanks also to Ruben Post for his editorial assistance.

LIST OF CONTRIBUTORS

Gwyn Campbell is Canada Research Chair in Indian Ocean World History and Director of the Indian Ocean World Centre at McGill University, Montréal. Born in Madagascar, he grew up in Wales where he worked as a BBC radio producer in English and Welsh. He holds degrees in Economic History from the universities of Birmingham and Wales and has taught in India, Madagascar, Britain, South Africa, Belgium and France. He served as an academic consultant for the South African government in a series of inter-governmental meetings which led to the formation of an Indian Ocean regional association in 1997. He has published extensively on slavery including, as editor: *Abolition and its Aftermath in Indian Ocean Africa and Asia* (London and New York: Routledge, 2005) and *The Structure of Slavery in Indian Ocean Africa and Asia* (Portland, OR: Frank Cass, 2004); as co-editor with Suzanne Miers and Joseph Miller: *Women and Slavery*, 2 vols (Athens, OH: Ohio University Press, 2007–8), *Children in Slavery through the Ages* (Athens, OH, and London: Ohio University Press, 2009) and *Child Slaves in the Modern World* (Athens, OH: Ohio University Press, 2011); and with Edward A. Alpers and Michael Salman: *Resisting Bondage in Indian Ocean Africa and Asia* (London and New York: Routledge, 2007) and *Slavery, Forced Labour and Resistance in Indian Ocean Africa and Asia* (London and New York: Routledge, 2005). He is currently completing a volume on *Africa and the Indian Ocean World* for Cambridge University Press.

Henrique Espada Lima is Professor of History at the Universidade Federal de Santa Catarina since 2001, where he teaches, supervises and conducts research on Historiography and Contemporary Labour History. He received his Doctorate in Social History from UNICAMP (Brazil). He held visiting fellowships at the International Research Center for 'Work and Human Life Cycle in Global History' (RE: Work) at Humboldt-Universität zu Berlin (Germany) and at Nantes Institute of Advanced Studies (France). Select publications include: *A micro-história italiana: escalas, indícios e sigularidades* (Civilizacão Brasileira, 2006); 'Freedom, Precariousness, and the Law: Freed Persons Contracting out their Labour in Nineteenth-Century Brazil', *International Review of Social History*, 54:3 (2009), pp. 391–416.

Michael Ferguson is a PhD candidate in the Department of History and Classics and member of the Indian Ocean World Centre at McGill University, Montréal. He is interested in the socioeconomic history of the late Ottoman Empire, particularly issues of identity, religion and integration of sub-Saharan Africans in the late Ottoman Empire and early republican Turkey. His publications include 'Enslaved and Emancipated Africans on Crete', in T. Walz and K. M. Cuno (eds), *Race and Slavery in the Middle East: Histories of Trans-Saharan Africans in Nineteenth-Century Egypt, Sudan, and the Ottoman Mediterranean* (Cairo and New York: The American University in Cairo Press, 2010), pp. 171–95.

Marc Kleijwegt is Professor of History at the University of Wisconsin–Madison. He is the editor of *The Faces of Freedom: The Manumission and Emancipation of Slaves in Old World and New World Slavery* (Leiden and Boston, MA: Brill Academic Publishers, 2006). He is currently working on a study of slavery in Petronius's *Satyrica*, a satirical novel from the reign of the emperor Nero. He is also co-editor of the forthcoming Oxford *Handbook of Greek and Roman Slaveries*.

Paul E. Lovejoy is Distinguished Research Professor in the Department of History, York University, holds the Canada Research Chair in African Diaspora History and is a Fellow of the Royal Society of Canada. He has served as Vice President of the Social Sciences and Humanities Research Council of Canada (1995–7), was Founding Director of the Harriet Tubman Institute for Research on the Global Migrations of African Peoples (2008–12) and is General Editor, Harriet Tubman Series on the African Diaspora (Africa World Press). Awarded an Honorary Degree, University of Stirling (2007), he has received the Distinguished Africanist Award, University of Texas (2010), the Life Time Achievement Award, Canadian Association of African Studies (2011) and the Faculty of Graduate Studies Teaching Award, York University (2012). He has published more than 30 books and over 100 articles and book chapters.

Russell R. Menard is Professor of History at the University of Minnesota. A specialist in the economic and social history of the British colonies in North America, his research interests include the economic development of the Lower South during the eighteenth century and the history of plantation slavery. He is the author of numerous publications, including *Sweet Negotiations: Sugar, Slavery, And Plantation Agriculture in Early Barbados* (Charlottesville, VA, and London: University of Virginia Press, 2006), *Migrants, Servants and Slaves: Unfree Labor in Colonial British America* (Aldershot: Ashgate, 2001), *Economy and Society in Early Colonial Maryland* (New York and London: Garland, 1985) and *Economics and Early American History* (Chicago, IL: Newberry Library, 1977).

Joseph C. Miller is the T. Cary Johnson, Jr, Professor of History at the University of Virginia. Trained as a historian of early Africa, his work on Angola – the major origin of the captives taken to slavery in the Americas – led to a monograph assessing the operations of slaving there in the context of the financial arrangements of Brazil's slave trading in the Atlantic, *Way of Death: Merchant Capitalism and the Angolan Slave Trade* (Madison, WI, and London: Currey, 1988). He has tracked the literature on slaving in world history through a series of annual bibliographies published since 1980 in *Slavery & Abolition* (through 2004, continued by Thomas Thurston) and compiled as a 'Bibliography of Slavery and World Slaving' viewable at http://www2.vcdh.virginia.edu/bib/. His initial reflections on the epistemology of the general field have been published as *The Problem of Slavery as History* (New Haven, CT: Yale University Press, 2012), and a survey of *Slaving and World History* is in preparation. He has edited a *Princeton Companion to Atlantic History* (2014) and served as President of the American Historical Association in 1998 and of the African Studies Association in 2006.

Olatunji Ojo is Associate Professor of African History at Brock University, St Catharines, Ontario and received his PhD in History from York University, Toronto. His research includes West African History (Social and Economic), African Diaspora and Gender. He is an Associate Fellow of Harriet Tubman Institute, York University, Toronto, and a member of the African Origins Names Database Project at Emory University, Atlanta. Select publications include (with Nadine Hunt), *Slavery in Africa and the Caribbean: A History of Enslavement and Identity since the Eighteenth Century* (London: I. B. Tauris, 2012); 'Child Slaves in Pre-colonial Nigeria, c. 1725–1860', *Slavery and Abolition*, 33 (2012), pp. 417–34; and (with Jennifer Lofkrantz), 'Slavery, Freedom, and Failed Ransom Negotiations in West Africa, 1730–1900', *Journal of African History*, 54 (2012), pp. 25–44.

Steven Serels is a Visiting Postdoctoral Fellow at the Center for Middle East Studies at Harvard University. He received his PhD from McGill University, after which he was awarded a Post-Doctoral Fellowship from the Social Sciences and Humanities Research Council of Canada. His research focuses on the development of regional and global trades in foodstuffs and on the historical causes and long-term legacy of food crises in the greater Red Sea and Gulf of Aden region. Select publications include: 'Famines of War; The Red Sea Grain Market and Famine in Eastern Sudan, 1889–1891', *Northeast African Studies*, 12:1 (2012), pp. 73–94 and 'Political Landscaping: Land Registration, the Definition of Land Ownership and the Evolution of Colonial Objectives in the Sudan, 1899–1924', *African Economic History*, 35 (2007), pp. 59–67.

Alessandro Stanziani is Professor of Economic and Global History at the EHESS and at the CNRS (Paris). He has worked on the history of competition, markets and food in France and Europe (eighteenth to twentieth centuries), the economic history of Russia (eighteenth to twentieth centuries) and bondage and forced labour in Central Asia, Russia and the Indian Ocean (sixteenth to twentieth centuries). He is the author of: *L'économie en révolution, le cas russe* (Paris: Albin Michel, 1998); *Histoire de la qualité alimentaire* (Paris: Seuil, 2005); *Rules of Exchange: French Capitalism in Comparative Perspective* (Cambridge: Cambridge University Press, 2012); *Labour, Coercion and Growth in Eurasia* (Leiden: Brill Academic Publishers, 2012) and *Bâtisseurs d'Empires, Russie, Inde et Chine* (Paris: Liber, 2012).

INTRODUCTION: DEBT AND SLAVERY IN THE MEDITERRANEAN AND THE ATLANTIC WORLDS

Alessandro Stanziani and Gwyn Campbell

Comparative versus Global History of Debt Slavery

Bondage in ancient Rome and Northern America has often been presented as forms of chattel or 'real' slavery as opposed to the 'mild' or hybrid forms of slavery, servitude and coercion found in so many different contexts in Africa, Asia and medieval Europe.[1] Such a distinction is problematic. Anthropologists, sociologists and historians differ considerably in their assessments of what precisely constitutes slavery, highlighting variously issues of social status (membership of or exclusion from the clan, family and local community), religion, legal status (forms of dependence, freedom of movement, hereditary nature of constraints), economic conditions and political, legal and procedural rights.[2] Researchers have pinpointed several variables in their attempts to find a definition of bondage, but without reaching a consensus.

The debate has sharpened even more over the last two decades as *cultural* and *subaltern studies* scholars have highlighted the relativity of notions of freedom and coercion. As a result, the critical question currently asked is whether the different forms of servitude found in various societies in Africa, Asia, the Indian Ocean world or the Americas can all be considered to constitute 'slavery'. If the answer is yes, then by implication slavery existed before and independently of colonialism. Conversely, if the answer is no, it means that these were forms of 'imperialist' dependence and bondage specific to a particular place.

The debate over slavery has spread beyond the confines of academia, and in so doing has become more virulent. One obvious example is the public allegations levelled by certain international organizations against countries and firms they accuse of practising and legitimizing hidden 'slavery'.[3] It is symptomatic and sometimes paradoxical to see cultural relativism espoused both by academics critical of 'imperialism' and 'colonialism' and now globalization and by local managers and multinational companies that exploit child labour. All these actors stress the different meanings of slavery in different societies to assert either the difference between Western colonial slavery and local forms of dependence (as is the case of those who criticize imperialism and globalization) or, at the opposite, to prove (multinational firm speakers) that informal and child labour in multinational firms cannot be defined as 'slavery'.[4] The aim of this book is not to favour any particular definition of human bondage but rather to identify the contours of debt slavery in specific historical and institutional contexts and explain why, in a given space and time, this rather than another form of bondage was conceived and put into practice.[5] By this, we are not seeking to relativize and deconstruct categories in order to assert, for example, that this or that form of slavery was an 'intellectual invention' of Western or African scholars. Quite the contrary, by viewing these elements in their proper historical contexts, we hope to provide an original explanation of the dynamics of forms of slavery. Instead of attempting to establish the moment when 'free labour' (and thus 'civilization') emerged, or conversely, stigmatizing the continuation of latent forms of slavery, we here attempt to grasp the dynamics at work in certain historical forms of bondage starting from the historically situated tension between freedom and coercion.

We do not intend to discuss all features of slavery, including issues of labour, race, gender, markets, ideology and institutions. Rather, we will focus on the link between debt and slavery. This focus has multiple advantages. It enables us to examine systems of servitude, such as that of ancient Rome, in which race did not play a major role, and compare them to modern slavery. Also, our approach, unlike conventional Eurocentric analyses that identify slavery and notions of 'freedom' exclusively with formal rules and structures of jurisprudence, permits us to examine in more nuanced ways non-Western notions of servitude, liberty and rights.

At the same time, unlike conventional economic histories of slavery that measure labour relationships and their evolution in terms of efficiency,[6] the relationship between debt and slavery at the core of this book leads to an investigation of the interplay between economy, society and institutions of slavery. The rise and decline of slavery responded not only to economic rationale but also to political and moral pressures. For example, anthropologists such as Marcel Mauss linked debt slavery to potlatch and reciprocity. For them, the obligation to reciprocate, instead of the search for profit or power, could lead to bondage – which represented a form of inclusion in, rather than exclusion from, society.[7] Critics of Mauss, such as Claude Levi-Strauss and certain structuralist and Marxist anthropologists, assert that dependency and power rather than reciprocity lie at the root of most forms of debt bondage.[8] Alain Testart, a leading figure in structural anthropology – the approach originally developed by Levi-Strauss – distinguishes debt slavery from both pawnship and debt bondage. For Testart, debt slavery is a form of servitude resulting from a situation of debtor insolvency.

It makes the debtor an outcast and this situation is institutionally preserved (by kin and village authorities), which is not the case for pawns and debt-bonded people. The main characteristic of pawnship is that the pawn is a form of collateral, not the debtor, while debt bondage is in principle temporal, for the debtor retains her/his status as a free person and can in principle reimburse her/his debt through work.[9]

The problem with these taxonomies is that slavery has not been the only form of bondage used to deal with insolvents and debt is not the only situation leading to such forms of bondage. Temporary debt bondage can be easily converted into permanent slavery and, at a macro level, a society that accepts debt slavery is a society that generates multiple forms of dependence instead of the simple opposition between free and unfree. Given such a splay of forms of bondage and personal dependency, it is difficult to clearly distinguish, as Orlando Patterson does, debt slavery linked to poverty and inequalities from debt bondage resulting from harvest failure.[10] Does this mean, as Patterson seems to argue, that debt slavery as a result of risk is more widespread in less commercially developed societies while debt as a direct cause of slavery was more common among the commercially more advanced people?

This argument might appear intuitively sound but does not stand up to proper historical analysis. Karl Polanyi, one of the major anthropologists of the twentieth century, is not only famous for his book *Great Transformation* (1944), but also for having stressed the multiple meanings of market and economic rationalities in different historical and regional contexts. Polanyi would have criticized such a clear-cut opposition between market and non-market economies, in particular as regards African slavery and societies. Markets present different logics and are embedded in different historical contexts so that there is no one single linear historical evolution from one to another. Thus, the Dahomey port trade that Polanyi studied reflects the encounter between capitalism and market economy, two different systems that both express a form of market.[11]

While some Africanists have from an empirical perspective justifiably criticized Polanyi and his analysis of Dahomey and slave trade,[12] the issues Polanyi raised are worthy of consideration, notably the questions: which forms of market correspond to which forms of slavery? Is debt slavery caused by market failure more or less widespread than that due to harvest failure? And to what extent in pre-market economies is it possible to maintain a clear distinction between debt bondage and labour relations, and how does this change in market systems?

Polanyi provided possible answers by suggesting that different forms of markets and market rationality coexisted in different historical contexts. However, he did not explain the passage from one to the other. Amartya Sen has offered an alternative solution based on his assertion that, even in pre-modern India and Africa, harvest failures were rare and the environment and market always interacted. In other words, a famine is always both a market and an environmental problem, and a bad harvest is, in itself, insufficient to provoke famine.[13] For Sen, in contrast to Polanyi, the clear-cut distinction between market and non-market is not overcome by proposing different forms of markets, but by a completely different paradigm. Sen argues that markets are not unique to advanced western societies but are widespread also in developing and pre-industrial societies. Hence, poverty and debt bondage are not exclusively linked to detrimental environmental factors or to pre-industrial societies. While debt bondage was, for Patterson, clearly linked to harvest failure and market inequalities, Polanyi stressed that it could arise in situations where different economic logics and markets coexisted, while Sen recognized that relatively well developed markets (and thus recognizably modern forms of debt bondage) also existed in pre-industrial societies.

Pranab Bardhan, like Sen a development economist, has suggested yet another model in stressing the limited separation in developing countries between labour and credit markets, and thus the major importance of debt bondage as a form of exchange between labour and credit. According to Bardhan, instead of expressing irrational attitudes, the interlocking relationship between labour and debt perfectly reflects the conditions of some developing areas where markets are imperfect and the division of labour is at its initial stage.[14] More recently, openly inspired by Bardhan, Gareth Austin has underlined the major importance of markets in pre-colonial as well as colonial Africa, and the specific connection between labour and credit markets as being at the root of debt bondage.[15]

A clear advantage of the Austin–Bardhan approach is that it avoids simplistic oppositions in terms between market and non-market economies, environment and society, Africa and Europe, and between different types of 'mentality'. Rather, differences are mostly explained in terms of historical trajectories of markets and institutions. However, the risk with Bardhan's model is that 'markets' are found everywhere and that we can hardly explain historical differences except in terms of institutions and their rationale. 'Bad' institutions limit markets and well-being while 'good' institutions enhance them. This point is crucial for our study for it raises the question, is debt bondage mostly linked to specific institutions (that might in themselves oppose market dynamics) or to markets themselves?

Answering this question requires overcoming ex-post justifications of institutions and investigating historical connections between institutions and markets. In particular, we need to address the question of understanding how reciprocity and power structures intervene in different historical contexts in the legitimization of various forms of debt slavery and bondage. For example, as shown by Joseph Miller's contribution to this volume, pawnship, international trade and the financing of the slave trade were not independent, but interrelated phenomena.

In this sense, we may turn upside down conventional views about the role of the relationship between markets and institutions in facilitating the development of (debt) slavery. Instead of asking which institutions foster slavery and which encourage and sustain the emergence of markets and free labour, we may use the historical variations and developments in debt bondage to reopen the debate on the relationship between forms of capital and the state. The clear-cut opposition made by Charles Tilly between capital-based and coercion-based political entities does not survive empirical scrutiny.[16] Italian city-states, where capital ruled supreme, were crucial actors in the development of medieval and early modern slavery. At the same time, ancient and non-European empires were not necessarily based on coercion, for they possessed both highly developed markets and forms of dependence that, often classified as slavery, in reality reflected much more complicated social and economic relations.[17] Over the *longue durée*, the global history of debt and bondage confirms what recent analyses[18] have already stressed – that the nation-state, in particular before the twentieth century, appears to have been more a political ideal than a historical reality. As forms of debt and labour depend on the structure of power and the historical forms of it, this means that we need to take into due account this interrelation. The relationship between debt and labour is not the same in decentralized societies,[19] in different forms of empire, in nation-states or in city-states like Venice.

Despite arguments to the contrary by luminaries such as Adam Smith, Max Weber and Charles Tilly, the currently dominant academic view is that capitalism is perfectly compatible with slavery, and with debt slavery in particular. The current debate concerns whether slavery and bondage are linked to specific forms of capitalism and, if so, how far back in time we may identify such a link. If the pre-Civil War American South or the modern European colonial enterprises mark the first links between slavery and capitalism, how can we qualify the relationship between markets and slavery in early capitalist medieval Europe, or pre-capitalist ancient Rome?

According to some recent interpretations, ancient Rome possessed markets in labour other than slaves just as Africa developed market relations in the pre-colonial and colonial eras.[20] Yet, this is insufficient basis to conclude that Imperial Rome was a capitalistic economy or to provide a definitive statement about the link between capitalism(s), markets and slavery(ies). Does the growth of slavery as an institution reflect market development or its absence?

It is impossible to satisfactorily answer such questions by applying a single general model or through simple descriptive juxtaposition of cases. We need to make connections and analyse entanglements in both space and time, as well as study local specificities and make wide-ranging comparisons in order to identify continuities and changes in debt slavery. We here start with ancient Rome, then pass to medieval Europe and the Mediterranean area, before concluding with Africa and the trans-Atlantic slave trade.

Ancient Forms of Slavery

Moses Finley, following Frank Tannenbaum, considered that only ancient Mediterranean and modern tropical and American societies possessed economies dominated by slave labour (thus being characterized by what some scholars such as Paul Lovejoy consider to be slave 'modes of production', all others being societies with slaves).[21] At the same time, Finley considered that whereas slavery developed at the core of the ancient Greek and Roman economies, it only dominated the periphery of post-1500 European-dominated economies. Also, in the ancient world slavery was considered to be a 'natural' institution and notions of freedom and abolition, as we know them today, were unknown. Manumission was thus part of a completely different system of values and practices. Unlike American slavery, Roman slavery was an open system, which means that slaves could marry free people; freedmen were Roman citizens, and marriages between widows and slaves were common. By contrast, American slavery was a closed system and inter-marriage across the slave–non-slave frontier was taboo.[22]

Moving from the general to the specific, Finley acknowledged that slave systems differed from region to region and over time, so that scholars need to carefully distinguish Athens from Sparta, and Republican Rome from first imperial and then late imperial periods. Also, within the Roman Empire, the conditions and importance of slaves in the Italian peninsula, Greece and Near East all differed.[23] Other scholars have pointed out that while initially the role of slaves was limited to domestic activities, in the imperial period it expanded to incorporate most economic activities.[24]

The reasons given for such differences and changes are various. Finley contended that while, during the republican era, slavery was practised on a small scale in both the agricultural and domestic sectors, in the subsequent period of imperial expansion, between the fourth century BC and first century AD, war captives and conquered people became the major source of bonds people – chattel slaves who were employed throughout the empire and in most activities. The real success of chattel slavery occurred during the 'golden age' of classical empire. In agriculture, for example, large estates developed based on slave labour. The success of chattel slavery was thus intimately linked to the dynamics of imperial expansion, its institutional order (the legal status of conquered people), and expansion of large-scale rural estates which, in contrast to urban artisanal workshops, depended increasingly on slave labour.

Finley's analysis has come under increasing criticism in recent years.[25] For example, Finley noted three pre-conditions for the development of mass chattel slavery in Rome: large private farms, labour shortages and a market economy. Prior to this, debt bondage in the small regional economies under Rome was common. However, imperial expansion created a Roman 'global economy' and the development of chattel slavery on a mass scale that encouraged the development of large slave-based estates. Nonetheless, recent empirical research has demonstrated convincingly that small productive units continued to be important throughout the imperial period, even in Italy, and that slaves were just one of a variety of forms of labour.[26]

Moreover, there is no empirical evidence that the rise of slavery in ancient Rome was linked to manpower shortages. Under both the Republic and in the imperial periods, domestic slavery was widespread, while bondage was maintained in the military, and in the artisanal and service sectors. Domestic slavery was more pervasive than agricultural bondage, being found not only in Italy and Greece but also in provinces such as Egypt where free labour predominated. Peter Temin has recently argued that a market for free labour was also common in the early Roman world and that slavery should be considered as part of a wider labour force, not a barrier to economic progress – at least under the Republic and in the early imperial era.[27]

Recent work has also stressed the mobility (despite legal restrictions) of both urban and rural workers, high manumission rate (affecting over each five-year period an estimated 10 per cent of slaves) and possibility for slaves to save and transmit money (*peculum*) and even property.[28] In this context, the link between debt and bondage is highly significant. In his contribution to this book, Marc Kleijwegt raises doubts about the conventional view that there was a close relationship between the abolition of *nexum* and the development of slavery. *Nexum* was a particular debt in which the lender offered his/herself and her/his work as collateral in order to obtain credit. Even if such servitude was likely to become permanent, Kleijwegt points out from his examination of Livy and other sources that they considered *nexum* to be different from slavery, as did debt-serfs who constantly claimed that their status was distinct from that of slaves.[29] Finley contended that chattel slavery started to become a major force in the Roman world only after the official abolition of *nexum* in 326 BC rendered impossible the exploitation of the labour of Roman citizens. However, no systematic investigation of the relationship between the abolition of *nexum* and the development of chattel slavery in fourth-century Rome has yet been undertaken. Kleijwegt argues that there is no evidence to link the abolition of debt bondage with the rise of chattel slavery, and that the abolition of *nexum is* misleading shorthand for a much more complex phenomenon.

Abolition of debt bondage occurred when the slave population had increased to such a degree that the supply of slave labour was surplus to demand. Owners reacted by manumitting their slaves through self-purchase at a high enough rate to replenish the state treasury. Also, a close examination of *nexum* clearly indicates that there existed a number of different categories of indebted Romans. Evidence from later Roman history suggests that individuals continued to be reduced to slavery as the result of their inability to pay off their debts. Different forms of servitude for debts thus persisted throughout ancient Roman history, despite the legal abolition of *nexum*. Kleijwegt's contribution in turn implies that the practice of debt-slavery and slavery, far from marking a major break between the Republic and the Empire, confirms the strength of continuities and the coexistence of a variety of forms of labour relations and bondage over the long run. We contend that this is the case not only in early Rome but also in medieval Europe.

From Ancient to Medieval Slavery

By the third century AD, forms of 'free' labour had become more significant in the Roman world economy than slavery. This was due in part to an end to imperial expansion in 14 AD and thus in the supply of slaves from newly annexed regions. However, this does not explain why slavery remained important until the fourth or fifth century AD. The explanation for this disparity is complex. In the early centuries AD, social mobility for the free population in the Roman world decreased and the hierarchical status of occupations became more rigid. The value accorded to clerks, warriors, merchants and others in higher status occupations increased, while those in the lower orders witnessed a decline in their status and living conditions. Thus peasant proprietors increasingly lost their land and entered the ranks of peasant tenants upon whom the state enforced strict restrictions in terms of geographical mobility and then in the access to rights. Paradoxically, however, slaves were acquiring increasing legal and social rights.[30]

At the same time, increased taxes in a context of stable yields and productivity reduced the profitability of large estates and the use of slave labour. Landlords sought a solution through imposing new forms of debt bondage on their tenants and they employed legal instruments to this end. The new political entities that arose in medieval and early modern times often found it convenient to refer to 'Roman law' as if it had constituted a comprehensive legal system in order to justify their actions, notably in conflicts with other political and religious entities, although scholars have over recent decades questioned whether such a unitary body of Roman law ever existed.[31] In this context, the conventional academic view that serfdom and slavery was legitimized through 'Roman law' is subject to major debate. Many legal scholars consider that in medieval Europe, as in ancient Rome, slavery was interpreted as an exception to the 'law of nations' characterized as *ius naturale*: Slavery was part of the law of nations but not of natural right, that is, in Roman law, the law of nature did not intervene to justify slavery. The problem with this argument is double: first, in Roman rules there was not such a clear-cut opposition between *ius gentium* and *ius naturale*; secondly, these categories were interpreted through the lens of modern (i.e. post seventeenth-century) Western legal culture.

A brief investigation of social practices may help clarify the issue of continuities and contrasts between ancient and medieval forms of slavery. Since the pioneering works of Charles Verlinden, it is now accepted that in addition to serfdom in the agricultural and domestic sectors, slavery was widespread in medieval Mediterranean Europe.[32] The traditional view that the two institutions were distinct has been eroded by growing evidence of complex linkages not only between medieval serfdom and slavery, but also between medieval and more ancient forms of bondage. For example, the medieval languages of Germany, Russia, Italy, Portugal and Spain hardly distinguished between slavery and serfdom. Indeed, in southern Europe, *sclavus* was often synonymous with *servus*, which indicated both agricultural labourers and domestic serfs. Thus, in Genoa and Sicily serfs and bondspeople were termed *servus* in legal documents, while in seventeenth-century Sicily some types of tenants were called *sclavi*. Only with the development of slave trade and the arrival of slaves of other ethnic origins, including Central Asians, Arabs and Africans, did the word *sclavus* come to refer exclusively to these particular groups.[33]

Even following the influx of foreign slaves, the living and working conditions, and hence the status, of servants and slaves who worked side by side sometimes became confused.[34] The terms used to distinguish servants and slaves had major legal, social and economic implications. Notaries in Venice and Genoa made careful use of words in order to identify the master's rights and the duties of the slave (or serf). However, it was not easily decipherable to others. Thus some Tatars who failed to comprehend the niceties of the medieval Latin in which Genoese slave contracts were written found themselves sold into slavery. Even upstanding wealthy citizens rarely understood the language of legal contracts, and in practice commonly ignored the principles of 'Roman law' invoked by lawyers.[35]

Moreover, Roman law was not the sole legal reference for slavery. Byzantine legal principles (the *prochirom legum*) were also important. They permeated the Norman rules adopted in eleventh-century Sicily which subsequently affected legislation about those of servile status in southern Italy. In Byzantine law, servile status was covered by a variety of words, each of which possessed several meanings that changed over time. The word *pais*, for example, could refer to a slave, servant or child.[36] Slaves were widely employed by public institutions in the army, public works and court, and private owners such as household servants and agricultural workers – although in agriculture they were progressively replaced by other forms of bondage, closer to serfdom and/or peasants/soldiers/colons.

In medieval Italy, much more than in ancient Rome (and unlike the United States), slaves could enter legal marriages, and buy and sell properties. However, forms and rules for manumission varied over time and according to place. There nowhere existed a unified code regulating slavery. For example, in Genoa, unlike

Venice or France, slavery was governed almost exclusively by guild regulations and the criminal law.[37]

In Europe until at least the fourteenth century the trade in slaves comprised chiefly war captives, some 'Slav' (a generic term for Balkan, Slavic and Tatar people), but chiefly Moors (North African nomads of mainly Berber and Arab stock). Christians captured Muslims and vice versa, eventually releasing them for a ransom. In Russia, Genoa, Venice and Constantinople, special magistrates were established to negotiate the terms of such ransoms, from which high rank prisoners benefitted far more than low status captives such as soldiers and seamen who generally remained in captivity or, if ransomed, were obliged to reimburse their ransomer through several years of unpaid work. This was often the case for Greek and eastern European Christians ransomed by Genoese and Venetian authorities. In the Mediterranean, ransoming and the exchange of war prisoners and/or their enslavement, practised from the eighth century, marked a sharp break from ancient Rome, where no ransom system existed for enslaved captives. By contrast, Byzantium limited ransoming and the exchange of prisoners of war to its relations with the Islamic world and such practices failed to influence, for example, the Russians and Bulgarians who converted to Christianity around the eleventh century.[38] Moreover, most of ancient Greece's slaves originated from the Balkans, through which major trade routes passed linking Venice and Genoa to the Black Sea and Central Asia.[39] As early as 1246, Mongols in the northern Black Sea ports of Maurocastro, at the mouth of the Dniester, and Caffa, in the Crimea, were selling Greeks, Bulgarians, Ruthenians and Rumanians to merchants from Genoa, Pisa and Venice, who in turn sold them to the Saracens. Indeed, in 1266, the Mongol khan authorized the Genoese to establish a colony in Caffa which they developed into a major market for Circassian, Tatar, Russian, Iranian and Polish slaves. The other chief fourteenth-century Black Sea slave mart was the Crimean port of Tana which the Venetians had colonized in 1333. Despite occasional political turbulence, Tana had better access to the Oriental markets than Caffa, importing chiefly furs, wine, grain, and slaves – the latter became increasingly important in the late fourteenth century due to Venetian demand for a servile workforce on Crete. During the early fifteenth century, due to growing Ottoman power, Venetian trade shifted to the western Black Sea (Maurocastro and the Danube estuary) and to Egypt and the Middle East. At Kilia, Tatar subjects were sold by their compatriots to Genoese, Venetians and Greeks from Constantinople.[40] In 1263, Genoa became the first supplier of slaves for both the armies and harems of the Mamluk sultans. Male slaves were also sent to the alum mines of Genoa at Focea and to Genoa and Spain. Women were particularly welcome for domestic service, while men were valued for ship work or sold to Spain, but the majority were kept in Genoa as domestic slaves. In early 1400, almost 10 per cent of Genoa's population (4,000–5,000 people) was unfree.[41] In Caffa, the revenue from the *gabella capitum* (custom tax per head) allows us to calculate the following number of slaves shipped to Genoa: in 1374 at least 3,285 slaves; in 1385/6 about 1,500; in 1387/8 about 1,600; in 1381/2 at least 3,800 slaves. During the fifteenth century, the *gabella* was farmed out. In 1411 one can assume that 2,900 slaves were sold, while from the 1420s until 1477 a maximum of 2,000 were sold each year. The fall of Constantinople in 1453 provoked a massive decline in the number of slaves sold to about 400 or 600 per annum, signalling a fall of about 80 per cent within a century.[42]

Despite the importance of the Central Asian slave trade, neither the Genoese nor Venetians organized expeditions specifically for that purpose.[43] This was probably due to the small scale and high transaction costs of the operations. It was simply not worth extending to Central Asia the credit and commercial arrangements in place on the Black Sea, and this was even truer for slaves, who constituted a minor and non-luxury item. The vast Central Asian caravan trade, solidly based on the interaction between non-pastoral nomadic activities and caravan merchants, was simply beyond the capacity of European merchants to influence. Nor did they need to intervene, for Central Asian societies grew increasingly politically stable and thus offered a secure context for trade relations. Islamization of the area accelerated this process without initially marginalizing Venetian and Genoese traders, who at first benefited from the decline of Byzantium.[44] At the same time, rivalry between Venice and Genoa prevented either one from controlling the Black Sea trade. By 1459, however, the Venetian senate was lamenting the scarcity of servile labour, as most Slavic and Tatar slaves were by then being sent to the Near and Middle East, mostly to Egypt and Turkey.[45] They therefore looked for alternative sources. Genoa, for example, acquired slaves in Islamic Spain and North Africa to sell in Seville and the Canary Islands.[46] It was at this point that Genoa tried to enter the market for slaves to the New World but was quickly overtaken by Spanish, Portuguese and finally British vessels.[47]

The fall of Constantinople and Byzantium had major consequences for Western Europe. The core of its world economy subsequently shifted from the Mediterranean to the Atlantic, and church–state relations were transformed. However, it also closed the eastern slave trade and led to the search for alternative supplies of slaves. Thereafter, Western Europe and the Islamic powers increasingly turned to two new sources of slaves – captives in Christian–Muslim conflicts and sub-Saharan Africa. In the following pages we will detail these two new sources of the slave trade.

Captives and Slavery in the Mediterranean

Another form of servitude in medieval and early modern Europe was debt bondage. Particularly widespread in south-eastern Europe, Byzantium and Russia,[48] it was also one of the most important characteristics of galley labour in the Mediterranean.[49] Debtors could work off the sum they owed and at least one third of labour on Spanish, Venetian and French galleys were so 'recruited'.[50] As they worked alongside war captives and criminals who were committed to galley labour, such practices can be considered part of a wider system of servitude linked to enslavement of war captives on both sides of the Muslim–Christian frontier in the Mediterranean.[51] Although there are currently no global evaluations of the number of Moors and Turks enslaved in Italy and Spain,[52] it is estimated that between 1 and 1.25 million Europeans were enslaved on the Barbary Coast between 1530 and 1780.[53] Mediterranean piracy and captivity represented for many captives not only torment, exile and the potential for apostasy, but opportunity and social mobility for others willing and able to exploit the porous racial and religious boundaries of the early-modern Mediterranean. Many captives were redeemed against a ransom. In exchange, the captive had to work some years for the individual or authority that had paid the ransom. This practice, widespread throughout the Christian Mediterranean world, represented a clear link between slavery, ransoming and other forms of bondage. Indeed the debt of the 'almost freed' ex-captive guaranteed a transitory phase that could last several years during which the concerned person was neither slave nor free. Financing redemption was a means of keeping people in bondage. Indeed, debt was commonly linked to emancipation in many different regions up to recent times, characterizing, for example, many cases of indentureship for black and white labour, the *rachats préalables* of slaves in French Africa, and Russian peasants after their emancipation in 1861.

To sum up, the traditional view that slavery, common in classical Greece and Rome, disappeared in medieval times has now been discredited. Research has demonstrated that debt bondage, serfdom and slavery existed in medieval Western Europe. This permits a new perspective on two major debates in the historiography: the nature of the relationships between Islamic slavery and medieval forms of Christian bondage and slavery; and European medieval and colonial slavery.

Debt Slavery in Islam and Pre-Colonial Africa: Forbidden or Forgotten Institution?

In Muslim societies, an early division was established between the core Islamic lands of the Middle East, which provided the markets for slaves, and non-Muslim domains, which constituted source regions for slaves – enslavement of non-Muslims captured in holy wars being justified under the Sharia. Military expansion under the Abbasid dynasty (AD 758–1258) brought into the Muslim polities an increasing number of slaves as war captives and tribute, and through commerce.

Islam's subsequent expansion into the Indian Ocean world, Africa and Central Asia encouraged further development of the slave trade, notably across the Sahara, along the Silk Road, and along routes connecting the Mediterranean to Russia and Central Asia via the Black Sea, and to and from India. Ralph Austen's (1987) estimates that between the seventh and nineteenth centuries some 17 million black slaves were traded to the Muslim world across the Sahara, the Red Sea and the Indian Ocean[54] have been revised downwards to about 11.5 million slaves: 6 million from 650–1500; 3 million from 1500–1800; and 2.5 million in the nineteenth century.[55]

There were in addition some 1.2 million Christians enslaved by Muslims from 1530 to 1780; 2 million (chiefly Ukrainians, Polish and Lithuanians seized by the Crimean Tatars) from the mid-fifteenth to the end of the seventeenth century; and another 2 million Circassians slaves who entered the Ottoman Empire between 1450 and 1700.[56] Women and children were more in demand than men and were also more likely to be incorporated into Muslim society. Boys were trained for military and domestic services, while adult men and less attractive women were assigned more menial tasks. Slaves were employed in all sectors, from domestic service to urban activities, agricultural labour and the army. Servile labour was common on medium and even small properties, and widely employed in irrigation, pastoralism, mining, transport, public works, proto-industry and construction. Slave status in Muslim societies was also hereditary in cases where both parents were slaves, but children of a servile mother by a free man were free under Shi'I Islam polities (although not in societies governed by Sunni Islam).[57] Self-enslavement for debt and sale of children, while forbidden under the Sharia, was in fact practised in some regions – the former in the Turkic steppe, the Caucasus and by the Kurds, the latter in south and Southeast Asia and Africa.

West Africa was particularly important to subsequent developments in the European trade in slaves. By the fifteenth century the acquisition of slaves through wars and raids was common along the Senegal river, as in the northern savannah, including Songhay, Mali, Borno and the Hausa states,[58] the consolidation of Muslim empires in Ghana, Mali, Songhay, Borno and Sennar pushed the raiding frontier considerably back, although when these empires collapsed the opposite tendencies emerged. Slaves were used in the military and government, taken as concubines or employed in agriculture. Throughout the borderland between the Sahara and the savannah, agricultural slaves were settled in villages under the control of overseers. They produced millet, sorghum, cotton and indigo, which were then sold to desert nomads. Their masters travelled to distant lands for gold, salt and other goods. These plantations transformed the inner Niger valley into a heavily populated and productive region. In East Africa,

Muslim expansion manifested itself not in territorial empires but in commercial city-states along the coast where slave trading rather than raiding was the main source of supply of servile populations. Concubines, domestic servants, officials and slaves in the plantations were the most widespread forms of bondage. We will discuss in detail pawnship and slavery in Africa in the next sections; before that, we need to explain forms of slavery and debt bondage linked to the 'rise of the West'.

Slavery in the World Expansion of the Seventeenth Century

It would be a mistake to consider that modern colonial slavery emerged only with the rise of the plantation system in the Americas. Long before that, sugar plantations using slave labour were developed in the eastern Mediterranean by both Venice and the Islamic powers. When the eastern slave trade was closed to the Italians they sought new sources of slavery and new places to establish sugar plantations. Venice established a plantation close to Tyr in 1123, while the Templars sought a similar enterprise near Tripoli. Similarly, when they occupied Sicily, the Normans founded sugar plantations there. All used slave labour, mostly war captives from Eastern Europe.

Following the fall of Constantinople the Italian and Spanish powers lost both their slave sources in the east and their sugar plantations in the Mediterranean. They subsequently developed new strategies. Bartolomeo Marchionni, a Florentine investor who in 1453 had fled Constantinople for Lisbon, established sugar plantations on the Madeira Islands to which he brought African slaves. The Portuguese developed other plantations on the Canaries, and the islands of São Tomé and Príncipe in the Gulf of Guinea. There already had existed a small but significant trade in black slaves purchased chiefly from northern Africa by Muslim, Genoese and the Spanish traders. However, from 1450 increasing numbers of African slaves were shipped to Sicily, Portugal and Spain, and others to the sugar plantations on the Portuguese-held Atlantic islands. Portuguese and Genoese merchants competed for control of the African slave trade, the Portuguese proving initially the more successful and establishing the pattern for later development of the trans-Atlantic slave trade. On the North African coast they established trading contact with Muslim traders and authorities, transferred slaves from the eastern Mediterranean plantations to the 'new' island plantations in the eastern Atlantic, and bought slaves with gold from West African authorities – exactly as the Muslim merchants did in the trans-Saharan trade.[59] As early as the second half of the fifteenth century, the Portuguese already traded 80,000 slaves per year along the Mauritanian, Senegambia and Upper Guinea coasts.[60] In this they benefited from an alliance forged with the kingdom of Congo, a non-Muslim state, which facilitated the export of slaves to Portugal and São

Tomé, from where slaves were also shipped to the Americas from the 1530s. Overall, between 1450 and 1600 some 410,000 slaves were exported from West Africa via the Atlantic basin, although in the mid-sixteenth century, following the collapse of the Congo kingdom, the Americas became their main destination.[61] However, America was also, at this early stage, the destination for another servile labour force – that of white indentured servants.

White Indentured Labour and Slavery in the Americas: Complementarity or Substitution?

From the early sixteenth century, the Spanish sought to produce sugar at Hispaniola, the Portuguese in Brazil. Sugar never flourished in the early Spanish Caribbean because of labour difficulties, alternative opportunities for investment in silver production after 1550 and the rise of Brazil as the premier American sugar colony after 1570. The Spanish and Portuguese initially sought labour for their New World plantations from local indigenous populations. Indeed, at first the Iberians relied on indigenous structures of production and labour relations, working through local intermediaries for the supply of provisions and services, including traditional rotating work gangs that built houses and churches, carried goods to markets and ports and panned for gold.

However, a different system developed on the European plantations in Brazil. Planters at first used enslaved indigenous captives as a permanent unskilled workforce, recruited seasonal labourers from Jesuit-run villages for planting and harvesting, and brought a few African slaves from the eastern Atlantic plantation islands to provide core skills and supervision. However, after 1600 the great majority of sugar workers were Africans. Profit and bondage merged in sugar and slavery. Brazil proved the model for Atlantic America. The Dutch, British, French and other Europeans adopted and adapted the system, which sustained centuries of profitable destruction in the Caribbean. At the same time, it would be misleading to conclude that in colonial Spanish America bonded and slave labour were the only existing forms of labour. Rural estates relied on seasonal work gangs organized by village leaders and paid in cash to plant and harvest crops. In mining, cloth making, commercial cultivation and increasingly in commercial grazing, work across Spanish North America was organized and paid commercially. Across rural Spanish North America, from the seventeenth century workers were recruited with advances accounted against future labour.

The situation was as complex in the Caribbean and North America where, faced with the irregular labour supplies and low productivity of Amerindians, two new sources of labour were looked to: white indentured immigrants and African slaves. As late as 1650, there were only 17,000 Africans in English America, amounting to only 2.5 per cent of the total population. Most Africans lived on the Caribbean islands. On the mainland, there were only 2,000 Africans in 1650. By 1700, however, the African population approached 150,000, more than a third of the population of the English mainland colonies. Regional variations were nevertheless important: the arrival of African slaves was fast in Barbados, slower in Chesapeake colonies.

It is incorrect to interpret indentured labour in economic terms simply as a temporary substitute for slaves in the aftermath of abolition. Indentureship began well before slavery and persisted during and after it. In the first period, from the seventeenth century to the 1830s, about 300,000 European indentured servants arrived in North America primarily to work on tobacco plantations and to a lesser degree in manufacturing. With the rapid development of the plantation system, African slaves gradually supplanted white indentured servants. However, responding to both push factors in Europe (industrialization, transformation of the countryside) and pull factors in North America, white indentured migration across the Atlantic remained significant until at least the 1830s.

Abolition of slavery gave new life to indentured migration which, in its second phase (nineteenth and twentieth centuries) affected 2 million workers, mostly Chinese and Indians, but also Africans, Japanese and Pacific Islanders, who were employed in sugar plantations and in manufacturing. Unlike white indentured servants during the first phase of indentured migration who largely remained in North America, many second-phase indentured workers, notably Indians, returned home: 70 per cent in Thailand, Malaya and Melanesia, and one third in Mauritius, the Caribbean, Surinam and Jamaica.[62]

Russell Menard argues that in North America, indentured servants and slaves were close substitutes, and that planters shifted from servants to slaves not because they preferred slaves, but due to changes in the supply and cost of the two groups. During the first half of the seventeenth century, Chesapeake planters found an adequate supply of labour in British indentured servants. However, around 1660, the supply of servants began to decline as in England the population fell while real wages rose – leading to improved opportunities at home. Consequently, after mid-century, migration to America fell.

However, other scholars argue that this shift reflected the planters' preferences for black slaves, whom they considered to be more docile and productive than white servants.[63] The issue is still different if we consider Barbados, where the development of sugar plantations transformed the island in the mid-nineteenth century. With the rise of sugar, monoculture replaced diversified farming, large plantations consumed small farms, blacks arrived by the thousands while whites left, destructive demographic patterns took hold, the island began to import food and fuel and the great planters rose to wealth and power. Sugar, because of its substantial scale economies and large profits, was most efficiently grown on big units and greatly increased demand for labour. Yet, this outcome would have been impossible without the transformations of African slavery itself.

The First African-American Connection, *c.* 1500–1700

The number of African slaves exported across the Atlantic steadily increased during the sixteenth (328,000) and seventeenth (1.3 million) centuries to reach a peak in the eighteenth century (6 million) and fall in the nineteenth century (3.6 million) when the Atlantic slave trade ended.[64] In the eighteenth century, the British carried about 40.5 per cent of slaves, followed by the Portuguese (31 per cent), French (18.1 per cent), Dutch (5.7 per cent) and North Americans (3.4 per cent). Between the time Britain banned the slave trade in 1807 and Brazil finally abolished slavery in 1888, the Portuguese dominated the Atlantic slave trade. The main areas of exports were Angola and Congo, followed by the Bight of Benin, the Gold Coast, Bight of Biafra and Senegambia.

However, the traditional export trade in African slaves north to Muslim countries continued to be significant, accounting for about 40 per cent of total slave exports from Africa in the seventeenth century, and about 30 per cent between the seventeenth and the early nineteenth century. Overall, between 1500 and 1800, the Muslim trade probably accounted for about 40 per cent of African slave exports.[65]

Most victims of the slave trade were enslaved as a result of wars, razzias, criminal punishment or impoverishment due to drought or other natural catastrophes. African commercial networks were fully integrated and forged strong links with external markets. The slave export trade was organized, in Muslim areas of Africa, by government agents, foreign merchants (mostly Muslims) and local traders, while Europeans dominated slave exports from the African west coast: the Dutch, French and English in the northern part, and the Portuguese in the south. Slaves were purchased chiefly with imported money (silver coins, iron bars, copper, some textile, shells, etc.), military goods and luxuries (textiles, mirrors, needles, liquors). Political instability and warfare enhanced both the demand for and supply of slaves. On the demand side, slaves were required for the army and to finance imports of weapons; on the supply side, population displacement and warfare encouraged razzias in which war captives and refugees were enslaved. The trade in slaves with Europeans was initially strongest with European enclaves in Africa, notably along the Guinea coast, and in Angola, Cape Town and Zambezia, which possessed between 60,000 and 100,000 slaves by the end of the eighteenth century.[66]

The abolitionist movement strongly influenced the slave trade in the Atlantic and in Africa. From 1807, when Britain abolished the slave trade, its slave traders suffered heavy losses, as did sugar planters and merchants because of reduced production in the West Indies, and investors in European sugar and coffee markets. Paradoxically, however, the number of slaves carried across the Atlantic initially increased as, encouraged by enhanced demand for sugar and coffee in North America and Europe, plantation production and demand for slaves expanded in Brazil and Cuba.[67] Moreover, Britain supplied at least 90 per cent of the manufactured goods used, and half the finance invested in the Cuban and Brazilian slave trade.[68] At the same time, the slave trade expanded elsewhere. During the first half of the nineteenth century, half a million African slaves were exported from East Africa and another 420,000 across the Red Sea.[69] Within Africa, British abolitionism initially depressed slave prices, but this stimulated internal demand, pushing the enslavement frontier ever deeper into the interior. The demand for slaves was augmented by the expanded production of so-called 'legitimate' cash crops such as palm oil and coconuts (in West Africa) and cloves (East Africa), which relied heavily on slave labour. Such developments also promoted an expansion in pawnship.

The Other Side of Debt Slavery: Financing Slavery and the Slave Trade

Pawnship and Trade in Africa

We here expand on the debate about pawnship and debt bondage in Africa (outlined above) in order to examine its relationship with international trade. Pawnship has been variously interpreted by different authors over time. Until the end of the nineteenth century, British colonial authorities considered pawnship to be such a 'mild' form of servitude as to be acceptable. Their attitudes changed during the Scramble for Africa, when they fell under the scrutiny of the abolitionist movement in Britain, and in the early twentieth century they banned pawnship as a form of slavery. Ever since, scholars have fiercely debated the nature of pawnship. For example, C. Meillassoux argued that pawnship and slavery were distinct, pawnship being a form of inclusion into society, and slavery a form of exclusion and alienation.[70] At the opposite end of the scale, I. Kopytoff and S. Miers contended that there was a continuum between slavery and pawnship and their entrenchment in practices.[71] Central to the debate is the question of whether pawnship developed in Africa before, or as a consequence of, the interdiction of slavery. This is an issue similar to those discussed above relating to ancient Rome and the early trans-Atlantic slave trade and emigration, wherein the debate focused on the link between respectively the decadence of debt bondage and the development of chattel slavery, and white indentured labour and black slavery.

The tensions between pawnship and slavery in Africa raise a similar issue: are these complementary or substitute institutions? Following Meillassoux, and explicitly referring to Finley (whom he criticizes), Gareth Austin argues that, just as there is no proven link between the abolition of debt bondage and the rise of chattel slavery in Rome, so in Africa there is no evidence of pawnship having developed as a consequence of the interdiction of slavery. Rather, slavery and pawnship were complimentary institutions. Unlike slavery, pawnship was an intrinsic part of the credit system, as pawns formed the collateral for loans. Moreover, pawnship was much more widespread among commoners than among chiefs, who used their power, wars and razzias to access slaves and money.[72]

Along similar lines, Lovejoy (in his chapter here and in his work with Toyin Falola) argues that pawnship evolved over time and interacted with other forms of financing, most of which were inseparable from the labour market. Because of the importance of women and children in pawnship, the flow of credit and the control of labour were closely linked to the institution of marriage. Yet pawnship assumed different forms according to region and time period. Before the abolition of slavery, pawnship facilitated the flow of some individuals into servitude, whereas following abolition it formed an alternative to slavery. The pawning contract, not the pawn, was the property of the creditor. Unlike slaves, who remained outsiders, pawns belonged to the society of their masters, and to a given extent pawnship was a means of inclusion, not exclusion. Nevertheless, pawnship and slavery share some common features. In both, the creditor/master had full control over the labour, and hence output, of the pawn/slave.[73] Ultimately, pawns could be enslaved *de facto* and *de jure*. Conversely, slaves could, like pawns, be used as collateral. This also explains why pawnship was nominally much less common in Muslim societies where debt bondage was forbidden. In reality, however, forms of disguised pawnship and debt bondage were widespread and Muslim traders who acquired pawns converted them into slaves. From the eighteenth century, in conformity with such practices, European traders explicitly asked not only for slaves, but also for pawns whom they transformed into slaves.[74] In the nineteenth century, both pawnship and slavery increased in Africa as rising external demand resulted in rapidly expanding production of 'legitimate' cash crops and minerals by cheap labour-intensive methods. The majority of such labour was obtained through enslavement, often through raiding by military states, and pawnship. This in turn drew the attention of the British abolitionist movement to pawnship, which they decried as a disguised form of slavery. By contrast, British colonial elites qualified pawnship as a form of mild bondage, domestic service and ultimately an exchange between labour and capital, and, as such, should be regulated by local customs. This interpretation has been, ironically, reiterated in African nationalistic and anti-imperialistic historiography, which maintains that there was a major difference between African slavery and pawnship, on the one hand, 'real' slavery (i.e. trans-Atlantic and white colonial slavery) on the other hand.[75] It was only at the turn of the nineteenth and twentieth centuries that the abolitionist viewpoint gained ascendency and legislation was passed against pawnship. However, far from disappearing, pawnship continued in a different form.[76]

In this context, the Yoruba provide a particularly interesting case study. Between 1815 and the 1850s, tens of thousands of Yoruba slaves were exported

to the Americas. The few available studies also indicate a major presence of
slaves and pawns in the Yoruba economy and society.[77] Agriculture was dominated by cash crop cultivation, while local manufacture supplied tools and goods
for household use. Slaves were used in the domestic economy, in manufacture,
transportation and military service. In his chapter in this book, Olatunji Ojo
highlights two major points: first, that pawnship coexisted alongside slavery
rather than emerging after its abolition; and secondly, that the economy of debt
and its link with bondage concerned not only poor families, but also traders
and planters, commonly in bilateral relationships of debt. Thus, in Yorubaland
adult males dominated the military and were more exposed to seizure in combat, whereas women and children formed the bulk of victims of non-violent
modes of enslavement such as credit default. Also, women and children lacked
adequate means to repel abusive creditors. A man with multiple slave wives and
children could offer one or more of them to creditors in payment of debt. More
women and children than men were pawned or seized for debt even when they
were not the actual debtors. They often became debt slaves because demand was
greater for them than for males and they were considered weak and easier to
control. In this context, monetary instability affected all social levels. Major
traders, exporters of legitimate trade products, suffered from this instability and
were often indebted to European purchasers. Occasionally, traders bought more
goods than they could afford. There was also the problem of currency instability caused by the transition from cowries to British coins which induced a high
incidence of borrowing on the part of soldiers who required weapons – which
in turn fuelled political and military conflict. The high cost of transportation, violence along trade routes and road closures often resulted both in the
relative scarcity of cowries in the interior and higher exchange rates. Monetization and currency fluctuations increased reliance on cash and lending to meet
numerous obligations, such as ransoming relatives from captivity, investing in
trade and paying for marriages, food, weapons, funerals, medication and fines.
While credit broadened market transactions, socio-economic instability made
it impossible for some borrowers to pay their liabilities. Because of this, long
overdue debts meant lengthy service in pawnship – which made the status of
slaves and pawns indistinguishable to most people. Certainly, creditors often
treated pawns who had served under them for many years as if they were slaves,
and sometimes enslaved them or sold them into slavery. Children pawned to
itinerant traders were particularly prone to enslavement. If kinship safeguarded
pawns from abuse, pawns removed from their towns and thereby separated from
their kin had little immunity from enslavement. Enslavement for debt continued
well into the colonial period and probably did not disappear until the end of the
First World War. The Yoruba case highlights the link between slavery, bondage,
credit and monetary issues. We have stressed the relationship between pawn-

ship, credit relations and external trade. This opens the road to a discussion of the long-standing debate over of the relationship between slavery and capitalism.

Debt, Slavery and Monetization: A Global Perspective

We have alluded above to the inadequacy of conventional theories of capital, state and coercion for the role of Italian city-states in medieval and early modern slavery, on the one hand, and the connection between empire building and capitalism, on the other. As Miller notes in his chapter, returns from slaving were multiplied by increasingly effective banking and lending strategies in Europe. This was effected initially by the Genoese, who created the financial basis for the first ventures into the Atlantic by the Portuguese, who in turn excluded their Genoese backers from the principal returns – namely gold dust from Senegambia and from Elmina on the Gold Coast – but encouraged them to invest in production on the island staging posts necessary to secure return of the precious metal to Lisbon. The arrival of gold and silver in Europe and Asia from the new American colonies contributed to finance commerce, including the slave trade in Asia and the Mediterranean in the early modern era. A fortuitous abundance of precious metals from the Americas also supplemented the initial introduction of Akan gold from Africa that formed the core of commercial liquidity in the Atlantic. Miller argues that the sequence of incremental historical strategies through which Europeans invested in the Atlantic economy as a whole, and also in purchases from the highly productive Asian economies of the Indian Ocean, were all based on credit. He contends that commercial debtors borrowed cash, or liquidity, which they repaid through cutting cash expenditure and maximizing cash returns, or returns in near-equivalent similarly liquid forms, on their investments. Whenever they could, they therefore appropriated resources, or factors of production – land, labour, raw materials – from outside the commercial sphere, that is from domestic communities that did not use cash. It was precisely because capital was relatively scarce in Europe, where it was mobilized chiefly for trade, manufacturing and agriculture, that European powers developed their colonies upon credit. Britain obtained financial credit as a by-product of the quest for specie that underlay the seventeenth-century development of the Atlantic. The agency was the Royal African Company, granted a charter in 1672 to establish an English commercial presence on Africa's Gold Coast. The Royal African Company was designed specifically to acquire gold in Africa. Europeans thus paid for their principal Atlantic initiatives up to the end of the seventeenth century, from the islands off western Africa through the Caribbean and continental northern and southern America with minimum investment of financial capital.

In the eighteenth century, a massive influx of Brazilian gold sustained monetary reforms and the development of the City of London, notably financial assets development and bank notes guaranteed by the Bank of England. The exploding

British-led commercial capacity that financed the rapid growth of indebted productive sectors of the American economies in the eighteenth century flowed even more momentously into Africa. Here suppliers and buyers alike over invested in the slave trade, just as they later did in legitimate trade. Thus, African debtors sold females they would have preferred to keep, in effect liquidating their human assets, and the planters bought women (and eventually children) to protect their investments in production even at lower levels of efficiency, provided they covered their operating costs, thus allowing their enterprises to slip back into debt. Loans backed by European commercial credit forced foreclosures on African debtors – which often extended to entire communities because of the communal ethos of collective responsibility to outsiders. Arguably, foreclosure on debts – backed by violence – became as important a source of captives as systematic militarization. By contrast, with British suppression of trans-Atlantic slaving proceeding incrementally, slavery in the United States and in significant sectors of southern Brazil became self-financing through the demographic reproduction of native-born populations of African descent who were retained in increasingly proprietorial ways. From this perspective, assets held in human form may be said to have financed not only the rise of slavery in the Americas, but also the beginning of its ending, as they contributed their value as assets to the creation and early growth of productive sectors in the Americas, independent of European (principally British) investment. The last section of this introduction will examine this process by looking at the role of debt during and after abolition.

Abolitionism in Context: From Slavery to Debt Bondage?

From Portugal to Brazil

In British colonies between 1832 and the early 1840s, a slave was obliged before becoming legally 'free' to go through a transitory phase of apprenticeship, in terms of both education and vocational training.[78] The normal six-year apprenticeship was raised to ten years for domestic slaves and twelve years for agricultural slaves. Apprentices worked forty-five hours a week for their former owners in exchange for food, clothing, lodging and medical care. Apprentices found guilty of absenteeism or other misdemeanours (according to standards set by the planters themselves) were handed out harsh penalties including physical punishment (suppressed under slavery during the 1820s) and often had their period of apprenticeship prolonged. Abuses were frequent.[79] Ex-slave-owners received compensation for abolition of slavery amounting in total to 20 million pounds. Many planters used the apprenticeship program as supplementary compensation and to this end sought to extract as much unpaid labour as possible. However, the final social and economic outcome of abolition differed from one colony to another according to the availability of land, previous forms of bondage and types of culture, new forms of labour, regulations governing the workforce (the different masters and servants acts enacted in different colonies), and systems of credit.[80] In Barbados, planters kept almost all the land, which they rented in part to ex-slaves who therefore largely remained on their original plantations. In Jamaica, Trinidad and English Guyana, many ex-slaves had formal access to land, but substantial numbers became indebted to their former masters, and thus found themselves back working on the plantations.[81] Nevertheless, ex-slaves who remained, for one reason or another, tied to their original plantation engaged in forms of protest that often resulted, as in the case of the sugar plantations of Jamaica, in reduced plantation output.

We complete our survey by examining the process of emancipation in Brazil and the Ottoman Empire, both of which provide significant contrasts to the more well-known patterns of manumission and emancipation in Britain, France and North America. Both the Brazilian and the Ottoman cases are often discussed in the historiography as major examples of 'delayed' abolitions – that in Brazil, for example, was considered to be due to the power of local planters.

In Brazil, slave imports increased during the nineteenth century, in particular after the British and US abolition of the slave trade. Effective anti-slave trade policies were adopted only from 1850, by which time the inflow of slaves had sharply declined. However, between 1850 and 1880, a buoyant internal market persisted for slaves.[82] Only from the 1860s did the abolitionist movement in Brazil become significant. However, other factors played as important a role in the decline of slavery. From the 1870s, many slaves signed official labour contracts, although even following abolition in 1888, the hirers of newly-emancipated ex-slaves commonly continued to physically and otherwise abuse them. In this context, changing legal status and the social practices of emancipation matter. In his chapter, Henrique Espada Lima analyses a sample of contracts engaged in by ex-slaves in order to pay for manumission. This practice was regulated by legislation drafted to promote a gradual extinction of slavery. Lima discusses how the relations between law, the labour market and the gradual disintegration of the slave system were directly connected to debt in the form of new types of bonded labour. It is conventionally assumed in the historiography that abolition of slavery in 1888 laid the foundations for the emergence of a free labour market in Brazil. However, recent research has demonstrated both that such transformations started in the 1870s and that forms of bondage persisted into the post-abolition era. Taking aboard such perspectives, Lima examines the development from the 1830s of contracts for indentured Asian and Portuguese immigrant labour. His conclusion is that the parallel between 'black' bondage and 'white' slavery was probably not just rhetoric; legislators and planters openly acknowledged their wish to impose the same types of control and discipline on indentured labour as they did on their slaves. From the 1850s, impending abolition and increasing monetization of the Brazilian economy had a major impact on labour relationships. Owners started renting out their slaves for hire, which in turn offered those slaves the access to currency and cash rewards needed to purchase their own freedom. Many offered their labour to their masters in return for the promise of manumission, while others became indebted to new employers who redeemed them and for whom they worked free in order to repay the cost of their manumission. The abolition act of 1888 erased compensations for manumission; at the same time, former slaves entered new relations of debt with their previous masters which were legally inspired by old forms of bondage.

Debt and Manumission in the Ottoman Empire

Having already discussed the role of Islam in the medieval, early modern and modern world, we here examine the development of Ottoman slavery in the age of abolition where continuities with previous forms of bondage are as striking. The historiographical debate concerns first and foremost the issue of whether Muslim societies demonstrated a coherent attitude toward slavery, with some scholars stressing the commonality of the Islamic world, while others emphasize the major role played by local authorities and jurisprudence, and, thus, the impossibility of treating the Islamic world as a unitary entity.[83] This volume does not pretend to enter this debate as such; rather, it will focus on the abolition process in the Ottoman Empire by examining the role debt played in the transition phase to abolition. During this period, the crux of the official Ottoman argument was that slavery in its empire and throughout the Muslim world in general was mild and thus fundamentally different from slavery in the Americas. Slaves were not employed on plantations; most were domestic servants, and they were frequently manumitted.[84] In part, this argument replicated official British and French positions on African pawnship, concubinage and slavery before the late 1880s.

However, it is now accepted that agriculture slavery was widespread in Ottoman and other Muslim societies and that 'real' slaves were an important component of the population. Also, the processes of abolition varied significantly from one region to another according to the social and economic role of slaves, and the strength over time of local and external abolitionist forces. In his chapter, Michael Ferguson studies the debate and practices of abolition in the Ottoman Empire exclusively with regard to African slaves. He argues that abolition was legitimized through the concept of social indebtedness; upon emancipation, a former slave was obliged through social and religious traditions to become a client of his or her emancipator *cum* patron. Social indebtedness was rooted in the traditional duties owed to their former masters by emancipated slaves – excluding those who had given birth to their master's child, married him or been married off to someone else. Indeed, as Ehud Toledano argues, slaves were well aware of the importance of maintaining ties to the household, and only when deemed absolutely necessary would they willingly break the bond.[85] The lasting ties formed by slavery, combined with Muslim traditions regarding the duties of enslaver and the enslaved following emancipation, can be called social indebtedness. It is this social indebtedness that, beginning in the third quarter of the nineteenth century, helped legitimize the Ottoman state's involvement in the process of emancipation and the lives of the emancipated.

The Abolition of Slavery in Africa

Anti-slavery movements that targeted chiefly 'Islamic slavery' converged in Africa with the overall movement for the 'abolition of slavery'. Public opinion and administrative rulers in Europe stressed the 'barbarian' and backward attitude of African elites willing to enslave other Africans and called for a 'civilizing mission' of the West which, it was envisaged, would pass through three main stages: 'slaves' had to be freed, the slave trade stopped, and an appropriate labour market established. However, on the ground, more pragmatic considerations prevailed. British officials sought to avoid confrontation with Islamic authorities, chiefly on the issue of concubinage, which was left intact – Islamic customary law being evoked to justify its legitimacy. In general, while the antislavery campaign was commonly cited as a pretext for imperial intervention, colonial policy actually sought to protect the local economy and society from the fallout that many administrators feared would ensue from rapid emancipation. They argued that it was essential to maintain discipline over the workforce and that the transition to free labour would necessarily take time. It would be irresponsible to let Africans become free agents overnight, to work when, where and how they chose. In both French and British Africa, administrators campaigned against vagrancy, theft, drinking and personal violence, although policy details differed from one colony to another, and within the same colony between districts and even villages. Colonial intentions rarely if ever translated into achievements. 'Emancipation' worked out for African slave owners and slaves in ways that the British and French rarely anticipated. Instead of becoming 'capitalists', 'landowners', 'proletarians' (as the British hoped in Kenya and Tanzania) or 'peasants' (as the French wished), most Africans worked as 'peasant-workers', moving back and forth between their own plots and plantations or urban activities. Serels' chapter studies administrators' use of indirect rule in Northern Sudan and, subsequently, indigenous debt, as motivators for indigenous participation in the colonial market. Since Marxist and Dependency Theorists began, in the 1960s, to re-examine the emergence of colonial African market economies, historians have linked the collection of taxes payable in money with state-led plans to create a docile labour force and cheap primary produce for foreign capital. However, variations in the ways in which colonial officials understood colonial tax regimes have been under-examined. Serels demonstrates that, during the first decades of the twentieth century, tax policy was shaped less by simple economic calculus than by the cultural assumptions of local administrators, which reflected their limited and partial knowledge of local conditions. While they did not conceptualize taxes as a means of forcing the indigenous population into the global market for labour and produce, administrators did incorporate coerced and forced labour as a central feature of their economic development programs.

Conclusion

It would be difficult to understand the history of debt slavery in the Mediterranean and the Atlantic worlds over the *longue durée* from ahistorical taxonomies of forms of slavery and coerced labour. Notions and practices of debt and slavery do not correspond to one single logic or classificatory principle. Chattel slavery and debt bondage are not necessarily substitutes. In ancient Rome, medieval Afro-Eurasia and the early modern and modern Mediterranean, African and Trans-Atlantic worlds, chattel slavery and debt bondage coexisted and sometimes transmuted one into the other. As such, they reflected long-term relationships between labour and credit on the one hand, and power, finance and territorial entities on the other. In the Roman Empire, debt bondage coexisted with forms of 'wage' labour and chattel slavery, the role and importance of which evolved with the passage from the Republic to the early, then to the Late Empire. In these changing contexts, debt bondage expressed the various mobile social and political hierarchies that lay between the 'centre' and 'periphery', between small and large productive units, and between domestic, agricultural and manufacturing labour. These flexible boundaries of labour, credit and bondage throughout the Roman period help us to understand their varied heritage around the Mediterranean and beyond, in the Byzantine Empire and Inner Asia during the medieval and early modern eras. The emergence from the twelfth century of new markets augmented the trade in slaves that connected all these areas. Forms of serfdom, slavery and bondage were widespread and together formed the foundation of the emergence of early forms of modern slavery in Islam, Russia and Europe. Debt played a significant role in the making of slaves, captives, recruits, soldiers, seamen, apprentices, indentured emigrants, pawns, eunuchs, galley slaves and colonists. Muslim and Christians both contributed to the development of slavery and debt bondage and their transmission from early modern to modern times in Africa, Asia and the Americas. Rather than pitch Europe against Africa and Asia, or national units against empires and city-states, the forces of coercion and capital overlapped in all these areas and polities. It was a matter of gradation, not of clearly opposed worlds. This is important in understanding the circulation of institutions such as debt bondage in so many different societies, regions and time periods. This circulation was also possible because markets were widespread not only in early modern and modern Europe, but also in Africa and Asia. The coexistence of capitalistic and non-capitalistic forms of markets (in Polanyi's terms), added to the importance of gift, as an obligation being not in opposition but complementary to market engagements, supported this commonality of debt and bondage across such varied geographical areas. Yet differences and hierarchies were also important. African pawnship was surely related to the export trade and to international capital circulation; at the same time, if the former was a necessary component for the development of the latter, it would be difficult to assert that a shift in the social and economic equilibriums in Yorubaland had the same impact on the City of London as the other way round. Nevertheless, it is important to underline that the relationship between Yorubaland and London was a two-way one. This was because, as indicated above, and underscored by Miller in his chapter, Africa – far from constituting a subsistence economy – possessed a well-developed market system. Thus, for example, famines in Africa were phenomena as related to market mechanisms as to environmental factors such as failed harvests, and market speculation occurred both in London and in Africa.

1 DEBT BONDAGE AND CHATTEL SLAVERY IN EARLY ROME

Marc Kleijwegt

In his book *Ancient Slavery and Modern Ideology* (1980) Moses Finley argued that chattel slavery only started to become a major force in the Roman world after the official abolition of *nexum* in 326 BC (or 313 BC, as some would argue) had made it impossible to exploit the labour of Roman citizens.[1] In other words, the drying up of one source of exploited labour led to a more intensified pursuit of another pool. In reviews of Finley's book scholars occasionally questioned the validity of this argument, but no systematic investigation of the relationship between the abolition of *nexum* and chattel slavery in fourth-century Rome has been undertaken so far.[2] Finley's argument has in fact become the standard interpretation of the development of slavery in early Rome.[3] In this chapter I shall try to do two things. Firstly, I shall argue that the abolition of *nexum* in 326 BC is misleading shorthand for a complex phenomenon on which we are very poorly informed.[4] What can be established with some degree of certainty is that the Senate responded to the excesses accompanying *nexum* rather than establishing its concern with the procedure itself. Secondly, I shall re-examine the evidence supplied by the historian Livy (59 BC–AD 17) for the number of captives enslaved by the Romans during the Third Samnite War (298–290 BC), which formed the basis for Finley's argument that chattel slavery rose to a level unprecedented in Roman history, and demonstrate that the argument is difficult to substantiate.

The procedure for the treatment of debtors in early Rome can be reconstructed as follows. Upon the acknowledgement of a debt in front of a judge, or the failure to repay an outstanding debt within thirty days after the debtor was condemned in court, the creditor summoned the debtor before the praetor, the chief legal magistrate. He subsequently proclaimed the debtor's failure to pay and laid his hands on him (*manus iniectio*) for the outstanding amount by grasping a part of the debtor's body. The debtor was not allowed to remove the creditor's hand and had to rely upon a third individual to step forward in his defence. If no one did, the creditor was allowed to take him home and bind him with sinew or fetters weighing up to 15 lbs (16.8 kg). The debtor was kept in these circumstances for sixty days. During this period the creditor had to appear before the praetor on three separate occasions and make a public announcement requesting for the debt to be settled. If after sixty days no one had stepped forward to release the debtor, the creditor was by law entitled to sell him across the Tiber or even put him to death.

Historians of Roman slavery translate *nexum* as debt bondage, but there are a number of unresolved problems with this definition, notably the lack of consensus among Roman legal historians as to what *nexum* was and at what stage of an individual's indebtedness it became operational. In his *De lingua Latina* (On the Latin Language; 7.105), the Roman polymath Varro (*c.* 116–27 BC) endorsed the view proposed by Mucius Scaevola which held that *nexum* was different from *mancipatio* ('the handing over of property to a new owner'; transfer of ownership). The *nexus*, the individual who was bound by *nexum*, did not become the full slave and property of the creditor, but entered into temporary bondage:

> a free man who, for money which he owed, 'bound' (*nectebat*) his labour in slavery until he should pay, is called a *nexus*, just as a man is called *obaeratus*, 'indebted', from *aes*, 'debt'.[5]

Livy, the author of a history of Rome from its foundation to the death of Drusus (stepson of the first emperor Augustus) in 9 BC, refers to *nexum* as something that can be entered into (7.19.5: *nexumque inibant*), which suggests that it was a form of contractual obligation. *Nexi* were given the opportunity to pay off their debt through work, without diminishing their status as Roman citizens. It can be inferred from Livy (2.24.6) that *nexi* continued to serve as soldiers in the Roman army and they must also be assumed to have retained their right to vote.

Varro compared the *nexus* to the *obaeratus*, a noun derived from the word for 'debt' (*aes*; Varro, *De lingua Latina*, 7.105), perhaps because his readers were more familiar with that term. It is tempting to assume that the two terms are equivalent, but the evidence is not conclusive.[6] Livy also uses two other terms which identify individuals burdened by debt: *iudicati* ('those who have been subjected to a ruling from a judge') and *addicti* ('those who have been handed over' to their creditors).[7] I want to suggest that these were individuals in different stages of the process of indebtedness as described above. *Iudicatus*, then, is reserved for individuals who were given thirty days to settle their debt after a ruling by a judge. The *addicti*, in turn, were those individuals who had already been subjected to *manus iniectio* and were given sixty days before they were sold into slavery or executed. It must be assumed that, although perhaps not slaves in legal terms, the *addicti* were frequently treated as if they were slaves, as will become clear from the discussion below.[8] It has been argued that the *nexi* entered into a voluntary agreement in order to avoid the extreme consequences of a judgement for default, but this begs the question why such an agreement was not offered to the *addicti* and *iudicati*.[9]

Livy discusses the problems caused by debt and enslavement for debt in a series of episodes which he characterizes as crucial moments in the ongoing class struggle between the aristocratic patricians and the non-aristocratic plebeians. The first episode is set in 495 BC and tells the story of a veteran who had been a distinguished commanding officer in the wars with the Sabines (2.23.4–6), during which his crops, his cottage, his property, and his flocks were destroyed. In order to pay his taxes he was forced to borrow money and when he was unable to repay the loan, his farm was taken from him and eventually his creditor had him led away, not into slavery, but to prison and the office of the executioner: *non in servitium, sed in ergastulum et carnificinam duci* (2.23.6). He was able to escape from his prison and managed to attract the attention of a sizeable crowd. To illustrate the extent of his suffering he took off his clothes to display the recent signs of a severe flogging on his back (2.23.7).[10] His story created uproar, and suddenly there appeared from all quarters other victims of the harsh law of debt, some of whom were in chains (*vincti*), and others not (*soluti*): *nexi vincti solutique se undique in publicum proripiunt* (2.23.5). This event eventually led to the decision of the plebeians to leave the city in the hope of putting pressure on the patricians to give in to their demand for political and economic reforms. Following long negotiations the plebeians agreed to return to the city after they had been allowed to elect two officials to act as their spokespersons.

Livy's story of the anonymous veteran makes clear that someone of his stature (a citizen and a former soldier), who defaulted on the repayment of a loan, expected to be led away into slavery (*servitium*) rather than be sent to prison and subsequently to the executioner's office, as was the *addictus*. By implication, *servitium* cannot be the same thing as the treatment that awaited the *addictus* after the sixty-day period had come to an end. The next issue concerns the composition of the *nexi* who appeared in the streets of Rome after the veteran's escape. As already mentioned, the translation states that some of them were in chains (*vincti*), while others were not (*soluti*). However, this interpretation is surely flawed, because it raises the question why, if all of them were *nexi*, should only some of them be enchained. Livy's words, however, could be taken to mean that two groups – those who were still in bondage (*vincti*), and those who had already been released from it (*soluti*) – responded to the veteran's speech, presumably to show their support.[11] The outrage the veteran's treatment produced surely demonstrates that *nexi* were not supposed to be kept in chains. The conclusion that the Roman people (and magistrates) were more upset by the fact that a veteran had been placed in an inferior category than by the suffering accompanying the practice of enslavement for debt seems unavoidable.

In Livy's account of domestic events in 385 BC the centre of attention was a centurion who had been condemned for debt (*iudicatum pecuniae*; 6.14.3–10). The politician M. Manlius Capitolinus, seeing the man being led away, delivered a rousing speech about the arrogance of the patricians, the inhumanity of the money-lenders and the sufferings of the common people.[12] Manlius made a successful emotional appeal by playing on the similar sounding words 'to save' (*servo*) and 'slavery' (*servitus*): 'tum vero ego' inquit 'nequiquam hac dextra Capitolium arcemque servaverim, si civem commilitonemque meum tamquam Gallis victoribus captum in servitutem ac vincula duci videam' (6.14.4–5: 'In that case was it all in vain', he cried, 'that I saved the Capitol and the Citadel with this right hand, when I watch my citizen and fellow-soldier being led away into servitude and chains, as if he were taken captive by the victorious Gauls?'). He paid the amount owed by the soldier to his creditor and freed the debtor (*liberatum emittit*). Manlius acted in the capacity of a *vindex*, a redeemer who stepped forward to settle a debt in the name of the debtor. Upon regaining his freedom the man explained that his financial difficulties were the result of the interest on his loan being so high that it swallowed up the principal (6.14.7). Manlius increased his popularity with the people even further by presenting for auction an estate of his in the region of Veii, stating that he would not own property while others were being dragged away into slavery.

A decade or so later Livy described the problems concerning debt as follows. The suffering of the common people had become even worse, because by then payment had been made compulsory and immediate. Livy's text states that 'since people in debt could no longer make compensation with their property' (*cum iam ex re nihil dari posset*), 'their reputation (*fama*) and body (*corpore*) were made over and assigned to their creditors by way of satisfaction'. It is not certain whether this means that debtors could no longer pay off their debts by selling their property or that people who were bankrupt were now immediately made into bondsmen.[13] 'Penalty had taken the place of credit' (6.34.2: *poenaque in vicem fidei cesserat*). As is illustrated by his choice of *fama* ('reputation') and *fides* ('credit', but also 'trust'),[14] Livy's terminology is more rhetorical than legal, which may suggest that the original source for this account offered a highly emotional reconstruction of events. He also appears to have collapsed several developments together without explaining what exactly caused them. Significantly, Livy identifies the debtors as *iudicati atque addicti* (6.34.2) and not as *nexi*. The financial problems facing a large part of the population were so severe that it had repercussions in the political sphere: Livy concludes that the plebeians had lost all interest in contending with the patricians for political office (6.34.4). The stalemate was only resolved a couple of years later, when the Licinian-Sextian laws of 367/366 BC allowed rich plebeians access to the consulship, the highest political office, while they offered the poorest plebeians some relief from their financial problems. Any interest already paid could be deducted from the original amount and the remainder discharged in three annual instalments of equal size (6.35.5).

The next important event occurred some four decades later – the abolition of *nexum* (8.28.1–9).[15] According to Livy, this momentous event was set in motion by the way in which the money-lender Lucius Papirius treated a young man, Caius Publilius, who had been forced to hand himself over for a debt owed by his father.[16] Papirius showed no sympathy (*misericordiam*) for Publilius's youth and beauty, but instead was driven to lust. He first tried to seduce the young man with lewd conversation (*incesto sermone*), then threatened him, but with no effect. Subsequently, Papirius had the young man stripped and scourged. After this ordeal, Publilius broke free, ran into the street and publicly declaimed Papirius. A crowd assembled and expressed their sympathy (*miseratione*) for Publilius and indignation because of his injuries. Livy stresses that the crowd 'was reminded of their own condition and that of their children' (*suae condicionis liberum suorum respectu*), which may be a reference to the fact that Publilius served as a *nexus* for a debt owed by his father and that the same thing could potentially happen to them and their children as well. They rushed to the meeting-hall of the Senate and requested the consuls to immediately summon the Senate. Once the Senate was in session, the people threw themselves at the feet of the senators and pointed to the young man's mutilated back. With no further delay the Senate ordered the consuls to introduce a proposal for the people's approval that only convicted criminals should be confined in shackles and prisons. A decision was also reached with regard to the repayment of loans. When a payment on a loan was not made on the agreed date the creditor could only lay claim to the debtor's property and not to his body. Finally, all individuals currently imprisoned were freed and in future it was forbidden to enter into *nexum* (*cautumque in posterum ne necterentur*; 8.28.9).[17]

Livy's account should not be taken as a true historical account of events leading to what is conventionally called the abolition of *nexum*. His history is a string of narratives illustrating the virtues and vices of the Romans against the backdrop of Rome's rise from shepherd settlement to world power. He frames his stories within a clearly defined interpretation of the past, which in this particular case is the struggle for political freedom by the common people. The episode of Publilius is represented as an event which reinforces the liberty of the Roman people, a clear reference to the freedom which the Romans had enjoyed since the establishment of the Republic in 509 BC, but which was still incomplete. Furthermore, Livy's history is replete with incidents that routinely involve sexual transgressions committed against usually young and female victims. Each incident leads to significant political and social changes. The story of Caius Publilius is a variant on this pattern only in the sense that the victim is a young man.

It is essential here to clarify the precise nature of the events of 326 BC, and for this we have to re-examine Livy's text in more detail:

Iussique consules ferre ad populum ne quis, nisi qui noxam meruisset, donec poenam
lueret, in compedibus aut in nervo teneretur; pecuniae creditae bona debitoris, non
corpus obnoxium esset. Ita nexi soluti, cautumque in posterum ne necterentur.

(the consuls were ordered to put in front of the people a proposal that no one should
be kept in shackles or in prison, except those who had committed a crime, for the
time during which they underwent punishment; and that for money lent the debtor's
property, but not his person, should be distrainable. In this way the debt-slaves were
released, and it was decreed that no one in future should become a *nexus*.)

Livy's text lists three separate regulations:

Only criminals are to be put in chains or in prison;

If a loan is not repaid the creditor can seize the debtor's property in order to
compel payment of debts, but not his person;

All *nexi* are freed and in future no one should be able to become one.

Relying purely on a translation can confuse the interpretation of key events. One
of the pivotal sentences in Livy's passage, that which introduces the history of
Caius Publilius, is: *quod necti desierunt*, which the Loeb-edition translates as
'for men ceased to be imprisoned for debt', and the Penguin edition has as 'the
abolition of enslavement for debt'. However, as in the case of the anonymous
veteran described earlier, that of Caius Publilius does not concern *nexum* per se,
but a situation whereby somebody who is repaying a debt is improperly reduced
to the inferior category of debtor. Livy's readers were well aware that whipping
was a criminal violation of citizenship that reduced Publilius to the status of a
slave, the only people in Roman society answerable with their bodies for criminal offences. A re-examination is also required of Livy's report on the proposals
submitted by the consuls to the people's assembly which ratified them as the
lex Poetelia. How do these measures clarify our understanding of the practice of
nexum given the two different categories of debt-bondsmen that possibly blurred
for Livy whose chief concern was that one group was systematically reduced to
the second? Assuming that Livy may have employed the terms in a non-technical
sense, we must treat his use of *nexus* or *nectus* with extreme caution.

The first measure proposed by the Senate and accepted by the people's
assembly stated that only criminals should be kept as prisoners, thus making it
impossible for indebted individuals to be kept in their creditors' homes. This benefited only wrongly imprisoned *nexi* who under normal circumstances retained
their status as Roman citizens while working off their debt. The other category of
debtors who were kept in chains, the *addicti*, benefited from this measure only if
proven not to be 'criminals'. However, the measure put an end to an excess rather
than abolish a particular procedure. The third measure declared that all *nexi* be

released (*nexi soluti*) and decreed that in future no one should become a *nexus*. This suggests that the verbal agreement called *nexum* should no longer be entered into, but how is the state capable of making sure that this did not happen?

I have reserved for last discussion of the second measure, because it suggests that what happened in 326 BC was the abolition of *nexum*. Livy states the following in Latin: '*pecuniae creditae bona debitoris, non corpus, obnoxium esset*', which I translate as follows: 'The consuls were ordered to carry a proposal that "for a loan (*pecuniae creditae*) the property (*bona*) of the debtor (*debitoris*), not his body (*non corpus*), should be distrainable (*obnoxium*)."' This means that the creditor could seize the property of the debtor to compel him to pay back the money that was owed, but he could not take his body. Whatever the meaning of this claim, Livy's own history provides clear evidence that the practice of imprisoning citizens continued unabated, which suggests that the same could be argued for debt bondage.[18] This appears confirmed by an event set in 216 BC, a century after the abolition of *nexum*. In the immediate aftermath of Rome's defeat against Hannibal at Cannae the dictator M. Iunius Pera issued a decree which promised exculpation and release from debt to individuals who were in prison for capital crimes or for not paying their debts, on condition that they agreed to serve in the army. Six thousand individuals answered the call and were given weapons that had been taken from the Gauls and displayed in the triumph of C. Flaminius of 223 BC (23.14.3–4). Livy labels the individuals who were kept in chains for not having repaid their debts *iudicati*, while Valerius Maximus calls them *addicti* (7.6.1).

Further evidence comes from Varro who refers to *obaerarii*, a term with a similar meaning to that of *addicti*. The supporters of Catiline, a renegade senator who attempted to overthrow the Roman government in 63 BC, consistently refer to debt and the cruelty of money-lenders as reasons for their willingness to join Catiline's movement.[19] Columella, the writer of an agricultural manual during the reign of Nero, launches an attack on wealthy individuals who possess more estates than they can visit and either abandon them to be trampled by cattle and wild beasts 'or keep them under cultivation with citizens enslaved for debt and slave chain gangs (*aut occupatos nexu civium et ergastulis tenent*)' (1.3.12).

The second part of Finley's argument maintains that in the years after the abolition of *nexum* in 326 BC chattel slavery increased dramatically. Rome was engaged in wars with the express objective, so Finley hints, to replenish one involuntary workforce with another. Finley viewed the labour demands of the Roman aristocracy as so extensive that they needed an alternative supply of compulsory labour to replace the debt-slaves. In order to substantiate his argument Finley points to the nearly 40,000 Samnite warriors which Rome acquired as captives between 298 and 290 BC, a figure which he labels in his own words 'as maybe not accurate, but also not complete'.[20] Finley took the figure of 40,000 from a work on mass enslavement in the Hellenistic-Roman world whose author had collated it from references in Livy.[21] The best way to show that this figure is unrealistically high is by drawing on research on the size of the late third-century Roman population undertaken by economic historians and demographers Elio Lo Cascio and Walter Scheidel. They independently assume that between 215 and 212 BC between 10 and 12 per cent of Rome's population served in the army. Scheidel estimates that in 215 BC Rome had a population of close to one million, comprising 690,000 women and children and 190,000 adult males.[22] In the light of these assertions, the claim, based on Livy's account – that during the Third Samnite War some 100,000 Samnites died on the battlefield and a further 70,000 were enslaved – must be deemed an exaggeration. Finley, however, uncritically accepted the numbers. In the absence of similar figures for the period before 326 BC it is impossible to firmly establish whether an increase in the number of slaves had also taken place earlier. However, slaves may already have been plentiful some decades before the 'abolition of *nexum*'. In 357 BC one of the consuls proposed a law which introduced, for the first time in Roman history, a tax on the manumission of slaves. The senators decided on the measure in order to replenish the empty treasury (Livy; 7.16.7). Thus the introduction of the law presupposes that the slave population had reached a considerable size and that owners were manumitting their slaves at a high enough rate to replenish the state treasury.[23]

Conclusion

The main purpose of this preliminary investigation has been to suggest that the abolition of *nexum* and Moses Finley's argument that its demise and the rise of chattel slavery in early Rome were connected merit re-examination. I have singled out two focal points which in my opinion are crucial for reassessing the relationship between debt bondage and chattel slavery, without entertaining the expectation that all the problems involving the procedure of *nexum* and its abolition have now been resolved. My first focus was the continuation of enslavement caused by debt in the period after 326 BC. It needs to be established in more detail whether the conditions for debt and slavery were the same or similar to those in place before 326, but for the moment it seems that there is enough evidence to make the claim that enslavement for debt did not disappear after 326. The continuing enslavement of citizens for debt makes it very difficult to entertain the idea that an important pool of involuntary labour had become completely dried up, necessitating the introduction of other forms of involuntary labour. I want to suggest that it is even more rewarding to re-examine the Samnite Wars in Roman history from the perspective of the rise of chattel slavery. For this argument Finley relied on the numbers of Samnites captured in war supplied by the historian Livy. However, the numbers must be deemed unrealistically high, especially when viewed against plausible reconstructions of the size of the Roman population around the end of the third century, almost a century after the Samnite Wars. By that time Rome had 190,000 adult male citizens and perhaps a military potential of close to 100,000 soldiers. The numbers of Samnite soldiers that were enslaved (40,000, if those taken in sieges are counted; 70,000, if all the captives are added up) and those that were killed in battle (100,000), both culled from Livy, suggest that the Samnites were completely wiped out by the Romans. I am quite prepared to believe that chattel slaves became more important after 326, but that the scale on which this happened has been exaggerated. Finally, I think it is unnecessary to argue that chattel slavery replaced debt bondage to supply the labour demands of the Roman aristocracy. Chattel slavery was already important enough in 357 BC to justify the introduction of a tax on manumission as a means to replenish the empty Roman war-chest. This last item complicates the belief in an abrupt transition from debt bondage to chattel slavery.

2 SLAVERY, DEBT AND BONDAGE: THE MEDITERRANEAN AND THE EURASIA CONNECTION FROM THE FIFTEENTH TO THE EIGHTEENTH CENTURY

Alessandro Stanziani

The history of bondage in Eurasia provides useful insights into the link between various forms of bondage and war captives, on the one hand, and slavery on the other hand. Two main sources are usually mentioned in studies of ancient, medieval and modern slavery: debt (widely conceived as a form of individual and/ or social obligation) and capture by war parties or belligerent armies. Roughly speaking, the first is somewhat internal to a given society while the second is generated through transgression of territorial boundaries.[1]

This taxonomy requires some important qualifications; for example, war captives may be offered for ransom, but they may also enter the category of slaves by being sold: sale of captives within the internal market of the victorious war party was quite widespread. However, this shift requires the agreement of the leaders of the clan or of the state. That is to say that the boundary between a war captive and a debt slave is flexible and depends on the relative power of military commanders, political leaders, slave brokers and slave owners in negotiating amongst themselves the disposition of war captives.

In turn, debt and 'obligated' slaves cover a much wider and debated category extending from debt bondage to voluntary or involuntary enslavement and finally to pawnship. In this respect, Eurasia and the Mediterranean provide a stimulating historical environment in which to discuss the appropriateness of the terminology adumbrated above and whether envisioning the phenomena encompassed by such wording is warranted historically.

The import of Russian, Tatar and Central Asian slaves into the Mediterranean is usually depicted as either an expression of colonial slavery on the one hand[2] or of Russian serfdom on the other.[3] The few available studies on this topic have focused mostly on imports by Ottoman[4] and European powers, but they have neglected Russian sources and the existence of forms of bondage and eventually slavery in Russia itself before serfdom. I will develop a fully integrated approach using previously untapped Russian sources (including translations from Persian, Chinese and Turkish- and Italian-Genoese archives in particular). In doing so, I will bring together the origin of war captives and their destinations, and in addition study local forms of bondage and slavery in Inner Asia. Over centuries, if not millennia, war captives, bandits and nomadic powers were the rule and not the exception in geo-political and economic equilibriums.[5] From the twelfth to eighteenth century, captives and slaves were part of the common world of the Mongols, Berbers, Ottomans, Chinese and European powers. All the groups took part in razzias and the trade of captives while making use of slaves. Indeed, captives and the slave trade were hardly isolated from trade in general. There was nothing like the trans-Atlantic slave trade in pre-modern Central Eurasia. From the eleventh to the nineteenth century we can identify three major routes for trading slaves and goods in this area: the Chinese–Russian, the Russian–Islamic–Mediterranean and the Russian–Persian–Indian routes. We will follow their expansion and evolution, concluding that the captive-slave trade and its timing necessitate a re-evaluation of major shifts in world history, namely, the presumed decline of nomadic powers on the one hand, and that of the Mediterranean to the benefit of the Atlantic on the other. Both of these outdated and constantly reiterated historiographical assumptions are Eurocentric and ignore the persistent institutional and economic power of Central Asia.

The sources for the study of bondage and the slave trade in Inner Asia raise distinct problems, since so much of the paperwork has not survived and those documents that have are in Middle-Russian palaeography. Despite official rules, war captives were not systematically recorded, and therefore their real number is substantially greater than what extant records tell us. We also lack sources from the Central Asian powers.[6]

This lacuna does not apply to the other important powers in the area under study, namely Byzantium, Venice, Genoa and, later, the Ottoman Empire, for these polities left an important archival legacy concerning war captives and the Eurasian slave trade. Ottomanists have already provided important studies on the trade in slaves between Crimea, Russia, Central Asia and the Ottoman Empire, in particular for the seventeenth to nineteenth century;[7] historians of medieval and early modern Venice and Genoa have also produced some remarkable studies. Sources from Genoa and Venice are not only in Latin (though not great in number), but also in pre-modern Italian. Much of our knowledge about the trade of Caffa is derived from the commercial deeds and contracts drawn up by the Genoese notary Lamberto di Sambuceto between 1128 and 1290.[8] A precise date for the foundation of the Genoese colony at Caffa on the Crimean coast cannot be given. The first historical reference to Caffa in the Genoese chronicles is the dispatch of three vessels by the consul of the port, Paolino Doria, to the aid of Tripoli in 1289.[9]

War Captives at a Crossroad of Empires

Central Asian Slaves for the Mediterranean, from the Thirteenth to the Fifteenth Century

The importance of captives and slaves in the expanding territory of Russia reflected changing power constellations in Central Asia, the southern Balkans, Crimea and the Mediterranean. The history of war captives in Russia and Asia is linked to that of the main trade routes and changing geopolitical situations over the centuries. The first phase spanned the thirteenth and fourteenth centuries and was mostly connected to the Silk Road; the second was from the fourteenth to the sixteenth century and followed a Russian–Iranian–Indian path; and the third was from the sixteenth to the eighteenth century and was linked to the expansion of Russia and the integration of Mongol khanates. Each of these waves had commercial and geo-political dimensions; our aim is to add the ransom-captive and slave markets to the picture and thereby shed new light on the entire process.

The origin of the words *esclaves* and *sclavus* in use in medieval and early mod-ern Italy reflects less the linguistic and legal heritage of ancient Rome than it does a link with the market for persons of servile status from the Slavic areas.[10] The slave trade had an economic prop in traffic from Central Asia to the Black Sea[11] and in the growing presence of Venetians and Genoese in this area.[12] It was not only in Venice, but also in Genoa that traders sold Circassian and Abkhaz-ian slaves previously bought mostly in Caspian and Black Sea ports. We have evidence from as early as 1246 that the Mongols sold Greeks, Bulgarians, Ruthe-nians and Rumanians to merchants from Genoa, Pisa and Venice, who in turn sold them to the Saracens. The Italians had purchased these slaves in the north-ern Black Sea ports of Maurocastro, at the mouth of the Dniester, and Caffa in Crimea, and it was in the latter that the Genoese received permission from the Mongol khan in 1266 to establish a colony. In Caffa, Genoese merchants bought Circassians, Tatars, Russians, Iranians and Poles, among others. The other centre of the slave trade in the Black Sea region in the fourteenth century was the Crimean port of Tana, which the Venetians established in 1333. In spite of the unpredictable attitude of the Mongol ruler of Tana towards Europeans, and resulting breaks in trading activities, Tana remained a place of high strategic value, ensuring better access to the Oriental markets and the Far East than the Genoese had in Caffa. The potentially high profits to be expected from trips to the eastern Black Sea area can be seen in the increased revenue of *incanti* for gal-leys bound for Romania in the first half of the fourteenth century and then again after the 1370s. The main trading goods were furs, wine, grain and slaves, the lat-ter becoming increasingly important in the late fourteenth century when Venice needed slaves for its colony on Crete. As a consequence of the growing Otto-man menace, the Venetian trade shifted to the western Black Sea (Maurocastro and the Danube estuary) and to Egypt and the Middle East during the first half of the fifteenth century. At Kilia, Tatar subjects were sold by their compatriots to Genoese, Venetians and Greeks from Constantinople.[13] Genoa, Venice and Catalonia were also in competition for the trade in slaves. In 1263, Byzantium reopened the trade between Egypt and the Black Sea, and Genoa became the first supplier of slaves for both the armies and harems of the Mameluk sultans. Male slaves were also sent to the alum mines of Genoa at Focea and, of course, to Genoa and Spain. Women were particularly in demand for domestic services, while men were valued for ship work or sold to Spain. In early 1400, almost 10 per cent of Genoa's population – some 4,000 to 5,000 people – was unfree.[14] The revenue from the *gabella capitum* of Caffa allows us to calculate the following numbers of slaves sold: in 1374, at least 3,285; in 1385/6, about 1,500; in 1387/8, about 1,600; in 1381/2, at least 3,800. During the fifteenth century, the *gabella* was farmed out. For 1411, one can assume a number of 2,900 slaves sold; from the 1420s until 1477, 2,000 per year at most passed through this port. The fall of Constantinople provoked a massive decline (to about 400 or 600 slaves per year). Thus, during a single century the numbers fell to around 80 per cent, with a decline already apparent before 1453; both the *gabella* incomes of February and June follow this trend.[15]

As for later trans-Atlantic slavery, in this case too it was war captives and people already enslaved in inland areas who were then sold to Genoa. Yet according to Genoese sources, 'voluntary' enslavement was equally widespread – that is, people who were still legally 'free' in Caffa and were seized there by Genoans. However, neither Genoese nor Venetian traders organized expeditions with this specific aim in Central Asia,[16] probably due to the small scale and high transaction costs of the operations. It was simply not worth extending into Central Asia the credit and commercial arrangements in place on the Black Sea, and this was all the more true for slaves, a minor market when compared to that of luxury items. The caravan trade, much too wide-ranging for European powers, was solidly based on the interaction between non-pastoral nomadic activities and caravan merchants. Increasingly stable communities in Central Asia offered a reliable environment for such activities. The Islamization of the area further drove this process – which did not, however, immediately marginalize Venice and Genoa; they even benefited at first from the decline of Byzantium, not only in terms of commercial trade, but also with regard to the captives market.[17] At the same time, the rivalry between Venice and Genoa prevented either from controlling the Black Sea trade. In 1462, after the fall of Constantinople, Genoese Caffa placed itself under the protection of Poland. From 1466 to 1474, intervention by the Genoese became particularly marked. Ultimately, Muhammad the Conqueror captured Caffa in 1475 and took control of the trade of goods and slaves from Central Asia. In 1459, the Venetian senate lamented the scarcity of slaves, mostly Slavs and Tatars, being sent to the Near and Middle East, in particular to Egypt and Turkey.[18] Genoa therefore turned to other sources, that is, to Islamic Spain and North Africa, where it acquired slaves to sell in Seville and in the Canary Islands. It was at this point that Genoa tried to enter the market for slaves to the New World but was quickly overtaken by Spanish, Portuguese and, finally, British vessels.[19]

At first glance this outcome would seem to confirm the traditional view in historiography of a progressive shift from the Mediterranean to the Atlantic.[20] According to this view, the decline of Venice and the Italian republic would have been linked to the rising power of Spain and the Western European powers (Portugal, the Netherlands, Britain, France), which was in turn connected to the discovery of the Americas. This view, while not totally incorrect, is nonetheless a prejudiced one insofar as it ignores what was transpiring in Central Eurasia, Russia and the Ottoman Empire.

Tatars, Russia, and the Ottoman Empire Slave Trade, from the Sixteenth to Nineteenth Century

The dissolution of the Golden Horde produced not only fully nomadic steppe societies such as the Nogays (a confederation of Turkic and Mongol tribes), but also city-states such as the Crimean and Kazan khanates. Turkic Kazakhs, Bashkirs and Tatars competed with Mongol Kalmyks. In the late fifteenth century, the alliance between Crimea and Muscovy continued to be based on their mutual interests against their respective foes, the Great Horde and Poland. With the disbandment of the Horde in 1506, Crimea, Moscow, the Nogays and Lithuania remained the major players in the region. Moscow actually began its real expansion eastward by conquering the steppe state of Kazan in the mid-sixteenth century. This marked the end of Muscovy's active participation in steppe politics for over seventy years; while this state continued to expand into Siberia in the north-east, during this period it turned its focus westward and began to fight against Polish and Lithuanian states. In pursuing this strategy, Moscow was first allied with Crimea against Poland; then it weakened its relations with Crimea while strengthening ties with the Ottoman sultan. At the same time, the nomadic Nogays, unable to resist the predations of the Kazakhs, abandoned their pastures east of the Yaik River and moved west, crossing the Volga into the pastures of the Astrakhan khan. The new khan of Kazan ravaged the provinces of Nizhnii Novgorod and Vladimir and moved towards Moscow. However, a confrontation was avoided insofar as Moscow and the Nogays had similar interests in the area. For Moscow, the Nogays were a critical force capable of checking Crimean raids and aiding in the conquest of Kazan.[21]

It was during this same period – as a result of their action against the Geno-ese of Crimea in 1475 – that the Ottomans made their presence more strongly felt among the Crimean Tatars and on the Pontic Steppe in general. By 1478, the Ottoman power established the right to appoint and dismiss the khans. It was thus with a single blow that Moldavian and Polish–Lithuanian access to Black Sea markets was brought to an end. By the beginning of the sixteenth century, the Black Sea had turned into an Ottoman lake.

Between 1555 and 1578, a number of events affected the Ottoman presence on the Black Sea. Firstly, Muscovy took Astrakhan in 1556. Trade ties between Muscovy and Britain commenced about the same time, and soon the English Muscovy Company was sending its traders into Persia in the quest for spices and silk. British woollens, hardware and firearms in turn whetted the appetite of the shahs. However, in Istanbul, despite initial concerns over Moscow's conquest of Kazan and Astrakhan, the issue of containing Muscovite ambitions did not become a priority as Istanbul was engaged with the Habsburg power to the west and Persia to the east. By the early 1560s, the sultan had adopted a more aggres-sive attitude and laid claim to Astrakhan, but war was avoided for the sake of the shared geopolitical and commercial interests of Moscow and Istanbul. Then, between 1575 and 1578, the Ottomans established their suzerainty over the Crimean khanate, while the long war of 1579–90 resulted in the establishment of Ottoman direct rule over much of the Caucasus. This was all the more important for Moscow because it suffered two humiliating defeats at the hands of Poland–Lithuania and Sweden in the 1570s and early 1580s. From that time onwards, the Nogays were increasingly divided and were ultimately debilitated by the arrival of the Kalmyks in the 1630s. This did not prevent them from launching raids into Russia, however, prompting Moscow to undertake a new initiative: the construc-tion of fortification lines in the south. This went along with colonization of the region and explains the refusal of central and local authorities to return fugitive peasants from central Russian areas to their legitimate masters.

Military instability in Eurasia during the sixteenth and seventeenth centuries – and not European expansion – reduced long-distance trade while benefitting the market for captives.[22] Muscovite rulers sought first to expand westward at the expense of the Polish–Lithuanian state. It was during this effort that they occasionally allied with one or another khanate to exploit their internal divi-sions; during a campaign in Lithuania in 1501, for instance, Crimean Tatars seized 50,000 Lithuanian captives.

During the second half of the sixteenth century, Russia once again moved eastward, into Siberia and certain Cossack areas, namely the territory of the Iaik Cossacks.[23] The resulting prisoners of war and captives held for ransom fed a consistent market for slaves. It is symptomatic that the Russian word for captive, *iasyr* or *esyr'*, was a direct transliteration of the Turkish and Arab equivalent used in Central Asia and the Ottoman Empire.[24]

In the fourteenth century, some 2,000 Slavic slaves a year were sold by Crimean Tatars to Ottomans, with that figure rising in the fifteenth century. The Tatars either bought them in Central Asian markets or enslaved them directly.[25] Slave-raiding forays into Muscovy reached crisis proportions after 1475, when the Ottomans took over the Black Sea slave trade from the Genoese and the Crimeans began slave raiding as a major industry, especially between 1514 and 1654. In 1529, half of the slaves in the Ottoman Crimea were identified as coming from Ukraine and Muscovy. Between 150,000 and 200,000 Russians were captured in the first half of the seventeenth century.[26]

Peace treaties did sometimes lead to the release of slaves, however. In 1618, for example, the Nogays signed a treaty with Moscow and released 15,000 Russian captives.[27] In 1661, the Kalmyks did the same for Russian captives they had previously acquired from the Tatars; in 1678, these same Kalmyks signed a treaty with Moscow and again returned Russian prisoners.[28] Certain rules governed the criteria for redeeming Russian captives. Thus, the Kalmyk Mongols agreed in 1661 to free Russians whom they had acquired through Tatars and in 1678 to return Russians whom they themselves had taken captive.[29] The Russians themselves were redeeming slaves from Turkistan as late as the mid-nineteenth century.[30]

The *Ulozhenie* of 1649 devoted a whole section (number eight) to the issue of ransoming Russian captives.[31] A ransom tax was introduced for this purpose in 1551 and remained in place until 1679. The ransom was stipulated in accordance with the captive's status; for example, the ransom for a high-ranking Russian boyar, B. V. Sheremetev, was estimated at 60,000 silver thaler. At the other extreme of the ransom scale, peasants were ransomed at about fifteen rubles per person.[32] Those who were not ransomed became slaves and were assigned various duties. In the Crimea, some were employed in agriculture or used as interpreters and guides to lead war parties into Russian territory. Those sold on the slave markets of the Ottoman Empire or Central Asian khanates were employed as craftsmen, labourers and domestics.[33] Fugitives returning to Russia often gained the protection of local authorities, provoking strong protests from Nogay leaders who laid claim to these very same fugitives.[34]

Conversely, above all during the seventeenth century, Russians seized war prisoners and captives for ransom from both Muslim and Catholic areas. According to the *Sudebnik* of 1550, captives were intended to serve the elite as administrative assistants or servants. Their maximum term of service was supposed to be until the death of their master, but they could also be redeemed by an agreement between the Russian state and their country of origin. If they had converted to Orthodox Christianity, they might be emancipated, although this was not mandatory. Such a decree might be issued by the state, as occurred in 1558 when the government ordered the manumission of any war slave who converted to Orthodoxy so that he might enter the tsar's service.

If war captives were not redeemed or returned to their country of origin, they then entered the category of full or limited *kholopstvo* (forms of bondage in Russia, ranging from chattel slavery to indentured contracts, debt bondage, etc.). Since the early seventeenth century, the state had tried to compile a register for military captives so that the central authorities could eventually return them to their home countries in cases of diplomatic agreement. However, several sources note the problems encountered by the Moscow authorities in ensuring compliance with these norms, and servitude for war captives persisted. After the conclusion of the Smolensk War in October 1634, the government ordered the release of all Poles and Lithuanians who had been seized. The effect of this provision was quite limited, however, and in 1637/8 another decree was promulgated on foreign military captives, insisting that they had the right to choose whether to return home or stay in Muscovy.

After the Thirteen Years War (1654–67), Lithuanian and Polish captives distributed to members of the upper and middle service classes were not registered by the latter, who tended, in practice, to treat them as genuine slaves.[35] In 1655, Poles, Lithuanians and miscellaneous others, both adults and children, were openly sold in the streets of Moscow.[36] As a result of this war, many people were sold in Russia, at times becoming *kholopy*.[37] The Nogays, who had joined the Muscovite forces, purchased German and Polish prisoners in Moscow.[38] It was not infrequently that Muslims were captured and occasionally sold in violation of Islamic law, prompting the Ottoman and Islamic authorities to send injunctions to Moscow in order to redeem them without compensation.[39]

In 1690, the Russian government returned to its position of 1556, decreeing that military captives were to be manumitted by the Slavery Chancellery upon the death of their owners. As in previous times, this process went along with a renewal of trade routes. From the late sixteenth century, delegations of traders had regularly travelled from Central Asia to Muscovy and – though less often – in the opposite direction. Bukharan interest in trade with Western Siberia also dates from the late sixteenth century. By the late seventeenth century, Muscovy was also trading with China, often through the mediation of Bukharan traders who were familiar with all the major routes between Muscovy and China. Some of these routes followed traditional itineraries, leading down along the Volga to Central Asia and then on to Xinjiang and China.[40]

In the early eighteenth century, though with less and less frequency, Russians were seized as captives or slaves. In 1717, the Kalmyks, this time temporarily allied to the Kuban Nogays, brought back 12,000 captives seized in the middle Volga provinces. At the same, in 1742, the Karakalpaks captured 1,000 Russian women and children in Siberia, and between 3,000 and 4,000 Russians are estimated to have become captives of the Karakalpaks.[41] This occurred at a moment in history when the Russian authorities were adopting an ambivalent attitude towards the Kazakhs, wishing as they did to dominate the area.[42]

However, by the end of the eighteenth century, the only slaves and ransom-captives in the Russian Empire were Tatars or Circassians. Quantitatively, the most important traffic in slave chattel and captives occurred with the Ottoman Empire. The Russian Empire interacted with Islamic regions where chattel slavery was common and regarded as the only legitimate form of coerced labour under Islamic law. Muslim Tatars of the Crimea raided widely for Russian subjects as well as other eastern Slavs, Poles and Lithuanians, and they exported most of their captives to the Ottomans.[43] In 1529, half of all the slaves in the Ottoman Crimea were identified as coming from Ukraine and Muscovy; the other half were Circassians.[44] From the 1570s, about 20,000 slaves were sold annually in the port of Caffa on the Black Sea.[45] Until the early seventeenth century, Russians and above all Cossacks also sold captives to the Tatars or directly to the Ottomans.[46] The Ottoman rules on slave trading distinguished between slaves who were brought from the Tatar and Circassian areas and those from Ottoman territories such as Azov and Taman. The tax on the latter was half of that on the former group.[47]

The Russian Empire also gradually incorporated areas where local populations had long practised various forms of servitude and slave trading.[48] Many inhabitants of the Caucasus – especially Christian Georgians and Armenians, together with heterodox Muslim Circassians – were sent as slaves to the Ottoman Empire, whether overland or across the Black Sea. For the first three quarters of the nineteenth century, the Ottomans imported between 16,000 and 18,000 such slaves every year.[49] Some male slaves entered the servile administrative elite of the Ottoman Empire, while many women ended up in the harems of the rich and powerful. Circassian families at times sold their own children to intermediaries, who transported them to Ottoman territory. Under British pressure, the flow of slaves from the Caucasus was suspended in 1854, but it grew again after the end of the Crimean War. Moreover, the brutal Russian conquest of Circassia led to an influx of between half a million and a million refugees into the Ottoman domain between 1854 and 1865, of whom perhaps a tenth were of servile status.[50] These massive migrations increased the number of agricultural slaves, which had been relatively few in number previously (with the exception of Egypt and Oriental Anatolia).[51]

Conclusion

Slaves were present in Russia and Inner Asia and were typically taken, as in other historical situations, in frontier raids in areas where boundaries were uncertain, or during military operations in the strictest sense. From a geopolitical standpoint, these forms of slavery were linked to conflicts within the Islamic world, between Russia and Central Asian powers, as well as to the conflicts that tore Europe apart in the seventeenth century.[52] At the same time, the existence of this phenomenon does not mean that this large geographical area was necessarily backward, for flourishing trade and vital markets developed despite raids and military expeditions. The markets for slaves and products were more complementary than synonymous, underscoring the fact that nomadic powers and territorial states were much more integrated with one another than is usually asserted in the historiography. One cannot simply associate captives and slaves with political instability or, for that matter, with stable powers, insofar as bondage could enhance or burden both configurations.

From this standpoint, the history of slavery in Russia and Central Asia emphasizes what previous studies on Mediterranean slavery have already done: the importance of pre-colonial slavery, in particular outside the trans-Atlantic route, and, therefore, the role these previous routes played in terms of the organization of labour, legal rules and trans-national powers. At the same time, the importance of numbers and the role of coerced labour points to major differences between pre-modern slavery and colonial slavery. The slave trade in Central Asia and Russia cannot be interpreted according to the trans-Atlantic paradigm; the main differences can be summarized as follows: (1) there was no plantation system; (2) there were no merchants and routes specialized in slave trading; (3) war captives played a dominant role; (4) there were not local conditions that enabled chattel enslavement, as was often the case in the trans-Atlantic trade, where war captives seized by African groups were sold to European traders; and (5) slaves played only a minor role in agriculture in comparison with domestic and elite slaves.

The slave trade in Russia and Central Asia was thus connected to the stabilization of territorial powers, the evolution of warfare and monopolies on violence. Indeed, the history of war captives in Russia is linked to that of the incredible expansion of Muscovy and Russia, and to the evolution of inner social relationships. Between the thirteenth and the sixteenth century, captives and slaves were commonly exchanged between the Khanates, Safavid Persia, Byzantium, India, Genoa, and Venice. Russia in particular was able to stop traffic in war captives and to eliminate contiguous nomadic power, but only at the turn of the eighteenth and nineteenth centuries, at a moment when it still tolerated the important traffic in Circassian slaves to the Ottoman Empire. This ambivalent attitude was coupled with the stabilization, on the one hand, of Russia on the Eurasiatic chess-board and, on the other hand, of legalized social hierarchies within Russia. The decline in war captives as a source of slaves followed in Central Asia and Eastern Europe the same path as elsewhere in the Mediterranean and in Asia: increasingly centralized states established a monopoly on power and evinced nomadic powers and pirates which had previously been used and even encouraged in geo-political games.

3 CLIENTSHIP, SOCIAL INDEBTEDNESS AND STATE-CONTROLLED EMANCIPATION OF AFRICANS IN THE LATE OTTOMAN EMPIRE

Michael Ferguson

In the nineteenth century, the Ottoman state began a process of reform and reorganization that involved a dramatic intervention into hitherto unregulated aspects of the lives of all people under its authority.[1] By mid-century, it had also become involved in the regulation of the slave trade and the fate of emancipated slaves. Indeed, although private owners were, and continued to be, responsible for most emancipations, state-initiated emancipations reached unparalleled levels from the third quarter of the nineteenth century. This essay examines why and how at this time the Ottoman state intervened and shaped the lives of many emancipated African slaves under its auspices. I argue that, while all aspects of Ottoman life were coming under greater official surveillance and regulation at this time, state intervention and its influence on the lives of emancipated slaves was unique in that it was legitimized through the concept of social indebtedness; upon emancipation, a former slave was obliged through social and religious traditions to become a client of its emancipator *cum* patron. These incursions into previously private social relationships were justified by the Ottoman state through a discourse of benevolence. When examining this intervention in the context of the broader changes in the nineteenth-century Ottoman Empire, it becomes clear that the discourse of benevolence was used, as in other aspects of Ottoman life, to justify and fulfil the objectives of maintaining order, expanding the army, creating a large tax base, solving labour shortages and removing other potential *loci* of power.

This chapter aims to push the debates about both indebtedness and slavery in the late Ottoman Empire in new directions. Firstly, I hope to move the discussion about indebtedness beyond solely the economic realm to one that cannot be quantified, but operates within a moral economy of overlapping religious and traditional practices. Admittedly, examining such a metaphysical thing is challenging as it inherently lacks concrete data to support it. Secondly, this chapter examines the history of slaves and slavery situated in the context of the rapidly changing late Ottoman Empire. Studies on this topic have treated slavery and

slaves in isolation, as an 'institution' divorced from late Ottoman society, politics, economics and culture. Likewise, many general studies on the history of the
Ottoman Empire fail to bring slaves and slavery into their analysis.[2]

Slavery, Emancipation, Clientship and Social Indebtedness

Before continuing it is worth acknowledging the traditional form of indebtedness in the Ottoman Empire most often studied, a type of economic indebtedness
known as the *mukātaba*. It has an extensive history stretching back throughout
the various empires in Muslim history (indeed it is discussed in the Quran) and
in the formative period of Ottoman historiography it was examined as part of
the history of labour and agricultural conditions.[3] The *mukātaba* is a contract
between two people wherein one signee is enslaved to the other for a set amount
of money. The enslaved is only set free when their dues, often in kind, are paid to
the other. This could be anything from harvesting a certain amount of crop, producing a certain amount of a handicraft, or general work for a specified amount
of time. This arrangement is rather unique in that it is voluntary, as both parties
work together to agree on the terms and conditions of the contract and thus
forms a type of voluntary indebtedness. One thing to note is that unlike simple
enslavement, this type does give the enslaved a certain amount of rights and protection, including, in theory, the prohibition of sex with female slaves. In many
cases entering a *mukātaba* contract might have provided a level of security and
stability. When the set out task is completed, the enslaved person is set free to
their own devices.[4] While this contract represents a formal and clearly recog-
nizable type of indebtedness, as this chapter shows, it is not the only type that
existed in the late Ottoman period.

The uniqueness of the Ottoman state's intervention into the process of emancipation and how its actions were legitimized through social indebtedness can
only be understood in the context of historical developments in the late Ottoman Empire, notably with regard to traditional methods of emancipation and
post-emancipation relations between master and slave. In the mid-nineteenth
century, the Ottoman Empire occupied much of the Eastern Mediterranean,
and portions of the Balkan Peninsula, Anatolia, the Middle East and North
Africa. The Ottoman elite ruled over a religiously and ethnically diverse popu-
lace including African slaves.

Unlike the enslaved Africans brought to the Americas, those brought to the
Ottoman Empire were mostly female and largely used as domestic servants or
became wives in elite households.[5] They originated from lands as disparate as the
territory around Lake Chad, the sources of the Nile and the interior of Indian
Ocean Africa.[6] Demand for African slaves dramatically increased in the nineteenth century for two main reasons. First, the expansion of the modern capitalist

world economy created a new Ottoman business class with a taste for luxury items, including slaves which had previously only been available to traditional elites.[7] Secondly, transportation innovations, such as the steamship, enabled merchants to move more slaves faster and across greater distances than ever before.[8]

Traditionally, slave manumission was largely a private affair. Only in cases of the death of a master, or the maltreatment of a slave, would an outside party, generally the local Muslim court, become involved. It was, nevertheless, widely practised and by the mid-nineteenth century a master would commonly manumit his or her African slave after some six to ten years of service.[9]

What is here referred to as 'social indebtedness' emerged out of the traditional obligations an emancipated slave – except those who had borne their master's child, married him or been married off to someone else – owed to their former master. The post-emancipation duties of master and slave are clearly laid out in both the Quran and early juridical texts which state that, upon emancipation, slaves should acquire the same full legal capacity as the freeborn.[10] However, they also imply an enduring, albeit informal, bond between the descendants of the master and those of the slave based on the gratitude of the latter for the act of manumission.[11] This bond, called *walā'* in Arabic, is often translated into English as 'clientship' which, however, fails to reflect its reciprocal nature. The *mawlā*, or the individual parties to a *walā'*, are described as 'higher' or 'lower' depending on their position relative to the other.[12] The bond between the two elaborated in various schools of jurisprudence, is immutable: no third party shall inherit or be transferred the rights of clientship.[13] According to one saying attributed to the prophet Mohammed, later expanded upon by jurists, this relationship should evolve towards something resembling biological kin relations. Failure to create these patron–client relations following emancipation is considered socially unacceptable.[14]

The social organization of the household facilitated the transition from enslaved to client. The household was a complex framework for organizing people, containing numerous and overlapping social, economic and political layers.[15] Jane Hathaway argues that this type of social organization was so prevalent that she refers to the 'hegemony of the households' in Ottoman provincial society.[16] The head of a household attracted and maintained clients in order to gain prestige and to cultivate social, economic, political and military influence (and thus power) for themselves and their family. Households varied in form, largely depending on the status and profession of its head. Moreover, slavery was, at its core, an important 'albeit involuntary ... means of linking individuals to households'.[17] Household clients included, but were not limited to: brothers and their families, sons and their families, male and female slaves, and wives and concubines.[18] According to Muslim tradition, the head of the household was also responsible for temporary care of orphans, travellers and the poor.[19] The household structure was designed to benefit its head in two ways: through the prestige of managing a large number of clients and as a key method of organizing their labour for his personal benefit.[20]

Post-emancipation patron–client relations were an almost natural outcome of slavery. In Ottoman society, slaves developed social, economic and emotional ties with the members of the slave-owning household. For the slave, these relationships compensated for the lack of kin relations, and only when deemed absolutely necessary would they willingly break the bond. Indeed, as Ehud Toledano emphasizes, the 'fear of losing a hard-earned reattachment ... played a major role in shaping the bank of options available to the enslaved in their new environment'.[21] This 'fear' generally continued well beyond emancipation. Failure to create a post-emancipation patron–client relationship represented for the former slave-owner and his household a loss of influence and could make the ex-slave vulnerable to poverty or re-enslavement, as going out into the world often proved to be risky, especially for females.[22]

Hence, the lasting bonds formed by slavery, combined with Muslim traditions regarding the duties of enslaver and the enslaved following emancipation, created forms of social indebtedness that, as will be shown, beginning in the third-quarter of the nineteenth century, helped legitimize the Ottoman state's involvement in the process of emancipation and the lives of the emancipated.

Ottoman State Intervention in the Slave Trade

Ottoman state intervention in the slave trade should be perceived as part of a greater process of change in the nineteenth-century Ottoman Empire. Beginning in the late eighteenth century, the Ottoman government decided to modernize and strengthen its army. This in turn necessitated major socio-economic and political reorganization, central to which was Western European political support and assistance in the form of experts, methods, techniques and capital.[23] Although by the mid-nineteenth century, the Ottoman state had begun the process of forging both a new professional army and modern state apparatuses with new power to exert direct influence over far flung provinces, they paid the price for European support. The Ottoman economy became more dependent on European trade and investment, and Western powers increasingly shaped Ottoman domestic policies.[24]

Western European, chiefly British, influence is evident in the pressure on the Ottoman state to participate in the abolitionist movement. The early nineteenth-century impetus had been on stemming the slave trade from West Africa to the Americas, but from mid-century the British began to pressure governments elsewhere to halt the trade in African slaves. By this time, Ottoman economic dependence on Britain, France and other western powers[25] was such that they had no choice but to listen to British remonstrations against the slave trade. Finally in 1857 they bowed to pressure: the Ottoman sultan issued an edict (*ferman*) which is considered the point at which the Ottoman Empire began to acquiesce to foreign abolitionist pressure. The Ottoman foreign minister explained the actions of his government to British authorities as follows:

> The [Ottoman government] is, in short, desirous of giving effect, as soon as possible, to a praiseworthy deed, so much in harmony with the dictates of humanity: indeed, as a preliminary to the acceptance of the principle of the abolition of negro slavery, the [Ottoman government] had already, from time to time, addressed suitable instructions on this subject to some of the provinces: but, as these were found insufficient, the definitive resolution has been adopted of abolishing the negro Slave Trade altogether, and of severely punishing those acting contrary to this interdiction. [26]

Significantly, however, the decree only sought to abolish the slave trade. It was believed it would have been too drastic to abolish slavery in one fell swoop for, as discussed above, slavery is not only permitted according to the Quran, but was also an important method of expanding a household and creating networks of dependence. Nevertheless, by the mid-nineteenth century, a strong, centralized Ottoman state was developing mechanisms, not only for halting the trade of slaves, under British pressure, but for shaping their future beyond emancipation.

State intervention in the emancipation process generally occurred when the British or other Western Europeans found slaves aboard ships or in Ottoman ports, or when slaves ran away to foreign (usually British) consuls claiming maltreatment. In both cases, the slaves were usually held by British consular officials who contacted local Ottoman authorities to request guarantees that they would be emancipated. If the Ottoman authorities determined the case to be legitimate, the slave or slaves would be manumitted by local Ottoman administrative councils, courts or police officers who issued the slave with an official document attesting to their new status, generally referred to as an *azatname*.[27] As manumission was traditionally done by slave owners, enforced if necessary by Muslim courts, state-issued manumission certificates clearly represents a significant innovation.[28] However, as British consular reports testify, local Ottoman officials were often unable or unwilling to participate in the rescue and emancipation of slaves – resulting in considerable tension between the two sides.[29]

Slaves who received their manumission certificate became technically 'free'. However freed slaves posed a problem for the Ottoman state which had to decide what to do with these homeless, poor and kinless people in a society based largely on clientship and households. Ottoman officials, with British approval, placed the majority of (mostly female) manumitted slaves as domestic servants in what they deemed 'appropriate' households whose heads agreed to pay them a wage and not re-sell them into slavery. In some cases, Africans rescued from slave ships and manumitted ended up being placed in the very households they had been destined for as slaves. Moreover, as Y. Hakan Erdem notes, official documents indicate that both the British and Ottoman governments 'had a poor notion of what was being done by its officials to free black slaves and take care of them'[30] and it is probable that once placed in a household, beyond the protection of British and Ottoman officials, many were re-sold and re-enslaved.[31] Thus, even in the era of state interventionist emancipation 'freedom' could not be guaranteed to officially manumitted slaves who continued to be incorporated within the traditional patron–client relationship in a household.

However, not all slaves were reintegrated into households. Some were 'freed' and simply left to their own devices. Perhaps this helps to explain the emergence of neighbourhoods of poor Africans in many large Ottoman cities including Chania on Crete, Istanbul and Izmir in the late nineteenth century.[32] This indicates that emancipated Africans had various strategies for gaining control of their destinies and ameliorating their conditions after emancipation – a subject which is beyond the scope of the current study.[33] However, by the late 1870s, the rise of this new urban underclass also prompted the Ottoman state to develop strategies to regulate those emancipated slaves located outside the traditional household nexus.

Ottoman State Intervention beyond Emancipation

The Ottoman state formed patron–client relations with emancipated slaves for a number of reasons. International treaties it signed for the suppression of the slave trade played an important role. In the 1857 decree, the Ottoman government promised to take an active role in feeding, housing and helping to settle emancipated slaves.[34] Subsequent treaties, including the 1880 Anglo-Ottoman Convention for the Suppression of the Slave Trade and the 1890 Brussels Act, further defined state obligations to former slaves.[35] For example, article III of the 1880 treaty states that 'the Ottoman Government engages to adopt adequate measures to insure the freedom of ... captured Africans, and to see that they are properly cared for'.[36] Moreover, British authorities repeatedly referred to this treaty when pressing the local Ottoman officials to take responsibility for the rescued slaves.

There are also indications that slaves directly sought state protection. For example, in 1837 a slave attached to the foreign minister's household petitioned the sultan for his freedom on the grounds that his master treated him poorly. His case was rejected because he had not yet reached adulthood and thus would not be 'safe' if liberated.[37] Again, in 1851, a slave in the service of another government official petitioned the sultan for his freedom. In this case, the sultan ruled in his favour and upon his manumission, he was enrolled in the army.[38] These instances reflect the influence of the imperial family which had a long tradition of manumitting slaves and giving them gifts, and often a salary and place to live.[39] However, it is clear that in the wider context of Ottoman reform and reorganization, state priorities formed the predominate factor in its new manumission policy. Thus, a detailed examination of the factors driving this new policy is in order.

Crucial to the maintenance of a strong central government in Istanbul able to effectively manage its population and resist foreign threats was the maintenance of internal order, a large tax base and, most importantly, a strong and able army. Sultan Abdülhamid II (1876–1908), during whose reign state-centred emancipation reached its climax, oversaw the largest shift in the methods and techniques of rule of the Ottoman state.[40]

First among the state's needs was effective military reform. The need to develop a modern, more effective army had been apparent since 1774, when the Russians inflicted upon the Ottoman Empire its first major defeat. Furthermore, the successes of the Mehmed Ali's army reform in Egypt through the help of western expertise and technology demonstrated first-hand the power of such an army, and at the same time showed the Ottomans it was possible to do it themselves.[41] This was often reinforced throughout the nineteenth century, especially after the war with Russia in 1878–88, when its army came within 50 kilometres of Istanbul.[42] As Selim Deringil has shown, these and other conflicts meant that late Ottoman Empire found itself increasingly short on useable manpower and thus the urgent requirements of defence meant that the sultan had to 'squeeze the population for the last reserves of fighting men'.[43]

The first aim was to expand conscription through eliminating many traditional exemptions for military service which were so extensive that Erik Zürcher argues that the Ottoman state's military capacity had been far less than its regional rivals.[44] Those exempted included women, residents of the holy cities of Mecca and Medina, and of Istanbul, students in religious schools and Muslim pilgrims, men who could prove they were the sole bread winner for their household, and non-Muslims.[45] Demonstrating the importance of the army for the Ottoman state, one top government official (Grand Vizier) advocated that the entire educational system should be reorganized 'according to the needs of the state' in order to facilitate enlarged conscription throughout the empire.[46]

Other programmes were enacted to control groups of people which had hitherto fallen outside of the watchful eye of the state. Uncontrolled, they represented at the very least a waste of potential resources or a hindrance to effective rule; and at worse, an alternative *loci* of power in the empire, and thus a threat to the state. For example, Eastern Anatolian nomads who had long lived largely unregulated by the government in Istanbul were forcefully sedentarized in order to make them easier to monitor and control. The state also sought to break up powerful households of hereditary feudal lords such as the Karaosmanoğlu family of western Anatolia.[47] Furthermore, an empire-wide spy network was employed to detect and expose opponents of the sultan and state.[48] Transport and communications innovations, notably rail, telegraphs, and steamships, also enhanced the state's ability to glean information from, and move troops to, the imperial provinces.[49]

The state justified its move into previously unregulated realms, in the form of a new ideology portraying the sultan as both spiritual leader of the Muslim world (caliph) and the patron of a benevolent state. Abdülhamid II revived the image of the Ottoman sultan as the caliph or rightful successor to the prophet Mohammed and leader of all Muslims – a claim which Ottoman sultans had not made publicly for some centuries. Further, he sent missions across the globe to promote this new image and employed learned men to produce Arabic literature describing how he ruled according to core Muslim principles. Abdülhamid II also used his clout as caliph to monitor and regulate the flow of *hajj* pilgrims to Mecca and Medina, and ensure that he remained the focus of religious praise, and the Ottoman state rather than Mecca the locus of political power.[50] In emphasizing his role as spiritual leader of united Muslim world, the sultan aimed to both stymie emerging nationalist and religious movements across the empire and inspire Muslims world-wide to resist European imperialism.[51]

Further, he promoted the image of a benevolent and paternalistic sultan. For example, his aides ensured the publication of newspaper articles detailing the sultan's philanthropic activities, such as natural disaster relief.[52] Thus, after an earthquake hit the Aegean province of Balıkesir, government newspapers detailed his personal involvement in rescue efforts and caring for survivors. In another newspaper article, following a rare Ottoman victory against the nascent Greek state in 1897, he is portrayed as a caring father to Ottoman soldiers.[53]

The Ottoman state's benevolence and paternalistic discourse reflects what Michel Foucault described as 'bio-politics', a deliberate promotion of the 'public good' in order to rationalize the permanence of 'complex organs of political co-ordination and centralization'.[54] The Ottoman state deployed bio-political techniques to claim the authority to intervene into many hitherto private and unregulated spheres of life. For example, the Ottoman government used concerns about destructive fires in densely populated urban centres such as Izmir as a means to justify the demolition of some of the older and poorer neighbourhoods of the city.[55] Its real motivation was to rebuild parts of the city on orderly lines to enable the government to monitor the inhabitants more effectively, and to maximize the flow of industry and commerce to the new port and railway stations.[56] In a similar fashion, the development of a centrally controlled, regionally deployed, *gendarmerie*, on the pretext of fighting lawlessness and insecurity in distant provinces, amounted to what Nadir Özbek terms a 'colonization of the countryside' by the Ottoman state.[57] Again, the elaboration of safety rules and regulations for miners working in the Zonguldak coalfield were aimed at disciplining and imposing state control over a hitherto unruly workforce.[58]

It is in this context that official interest in the emancipation process should be considered. The accepted view, represented by scholars such as Erdem, Abdullah Martal and Toledano, is that a benevolent Ottoman state was forced to intervene into erstwhile private processes of manumission because of the growing numbers of slaves being rescued or seeking refuge at foreign consuls. Wishing to 'ensure that the emancipated slaves do not remain in a state of misery for an extended period of time'[59] the Ottoman government ensured their future protection and security through their 'responsible placement' in elite households and elsewhere.[60] The state thereby created a new and direct dialogue with the ex-slaves.[61]

However, it is here argued that the language of benevolence was used to justify Ottoman state intervention into the lives of emancipated Africans in order to prevent the emergence of an unruly population, to access additional manpower for its army or indeed to fill the roles of slaves and, above all, to help make sure they contributed to the Ottoman state's strength and stability, and not be a hindrance upon it.

While the state employed the same techniques of regulation and control on the kinless, patronless, emancipated Africans as they did other elements of society to accomplish its above described goals, there was one key difference: the state's interventionist actions were legitimized through the traditional concepts of post-emancipation patron–client relations and social indebtedness. According to prevailing religious and social practices, the slave was, following emancipation, indebted to her/his former master. When the Ottoman state became an emancipator of African slaves in the third quarter of the nineteenth century, it also assumed the role of their patron. The former slaves thus became socially indebted to the state.

Examples of State Intervention in the Lives of Emancipated Africans

As social indebtedness is not an easily definable quality, quantity or state of being, it is unlikely that cases exist where its role in shaping post-emancipation lives of former slaves is clearly spelled out. As a result, reading between the lines is critical to see how this process unfolded in specific contexts. Thus the following examples represent instances where it appears social indebtedness shaped the actions of the Ottoman officials on the ground.

In early 1880, after taking refuge in the British Consulate in Istanbul, some twenty-five or twenty-six runaway female African slaves, one with a child, had been sent to the local Ottoman officials to obtain the requisite document attesting to their freedom. However, upon arrival they were detained in what one British consular report calls a 'prison'.[62] This was no doubt one of the newly formed 'guest-houses' (*misafirhane*), required by the 1880 treaty, wherein the Ottoman government had promised to care for emancipated Africans.[63] After clandestinely sending a 'petition' back to the British consular officials begging for their help and claiming severe maltreatment, the British consular officials began to pressure the local Ottoman authorities to release and grant these women freedom. Local officials responded by explaining the women 'were kept only as guests until '[t]he [central government] should have had decided what to do with them'.[64] As an agent of the benevolent state, the Ottoman official added that if they were set free 'they would not know what to do with themselves and would remain starving in the streets'.[65] Thus the Ottoman official seems to believe that they were helping the women in keeping them detained in such poor conditions. After the women were finally released and given their documents, the Ottoman officials reiterated that they had been keeping them until they figured out what to do with them and added that letting them go on their own would result in their selling themselves back into slavery or fall into prostitution.[66] Thus even though in this instance the emancipated slaves were eventually released by the Ottoman officials, they made it clear that it was in fact not good for the emancipated Africans' well-being or for public health. Thus a bio-political argument was employed to keep the slaves under state protection to eventually make use of them how they saw fit. However it appears British pressure forced them to release the slaves to their own devices.

From as early as 1877, provincial authorities had been receiving orders and funding to help house and care for ex-slaves.[67] However it was a few years later when the state changed its policy on emancipation and sought to make use of emancipated slaves in far flung provinces in whatever way it directly required. It was a request from the governor of Benghazi[68] in 1884 asking the central government in Istanbul for assistance for the growing number of emancipated Africans there that triggered a response that represents the beginning of the state's interventionist policy.[69] The central government did not agree with local authorities that the male slaves should be enrolled in local public works such as salt transportation and risk re-enslavement. They thus informed the Benghazi authorities to send the emancipated Africans to Istanbul and Izmir where the men would be enrolled in military bands and artisan battalions, and the women would be employed as salaried domestic servants.[70] From this point on a growing number of rescued slaves were ordered to be sent to Istanbul or Izmir in this fashion, to fill whatever roles needed.

Another case demonstrates the Ottoman state's desire to be the sole caretaker of emancipated slaves, despite the emergence of effective local programmes. In the spring of 1884 the British Consul at Chania on Crete described to his superior in Istanbul the actions of the local Ottoman governor which, while not written as part of the British–Ottoman Convention against the slave trade, did have a positive effect on rescuing and settling slaves there. It was reported that after finding suspected slaves aboard ships in the port, the Ottoman governor had them 'lodged in the house of the Sheikh of the Benghazi Arabs who are domiciled at the outskirts' of Chania.[71] After a day of living under the auspices of the sheikh's household, they declared themselves to be slaves and sought to stay on Crete and had already found employment either with or through the sheikh. The British consul approved of these actions by the Ottoman governor and declared that this 'worthy Sheikh' asks no compensation and is ready at all times to co-operate.[72]

A year later, in the autumn of 1885, a similar situation was reported by the British Consul at Chania, with a rather different response from the Ottoman governor. Enslaved African women had arrived onboard a boat coming from North Africa bound for Istanbul. This time, however, the rather than taking the suspected slaves off the boat and sending them to stay with the 'Sheikh of the Bengazi Arabs' overnight, the Ottoman governor explained to British officials that if he did so, he would be 'exceeding his instructions' from Istanbul. The British consul regretted that the central government in Istanbul was interfering with the local programme aimed to help ameliorate the condition of emancipated Africans there. The consul noted to his superior that 'if the Ottoman government cared to put a stop to the traffic in slaves' it would permit 'the temporary detention of suspected slaves with their African countrymen established in [Chania]'.[73] After British representatives attempted to pressure the government in Istanbul to keep this programme in Chania going, Ottoman officials in Istanbul issued a decree stating that slaves given to

> the Arab Sheikh nominated by the [British] Ambassador ... is beyond the clear and natural limits of the [1880 treaty], and that the [Ottoman government] can never recognize the existence of such a Sheikh in Crete nor approve of his interference into these affairs.[74]

The response also states that only the centrally-controlled Ottoman police are capable of conferring manumission upon rescued Africans and that they alone will issue Istanbul-approved documents that prove a person's status. From the state's perspective, the African women who in 1884 on Crete were rescued and likely integrated into the local sheikh's household represent a lost opportunity. By falling out of its purview, the state was unable to benefit from being their patron after aiding in their emancipation. Demonstrating how committed the Ottoman state was to its interventionist programme, just months before this disagreement in Chania, the central government in Istanbul reiterated its policy to its governor in Benghazi, once again stating that if he was unable to place rescued female slaves 'under good guarantees' as domestic servants there and if the men could not be suitably incorporated into the military bands in a 'proper situation', then they should be sent 'at Government expense, to [Izmir] or [Istanbul], in order that they may be suitably settled there by the local authorities'.[75]

Another aspect of this state intervention involved putting emancipated Africans in the army, as has already been mentioned above. In 1893, the British consul at Benghazi saw this approach being implemented for himself:

> In the course of last year I suggested to [the governor], who has musical tastes, the utility of his incorporating in the military band some of the emancipated Blacks who

idle about the streets of Bengazi in a very miserable condition, as many of them have a good ear for music, and are also physically capable of being enrolled in other branches of the Ottoman army. Nothing came of my suggestion till the commencement of this month, when on morning I saw a number of Blacks in military uniform being drilled, and apparently well clothed. On inquiry I found that the [governor] had filled up several vacancies in the band with Blacks, and had drafted the taller and stronger men into a battalion of the regular troops.[76]

Soon thereafter, the same consul reported that increasingly fewer slaves were taking refuge at his consul because the local Ottoman army had enrolled 'over 200 blacks' in its ranks.[77] The British consul makes clear that these actions were a result of benevolence as the Ottoman army was helping emancipated Africans who 'idle in the streets ... in a very poor condition'. However, in light of the Ottoman state's demand for evermore soldiers and the precarious nature Ottoman rule in North Africa, the conscription of these emancipated Africans was arguably based more on maintenance of Ottoman power than benevolence.[78] By 1890, the sultan began declining funding requests from provincial authorities and instead requested they send 'as many as possible' to be enrolled in the army in Istanbul.[79] Once again, the practice of caring for ex-slaves had turned into a pragmatic process of using them as the state required.

One of the more notable examples of how Ottoman benevolence and care was used to further its own needs occurred in and around Izmir. Izmir was at this time the second city of the empire, with a large port and productive agricultural hinterland.[80] As discussed above, part of the 1880 and 1890 treaties, the Ottoman state was required to construct guest-houses for emancipated slaves all across the empire. They were, however, designed solely as temporary shelters until they could be transported to the main guest-house in Izmir. Once in Izmir, the state planned to put the men in vocational schools, artisan battalions and military bands, while the women were to be placed in appropriate households as salaried domestic servants.[81] Many of these slaves were to be trained in a facility originally founded in 1861 to house and educate orphans in trades such as tailoring, rug making, metalwork and operating printing presses. However in honour of its new sultan and patron, Sultan Abdülhamid II, the school was renamed in 1881 Hamidiye Mekteb-i Sanayi (the Hamidian School of Industry).[82] It was estimated it would hold up to 200 emancipated slaves.[83] Despite it not being clear how many slaves actually went through the Izmir guest-house, it is known that by 1893, Ottoman cities far and wide were commanded by the state to send 'as many as possible' emancipated slaves to Izmir. It appears that, responding to this order, local governors even began transferring slaves that had married, started new lives, had integrated into households and hence were not really in need of the state-run institution's training and settlement programme.[84] Thus in 1893 the sultan sent out another order clarifying that he only wanted unmarried, recently emancipated slaves to be sent.[85] It is easy to see why the Ottoman state wanted emancipated Africans in this specific condition: homeless, kinless and patronless, they were the type most easily brought under its influence. However, state expenditures were low in the following years and the Izmir guest house never received the adequate funding from authorities in Istanbul to operate at full capacity. It is known however that men 'almost immediately found employment' upon arriving.[86] Just where they found employment is unclear. Perhaps they found work in one the trades the school was associated with, as was the intention. Many also likely became porters, as photographic evidence shows a significant number of the porters in Izmir's bustling port at this time were Africans.[87]

Another key aspect of this 'Izmir plan' took place in Izmir's rich agricultural hinterland. Since at least mid-century, the Ottoman state had been settling refugees there in an attempt to solve growing labour shortages.[88] This land was a bountiful source of cotton, tobacco, figs and other crops for not only the Ottoman Empire but for the global market.[89] In the mid-nineteenth century, new railways connected this fertile land directly to Izmir's port.[90] In periods of economic growth, the relatively high amount of available agricultural land combined with a general scarcity of labour meant there were periods where labour was in extremely high demand.[91] In order to further provide for the growing needs of this rapidly developing agricultural region, officials devised a plan to forcefully marry and settle emancipated Africans on this land. The state also constructed houses for them and provided some farming tools.[92] Some emancipated female Africans were also sent on their own to these farming villages to work as domestic servants in the households of wealthy farmers.[93] Much of the land they were settled on was likely state-owned farms, as records show the vocational school in Izmir discussed above intended to send its graduates to work on Ottoman imperial farms in the hinterland.[94] Thus it appears that in this instance that, in return for emancipation, the government not only used the Africans labour power, but in some cases even attempted to control their reproductive capacity – something which often defines slavery. This example of the state marrying emancipated Africans and transferring them to a region crucial to the economic output of the empire is one of the clearer instances of the state taking control of the lives of ex-slaves for its own gain. It is still not clear to what extent these settlements were successful, thus more research is required to gain a clearer picture of this unique moment in the history of indebtedness in the Ottoman Empire.

Even those emancipated Africans who were reconfigured into salaried domestic servants and reattached to households indirectly served the needs of the Ottoman state. Not only did they address labour shortages in domestic service for elites brought about by the reduction of available slaves, but in being reconfigured as wage labourers they were helping to expand a cash based economy, something desired by the Ottoman state and its European financial backers at this time.[95] Furthermore, as wage labourers, they were largely unattached to households and could be let go in times of economic downturn. Ironically, without the bonds of clientship tying them to a former master, their futures now lay in the invisible hand of the marketplace.

Conclusion

The Ottoman state's unprecedented intervention into the lives of enslaved and emancipated Africans is a marked change from the traditional transition from enslaved to free in the Ottoman Empire. The state's goals of the maintenance of order, the expansion of the army, the creation of a large tax base and the removal of other potential *loci* of power in the empire were aided through the shaping of the lives of emancipated Africans. This was accomplished by use of the same discourse of bio-politics and benevolence which the Ottoman state used to justify its intrusion into all aspects of late Ottoman society. However, in the case of emancipated slaves, state intervention was facilitated by the traditional concept of post-emancipation patron–client relations referred to here as social indebtedness.

It must be kept in mind that the majority of emancipated Africans were reincorporated back into the very households they had served as slaves. Those slaves that were emancipated by the state and subsequently fell under its influence were in the minority. Furthermore, this government control was not implemented by well-defined policy. Finally, it must also be noted that there was often a difference between the intentions of the Ottoman state and what actually occurred on the ground. As mentioned above, local Ottoman officials were at times either unwilling or unable to acquiesce to the orders coming from Istanbul.[96]

This study has attempted to show these events from the Ottoman state's perspective. This of course, was not the only one. As a result of the lack of source material, the voices of the enslaved and emancipated in this process are largely silent. This process involved a negotiation between the state and the emancipated Africans. As has been noted in the historiography, the enslaved and recently emancipated actively took the initiative to ameliorate their situations when the opportunity presented itself. Thus responses from the emancipated Africans to this process were neither passive nor monolithic. In some instances, state control was welcomed and accepted as a chance to improve their condition, while by others it was contested and resisted. Finally, what 'freedom' meant for the Ottoman state, the emancipated Africans and indeed Ottoman society at large remained and indeed remains unclear.[97]

Acknowledgement

This project has been supported by the Social Sciences and Humanities Research Council of Canada (SSHRC).

4 PAWNSHIP AND SEIZURE FOR DEBT IN THE PROCESS OF ENSLAVEMENT IN WEST AFRICA

Paul E. Lovejoy

Pawnship was a legal category of social and economic dependency in which a person was held as collateral for a loan.[1] Pawning of individuals constituted the transfer of productive assets as security until the debt was fully repaid. Pawnship stands in contrast to a mortgage, where assets are only transferred in case of default. The labour of the pawn, at least in non-Muslim settings, constituted interest on the debt and theoretically was intended to cover the cost of subsistence and accommodation but did not contribute to the principal. Usually, the pawn lived with the creditor, who was responsible for subsistence. Commercial hostage-taking was an extension of pawning, in which one or more individuals were held as security for a debt or an expected payment.[2] In West Africa, pawnship derived from the concept in which something, or as was often the case, someone, is held as collateral for a debt. The way pawning operated was different than the pawn shop as a place where an individual can receive a loan against a valuable object, such as jewellery, but with the possibility that the pawned object can be sold after a specified period of time if the loan is not repaid. The use of human beings for this purpose was contested and subsequently declared illegal, following the League of Nations enquiries in the 1920s. Nonetheless, there has been considerable confusion over terminology. The problem arises because of the various types of dependency that were to be found in Africa. In fact there was seldom any confusion with respect to slavery. Anyone who could be sold or who had been purchased was a slave. However, other relationships of dependency have not always been clearly defined. Pawns were not slaves, although as demonstrated, pawns might be enslaved if there were no mechanisms to establish clientage to the creditor and if individuals were not subject to political authority that protected individuals from enslavement.

Pawnship was clearly institutionalized in West Africa and as such was related to access to credit in many places, particularly in non-Muslim areas, whether or not there were centralized states or societies and communities organized through secret societies. People were pawned to provide security for what was owed, but in some places so were trees, gold and other commodities, and hence the institution was similar to the underlying principle of modern pawnshops. Kola trees were pawned in the producing belt in the interior of Sierra Leone and Liberia, where the Poro society was the governing institution involved in the enforcement of credit arrangements. Similarly, gold was used in pawning arrangements at the European castles on the Gold Coast in arrangements with local merchants. Human pawns, valuable commodities with productive potential, were used as surety for debts that could only be retrieved upon full repayment of the debt, and usually involved a service fee. Interest could and often was built into the evaluation of the loan and repayment amount. In the case of the pawning of people, there was an added cost. As individuals, the cost of maintenance was a factor, and therefore the labour of the pawned individual was the property of the creditor, although within carefully proscribed arrangements arising from interpersonal relationships between creditors and debtors, who might even be relatives. The servicing of the debt that was involved in feeding, housing, clothing and educating the pawn fell on the creditor, which was transferred into the economics of the transaction through evaluation of the cost of the debt and its expected repayment schedule. Often children were pawned, whose labour was marginal except through their roles in apprenticeship and in fulfilling household chores, including looking after smaller children. The long term commitment and obligations to the house could be beneficial and certainly helped to offset costs. In the case of girls, especially, pawnship could lead to marriage to someone within the household, which could preclude payment of bride wealth and hence conserve scarce resources within extended families. Acquisition of wives through pawning arrangements lessened or eliminated bride price payments and labour commitments.

We have to remember that 'indebtedness' arises from the inability to pay for something that has value but this implies access to credit and the commitment to pay off the debt under specific conditions. In the case of pawnship, how was credit obtained, how was it secured and how could indebtedness lead to slavery, or in fact did it protect individuals from enslavement? These are the questions addressed in this essay. Pawnship was certainly intertwined with slavery, but pawnship was intended to prevent – and it certainly did restrict – the process of enslavement rather than facilitate the generation of slaves.

On the one hand, pawnship operated as an institution that was crucial in commercial transactions, not only in slaves but also in other commodities, and to this extent pawnship facilitated the slave trade and the reliance on slavery in the domestic economy and in the export sector. Pawnship as an institution was part of the process of enslavement because it underpinned credit arrangements that facilitated the slave trade. Pawns as individuals, on the other hand, did not inevitably slip into slavery, and almost everywhere in West Africa, as far as we can tell, there were methods of protection against such a transition, although we also have cases of pawns being enslaved. The analysis of pawnship inevitably addresses the connection between credit mechanisms and the modes of protection, including legal constraints and moral and religious codes of behaviour. Pawnship was an institutional response to the need for credit and the means of guaranteeing repayment of debts. That some pawns found themselves reduced to slavery reveals tension in the institution as to how it operated.

The relationship between indebtedness in West Africa during the period of trans-Atlantic slavery and its aftermath and the institutions of pawnship and slavery was complex. It is not clear to what extent indebtedness was a means by which individuals could be reduced to slavery and sold into the trans-Atlantic trade. The institution of pawnship was sometimes related to seizure for debt and sale into slavery and sometimes not. In West Africa, at least in the eighteenth and nineteenth centuries, pawnship served to protect people from enslavement, while in central and eastern Africa, pawnship seems to have been largely a fiction to disguise seizure for debt and subsequent enslavement. Hence the concept of pawning has been applied in conflicting ways that warrant comparison. This paper is intended to explore the distinction between pawnship in which people were protected against arbitrary seizure or 'panyarring' and the use of the concept of pawnship to justify the seizure of relatives of individuals who were in debt and therefore represented a form of foreclosure. The two divergent practices, both under the name of pawnship, protected individuals from enslavement in the first instance and justified their sale into slavery in the second. Historically, it appears that pawnship as practised in much of West Africa, from the Senegambia as far as the Bight of Biafra, developed as an institution to prevent arbitrary seizure for unpaid debts. Individuals were held as pawns to assure that debts would be paid, and while occasionally pawns were sold into slavery, this was not considered legal and could result in retaliation.[3] In West Africa trees could be pawned in some places, the harvest adhering to the creditor until the debt was repaid, while gold was also pawned on the Gold Coast as early as the seventeenth century.

As practised in West Africa, at least, pawnship prevented the arbitrary seizure of goods or people in relation to debts. The pawn served as the guarantor that the debt would be repaid. Arbitrary seizure was institutionalized as 'panyarring'. Whereas pawnship identified a specific individual as the representative of the debt, panyarring was a coordinated action that was directed at a community which was held collectively responsible for the debt, crime or violation. Panyarring has sometimes been confused with kidnapping, which can be defined as arbitrary seizure of individuals for purpose of ransom or sale into slavery for profit, but for which there is no claimed justification for seizure.[4] The distinction here is between illegal seizure of people without cause, which is kidnapping, and the seizure of people or goods that was based on a collective action, both in its implementation and in its impact. Because panyarring was collective, it was often conducted through male associations and secret societies, such as the *asafo* houses on the Gold Coast, the *Ekpe* leopard society in the interior of the Bight of Biafra and *Poro* in the interior of Sierra Leone. Panyarring and pawning were inevitably linked; panyarring enforced foreclosure, while pawning limited panyarring. Pawning provided collateral to ensure that debts would be paid without resort to violence, while panyarring forced payment when debts were not secured. In practice, arrangements for pawning were the antidote to panyarring, and it is possible that pawning came into use as a means of countering the destruction that was inevitably associated with panyarring. In central and eastern Africa, however, the seizure of 'pawns' and their sale into slavery was not arbitrary but rather directed at the kin unit of the debtor, which was held collectively responsible for the debt and thereby had to tolerate the removal of a pawn and the subsequent sale of the individual into slavery.

In West Africa, pawnship described contracts that were enforceable by law and regulated by customary protection. Although there were violations, pawns could not be reduced to slavery and had to be treated as well as other members of the household in which the pawn was held. Pawnship involved face-to-face relationships with people who were known to the family of the pawn, who was thereby protected to varying degrees and hence could not be sold or disposed of in any other way. Death or injury could result in legal and extra legal consequences. Slavery, by contrast, had none of these protections and was the result of war, kidnapping, panyarring, legal decisions and even the reduction of debtors into slavery. However, it is necessary to identify where these various practices were to be found, and to establish how pawnship specifically operated as a system of collateral in credit relationships, rather than as a mechanism for the reduction of individuals to slavery. Moreover, while pawnship protected people from slavery, pawnship was a form of servitude related to debt but was an institutional form of servitude that was not slavery. The process of enslavement in West Africa, at least, had mechanisms that safeguarded members of families from slavery, even while allowing forms of servitude that related to flows of credit and facilitated individual needs to pay funeral expenses, marriages, legal fees and religious obligations. Pawnship had legal sanction that was enforceable. Hence there were institutions to protect pawns and compel payment of debts. Pawnship demonstrates an extreme form of dependency, one in which an individual was expected to represent the debt of another person.

We seem to know what debt and slavery are, and hence the nature of credit, but I am not convinced that the term 'pawnship' is always used with any confidence as to its meaning. This collection examines whether or not there is a connection between the process of enslavement and factors of debt. This is clearly a very complex issue, especially because on the surface there should be very little connection. The process of enslavement in the great majority of cases was instituted through violence that had nothing to do with credit arrangements or market transactions but rather was identical with theft. Even the birth of children into slavery was a form of theft, a denial of rights of freeborn, without cause or recourse. Enslavement for debt and pawnship are mentioned in the records that were kept in Sierra Leone for the reasons that those taken off slave ships had been enslaved, although the distinction between enslavement for debt and pawnship is not usually clear. Contemporary documents refer to formerly enslaved individuals found aboard slave ships that were seized and condemned (by the Court of Vice Admiralty before 1819 and the Courts of Mixed Commission thereafter) as 'recaptured' people who were subsequently placed in conditions of apprenticeship as 'Liberated Africans'. Enslavement for debt and pawnship are both mentioned, but such cases represent only a small proportion in comparison with evidence that most people were enslaved through war, raiding and kidnapping – in effect, violence. Hence most cases of enslavement had little if anything to do with debt, except that the extension of credit was often important in the trade that resulted in the purchase and sale of enslaved people. Enslavement itself was a product of confiscation not a relationship derived from the extension of credit or indebtedness. Nonetheless, individuals could be enslaved through foreclosures on debt in the form of 'panyarring' or outright confiscation. Perhaps people did place themselves in a form of indenture that was governed by debt and its administration, and might thereby end up in slavery. Moreover, people were held for ransom, which friends and relatives had to pay if they could and if they were willing, but the ransom amount was not a voluntary debt but an exchange arising from violence and the threat of enslavement. Patron–client relations could be premised on debt, but this did not usually result in a process of enslavement, nor did many forms of debt bondage, including share-cropping that tied people to land and production.

Because pawnship arises from credit relationships and therefore serves as collateral for debt, it was different from indentures and other forms of debt bondage. An indenture involved paying off a debt in a specified period of time, labour constituting the form of payment. E. Adeniyi Oroge even referred to pawning as 'indenture' because such arrangements could blur into patron–client forms of relationships.[5] Indenture was a form of debt bondage in which a person had to pay off a debt, but pawnship differed from indenture in that the labour performed by the pawn did not contribute to the payment of the debt, which had to be paid in its entirety before the pawn was released. In cases described as 'self pawning', the pawned individual did not live with the creditor but lived on his/her own as the only way of earning money to pay off the debt, and in such cases, the debt was a form of indenture that had to be indemnified. Such arrangements were nonetheless conceived in the context of pawnship.

The idea that the labour of the pawn could not pay off the debt was essential to the institution of pawnship. In Muslim areas, at least in the nineteenth century, slaves could be allowed to work on their own account, paying a set fee to their masters, but this fee was not considered a payment towards their freedom. The practice was known as *murgu* in the Sokoto Caliphate.[6] While this fee was considered a debt that had to be paid, the payments gave slaves the opportunity to work on their own account, keeping any earnings above what had to be given to masters. The cost of emancipation was a separate calculation, and hence like the principal on the loan behind pawning, the cost was not related to the labour of the individual. As Olatunji Ojo observes, the average daily wage of an adult worker in Egbaland in 1845 ranged between 120–160 cowries (4–5*d*), rising to about 200 cowries (5*d*) in 1860; in north-east Yorubaland, the daily rate was 400–650 cowries per day in the 1850s and 1,000 cowries in the late 1870s.[7] Similar rates of pay were common in the urban centres of the Sokoto Caliphate where slaves under *murgu* contracts had to pay fixed amounts weekly or monthly and provide for their own food and accommodation. *Murgu* and similar practices forced people to sell their labour and earn cash, which in the Sokoto Caliphate was transferred in the form of cowrie shells.

Intrinsically, pawnship did not lead to slavery but rather was legally distinct, at least in theory. Pawnship could technically carry into a second generation, if the original debtor died without repayment. The time limit on the debt was not fixed. Hence any process of enslavement arising from pawnship has to be explained in historical context. Moreover, pawnship cannot be equated with poverty in which indebtedness is the principal characteristic. Rather, instances of pawnship are as likely to arise in situations of extensive public display, such as funerals, weddings and accession to political and ritual office, as from necessity arising from poverty. Pawnship was often used to sanction commerce and facilitate interactions based on trust, despite the denial of freedom to the person who was actually being held in pawn. The pawn's expectations that the debt would be paid and they would be redeemed arose from continued links to kin and the maintenance of identity, which stands in sharp contrast to the experience of slaves. Nonetheless, pawns did become slaves, and indeed slaves were even pawned, just as trees and land might be.

Similarly, let us consider the idea of ransom. The practice was common along the long frontier between Muslim and Christian countries, centred on the Mediterranean, but also extended across the Sahara so that it was widespread in West Africa, especially in Muslim areas. Indeed, the practice was common throughout the Muslim world, extending into the Indian Ocean. The most well-known pattern of institutionalized ransoming related to the so-called Barbary pirates, in fact licensed Muslim adventurers whose 'piracy' had been systemized, ransoms being handled through resident European consuls in the Muslim domains of the

Maghreb.[8] Like pawning, individuals being held for ransom were in the hands of the claimants, and at their disposal to be sold into slavery, confined to harems, prison or engaged in some productive activity, the output of which remained with the captors. The difference primarily related to the nature of the indebtedness. In ransoming, there was no debt, but rather a claim for compensation for which there was no commercial gain for those who paid. The practice of ransoming was more compatible with kidnapping than with pawning. The demand for ransom differed from panyarring in that individuals seized for ransom were expected to pay through third party intervention, while individuals and goods seized during panyarring were the actual payment of the claim for compensation.

In West Africa, at least in non-Muslim states and societies, pawnship had three functions – first, pawning was fundamental to credit mechanisms that promoted the process of enslavement and the trade in slaves; secondly, holding pawns pre-empted the risk of panyarring; and thirdly, individuals held in pawn sometimes became slaves if they were sold, often illegally, on the market, thereby severing any contact with kin. It is important to distinguish between these aspects of pawnship. Pawnship was fundamental to trade and some pawns became slaves. Pawnship was embedded in social and political structures that enforced compliance and facilitated the flow of credit and thereby reduced the risk of violence. Its institutional embedded-ness can be understood as a rational application of transactional economics. In discussing the relationship of pawnship to slavery, therefore, it is important to understand that pawnship and indebtedness were not the same. Pawnship normally and legally was based on customary laws that prohibited the reduction of pawns to the status of slave. Pawns did become slaves, but whether in a legal and acceptable manner according to local ethical standards is another matter. The challenge is to address issues of chronology, development and change over time in how pawnship operated in West Africa.

Despite the clear restrictions on the reduction of individuals who were being held as pawns to a condition of slavery, it is clear that pawns sometimes did find themselves being sold as slaves. As Ojo shows in his study of women, slavery and indebtedness in nineteenth-century Yorubaland in the period of the 'illegal' slave trade from the Bight of Benin, that is, the trade after British abolition in 1807, pawnship was an important institution associated with trade and marketing.[9] Ojo underscores the importance of credit in the conduct of trade, not only in connection with the export trade in slaves and then palm oil but also within Yorubaland itself. In particular he demonstrates that *ele* or *eda* ('extra' or an instalment) was charged on loans, often at usurious rates of 100 per cent per year, and with a portion of the interest often taken out before the loan was given. In some cases pawns were used as security on these debts, but under what conditions is not always clear.

Ojo indicates that 'redemption and ransoming fees' for captives often resulted in the need to raise capital through pawning, which he defines as 'mortgaging the services' of the individual. According to Ojo, in nineteenth-century Yorubaland, the link between pawnship and freedom from slavery meant that family members sometimes had to become pawns in order to secure freedom for someone else in the family who had been enslaved in war or in some other manner.[10] The confusion between slavery and pawnship arose from the necessity to raise capital to free enslaved family members, but the confusion arose over the relationship between pawnship and slave redemption, not the enslavement of pawns. Because of this confusion, Christian converts often opposed European efforts to prevent pawnship. As noted by Rev. Samuel Crowther in 1856, pawnship was important as a means of raising money that was needed to 'ransom their captured relative[s] from going into foreign slavery[;] thus thousands have been kept back from being removed out of the country', and he thought the 'system of pawns as it's practiced in this country has proved beneficial to thousands of families since slave wars broke out with unbounded fury'.[11] In order to secure the release of individuals who had been kidnapped or captured in war and therefore were in danger of being sold as slaves, pawned individuals were more likely to be female than male, young rather than old. There were credit agencies, known as *ogo*, which enforced repayment of debts through the practice of *emu* (pan-yarring), and pawns were often used to protect families against such arbitrary seizure, which could result in enslavement. As Ojo noted, the person with the title of Ologo or Asa carried a staff of the king or *ogboni* to the house of the debtor, indicating debts were owed. The Ologo could destroy property, which meant that people could lose more than what they owed.

Various studies of pawnship, especially from Sierra Leone and other parts of the upper Guinea coast, the region that became Liberia, the Gold Coast, the Bights of Benin and Biafra, Gold Coast, as well as the western Sudan indicate that the practice of pawnship was widespread. These studies demonstrate that the gendered nature of pawnship was extremely important. Girls and women were offered or simply taken in many cases because of the possibility that a personal relationship would develop in the household of the creditor that would lead to marriage to the pawned girl, thereby erasing the debt. This was an important consideration for the debtor, and involved no bride price payment on the part of the husband other than foregoing the debt. Even then, the husbands of pawned women might keep any earnings of the wife as a claim against the original debt, in contrast to the income and property of wives for whom a bride price had been given.

It is possible to attempt to periodize the study of pawnship in order to remove the subject from the arena of a timeless anthropology. Early studies of pawnship focused on recognition of its importance, not on attempting to understand the institution in its historical context. It is now clear from a study of pawnship in the Bight of Biafra, and especially at Old Calabar, that we can discern various changes over time. In the interior of the Bight of Biafra, the male association known as *Ekpe* performed the functions of foreclosure on debts and also of protecting pawns, while in the interior of Sierra Leone, *Poro* did the same. Both associations were 'secret' in the sense that members who were initiated into the various grades of the associations learned specialized codes, rituals and other knowledge to which outsiders did not have access.[12] Pawnship was adapted to the needs of the Atlantic slave trade to guarantee credit arrangements, and hence *Ekpe* members became concerned with protecting pawns held on board European ships until commercial transactions were completed, so that ships would not sail with pawns on board. Without allowing for such modifications in how pawnship functioned, we are left with a static view.[13] The chronology is important. At this point, there are no references to pawnship before the 1730s in the Bight of Biafra, when the system seems to have already been in operation at Old Calabar. What we do know is that the *Ekpe* society was functioning from at least the mid-seventeenth century and that pawnship was governed by *Ekpe*. There is a problem here of methodology and interpretation – how much can we extrapolate backwards; how do we avoid generalizations without due consideration of limitations of data and efforts to correlate the practice of pawning with the phases of the slave trade.[14]

There is no evidence that Europeans belonged to *Ekpe* in the eighteenth century, for example, although there are claims to the contrary. Our evidence indicates that Europeans only began to join *Ekpe* in the 1820s, although it is possible that they were admitted a decade or more earlier. Europeans were specifically excluded from membership in *Ekpe* before 1808 for reasons relating to the institution of pawnship, because people were being held as collateral for debts. European ships accepted pawns as security for goods advanced on credit in some places, such as Old Calabar, on the Gold Coast, and apparently also in certain areas on the upper Guinea coast, but in some places pawns were not acceptable to European ship captains, such as at Bonny and Ouidah. Apparently pawns were useful in the slave trade to the Americas in places that lacked centralized authority that could otherwise guarantee the payment of debts other than through the use of pawns. In these situations, moreover, the nature of pawnship was different from local practice, because slave ships demanded that the term of pawning be fixed to the date on which ships sailed. If pawns had not been redeemed by the agreed date, they might be taken to the Americas and sold as slaves. Nonetheless, the many disputes and various instances of retaliation visited on slave ships reveals that the extent of agreement over this issue was contested. In most cases, apparently, ship captains chose to exchange pawns that they were holding with neighbouring ships for slaves to avoid confrontation. In cases where ships sailed with pawns, local merchants sometimes retaliated against other ships flying the same flag as the absconding ship.

It is unlikely that most pawns in local credit arrangements were held in miserable conditions, because those being held in pawnship were supposed to be guaranteed treatment similar to that for family members.[15] The degree of comfort and poverty was certainly relative, but in principle, unlike slaves, pawns were customarily assured of comparable conditions of life as full members of the family of the creditor. Since pawned individuals were clearly identified with a kin group and a place of residence, which was not usually too far away, pawnship was not simply an institution of labour control or mechanism for exploitation. If pawns ran away, they had to be replaced. The death or injury of pawns had to be investigated. Moreover, there was almost always an age distinction, because children were most likely to be pawned. When adults were pawned, the relationship was implicitly different due to the level and nature of work that was associated with the pawning arrangement. While an individual was in pawn, his labour belonged to the creditor. Children were assigned tasks that were often domestic in nature, but everyone worked in the fields. The sustenance of the pawns was the responsibility of the creditor, as was accommodation, which further limited any profits that might be gained from holding individuals in pawn. Pawnship was as much a system of investment, in which resources were tied up in the form of the pawning relationship, the cost of the pawn eventually to be realized.

Islamic law as interpreted in West Africa was not clear on the legality of pawning. The Arabic term *rahn* referred to mortgages and the property that could be held as security for the loan, which could be a slave. There are equivalent terms in Kiswahili and Hausa, and perhaps other languages. According to at least one interpretation of Islamic law, anything that could be legally sold could be mortgaged or pawned, including slaves. However, pawning of freeborn people and the seizure of free persons for debt was illegal. Free people could not be pawned because they were not commodities. The *umm walad*, the slave who had a contract for manumission, especially a concubine (who as a slave was promised freedom if she gave birth to her master's child), and anyone who was promised manumission after the death of the master, could not be pawned because the individual had acquired some aspects of freedom that already were being guaranteed – which meant that the individual could no longer be considered a mere commodity.

Technically, moreover, the person who received a pawn as collateral could not use the pawn for advantage. If the pawn was a slave, the creditor could not use the services of the person; if it was a horse, he could not ride it. It was possible to employ the pawned slave if the slave was given a salary. The person who placed a slave in pawn was responsible for the needs of the slave, including food, clothing, medication and marriage obligations. If the pawn was a female slave and the one who received her had sexual relationships with her, he was subject to legal sanction, had to pay a dowry and the contract of pawning was declared null. In some cases, the guilty party had to pay half of the tenth of her price (one-twentieth) for each time he had had sexual relations with her. If she had been a virgin then the compensation was one-tenth of her price for each engagement, but any offspring were considered to be slaves of the owner. If the pawned slave escaped or died, the creditor had to be compensated. If the pawn was allowed to marry a slave woman belonging to the person who held him in pawnship, the creditor legally could still have sexual relations with the woman, because the creditor owned the woman and the right of sexual access took precedence over the marriage contract. Finally, female pawns were not allowed to marry creditors because the pawning contract would thereby be annulled. Whether or not these prescriptions were recognized locally, the differences between the practice in non-Muslim areas of West Africa are striking, both in relation to the product of the labour of pawns and the sexual access that potentially could lead to marriage and annulment of the debt.[16]

The accounts of Abū-l-Ghayth b. Ahmad al-Tuwātī, who was the wealthiest merchant in Katsina in the Sokoto Caliphate from the 1820s to 1850s, demonstrates that both property in the form of houses and slaves were used to secure debts. According to his account book, al-Ghayth accepted property, including slaves and real estate, as collateral. For example, in one case he received a slave girl in lieu of a loan of 15,000 cowries, the currency of the central Sudan.[17] The repayment date was specified as the month of Dhū-l-Hijja, but until then, Abū-l-Ghayth was not supposed to collect interest on the loan through the labour of the slave girl, Akakba. She was not supposed to work either in his own household or as a domestic whose services could be rented out. In effect, she was not in a condition of pawnship as understood in non-Muslim societies. The girl had value only as a slave, and if she was rented out as a domestic servant to someone else, the profit of her labour would benefit the loan provider, but illegally.

The interface that turned pawns into slaves was located in areas where Muslim merchants were trading with non-Muslims. The data for West Africa shows a persistence of pawning into the colonial era, in which cultural 'misunderstandings' prevailed in the reduction of pawned children into slaves for the Muslim market. Children were pawned in West Africa who were subsequently sold as slaves, confirming the divide between Islam and dependent and subordinate societies. This Muslim and non-Muslim divide may have resulted in misinterpretation and misunderstanding over someone who was pawned being enslaved, and therefore presented problems of legal enforcement. There are questions of how interest was collected on debts and how pawnship was interpreted and implemented through the specific nature of contracts based on time limitations.

It is imperative to distinguish between indebtedness, in which people are poor, even destitute, and pawnship, in which individuals are held as collateral for debt, but are not themselves in debt, only the representation of debt. This important distinction is an underlying feature of pawnship – i.e., that a person is held in lieu of the debt. This is not in itself indebtedness, only a manifestation of how debt can be secured and the human consequences of such forms of insurance. An evaluation of the institutions of enforcement and protection in relation to pawnship reveal how kin protected pawns, restored individuals from pawnship and arranged marriages to offset pawning arrangements. In these ways, it was possible to prevent the sale of individual pawns into slavery. In areas where state institutions were absent or weak, there were other mechanisms to protect pawns from being exploited. In some places, so-called 'secret societies' protected the rights of pawns. Pawnship experienced resurgence under colonialism during the global depression of the 1930s, when the institution was tied to the mobilization of rural workers, dependent kin and child labour, as Martin Klein and Richard Roberts have pointed out for the western Sudan and which was confirmed for the area of the former Sokoto Caliphate by Lovejoy and Jan Hogendorn.[18]

Conclusion

The study of pawnship addresses indebtedness in the economies of West Africa and the vulnerability of people to slavery. I have not been able to document the process of transformation or to establish clearly when change occurred, but I would like to suggest some possible benchmarks. There seems to have been a divide between Islamic and non-Muslim societies, on the one hand, and between the Atlantic world and specific parts of western Africa, on the other. Muslim merchants appear to have recruited slaves through manipulations of pawnship almost seamlessly, while pawnship seems to have greased the credit mechanisms of trans-Atlantic slavery, but not always and not everywhere. We need to know a lot more about the slippage from pawnship into slavery, which in hindsight reveals local confusion, documentary contradiction or projection of theory into vague description. In the past, distinctions were made between what was considered legal activity and illegal activity, although interpretation could indeed be contested. Nonetheless, slavery and pawnship were perceived as different.

If pawnship is defined as a system in which collateral is provided to guarantee the repayment of a debt, there are important differences in the practice in West Africa, the legal meaning in Islamic law, and the way the term has been applied in east and central Africa. We would be more accurate to talk about enslavement for debt in East Africa and pawning of individuals in West Africa, recognizing that they were not the same. We would recognize that pawns in non-Muslim areas of West Africa provided the interest on the debt through their labour, which was prohibited in Islamic law. These conditions and situations have little similarity to what Mary Douglas described as 'blood-debts' arising from social and economic disputes between kin groups and communities.[19] In West Africa, individuals were seized or held as compensation through panyarring and war, and while they might be considered to be 'pawns', it would be more accurate to see their condition in which kin groups and communities were being held collectively responsible for compensation and reparation. The blood-debts of central Africa more often related to alternatives of revenge and human execution that arose from perceived wrongs, such as murder, adultery, failure to repay a loan, or any other recognized act that required retribution. The threat of indebtedness was sufficient to justify the sale of individuals into slavery as a means of settling debts, no matter how incurred, but pawnship as practices, even if sometimes only in theory, was designed to prevent enslavement.

In examining the historical development of pawnship as an institution, we need to identify references to its use in the Atlantic trade, when and where. We need to know more about the relationship between human pawnship and the practice of pawning trees, land, gold and other commodities, which could reinforce other relationships, including patron–client arrangements, marital contracts and kinship connections, whose resurgence during the colonial period, and especially during the Great Depression of the 1930s, is well documented. The methods of enforcement and protection involved secret societies, centralized states, reliance on panyarring and the use of intimidation, threat and force. Hence there seems to be very little connection between pawnship and the process of enslavement, in which the pawned individual becomes a slave. Finally, we need to examine the interface between Muslim trade and marketing and the friction between 'protected' people and other non-Muslims that arose from an institutionalized cultural misunderstanding. Enslavement and pawnship were clearly different in non-Muslim areas of West Africa, and where Muslim law was enforced or recognized, only slaves could be pawned, not free people, because slaves were considered property.

Acknowledgements

I wish to thank Mariana Pinho Cândido, José C. Curto, Yacine Daddi Addoun and Gwyn Campbell for commenting on an earlier version of this paper, and Olatunji Ojo for providing me with details that are incorporated in the chapter. I owe a special debt to David Richardson and Toyin Falola, whose collaboration underpins this paper. The research for this study was carried out under the auspices of the Canada Research Chair in African Diaspora History.

5 THE BUSINESS OF 'TRUST' AND THE ENSLAVEMENT OF YORUBA WOMEN AND CHILDREN FOR DEBT

Olatunji Ojo

Slave-wives have been sometimes sold off with their babies born to their masters to pay debts.

James Johnson, Ibadan, April 1877[1]

In his journal of 16 April 1864, James Thomas, the agent of the Church Missionary Society (CMS) at Gbebe, a town in the north-eastern Yoruba district of Bunu, near the confluence of River Niger, reported that his congregation paid eight bags of cowries for the redemption of a woman and her son to prevent their enslavement for debt. The woman, Elizabeth Alady, was seized during a Nupe raid on an unnamed Yoruba town around 1850 and later taken as a slave wife. In 1864, three years after she gave birth to a son, the master-husband and his freeborn wife were convicted of a crime and ordered to pay the value of two prime slaves in fine. This was an exorbitant fine for the poor couple. Because they had no means of paying what amounted to debt, the court seized Alady and her son and sold them into slavery in order to pay their debt. However, the local CMS redeemed mother and child before the buyer could take them away.[2] This case illustrates an interface between debt and the enslavement of women and children in Yorubaland. Although most accounts of enslavement tactics in nineteenth-century Yorubaland have focused on warfare and kidnapping, many women and children were enslaved for debt. If Alady's initial enslavement was through warfare and her son was born into slavery, their re-enslavement was due to a debt owed by a third party (that of their master) and can be considered as a kind of 'credit default'. This chapter explores how debt underpinned the enslavement of women and children in nineteenth-century Yorubaland. First, it argues that credit operations, the genesis of most debts, drew more Yoruba women and children into slavery than hitherto recognized. Secondly, it discusses the diversity of debts and how debts drew women and children into slavery because of their age and sex. The chapter is divided into two parts. Part one discusses the organization of commerce and capital mobilization in nineteenth-century Yorubaland. Part two analyses the impact of socio-economic ruptures on credit transactions and how debts led to enslavement. In the section I offer new knowledge on the institution of pawnship in Yorubaland as it relates to the treatment of pawns and the thin line between human pawning and enslavement. Throughout, I differentiate between women enslaved for their own debts and others, including most if not all children, enslaved for other people's debt. For example, if a man faced enslavement as a form of judicial punishment or because he was unable to pay a fine, he might choose and be permitted to substitute for himself a slave, often a female slave gained through warfare, and also his children by her. The risk of re-enslavement women and children faced challenged Yoruba traditions which generally affirmed that 'any slave woman taken as a wife [by her freeborn owner] becomes *ipso facto* a free woman' and her children were accorded the same rights as freeborn children of the same father.[3]

Commerce and Credit in Nineteenth-Century Yorubaland

From the eighteenth century commercial credit (*awin*) was a major feature of Yoruba trade. With reference to the 1810s, Osifekunde, an Ijebu slave in Brazil, informed a French writer that '[b]arter or the exchange of goods for goods is hardly ever carried on except at wholesale'. Rather markets operated 'through the medium of a currency'.[4] However, not everybody paid cash for goods and services. Commerce also involved extensive 'trust', meaning that traders had the option of postponing payments for goods bought. In 1861, the *Iwe Irohin Yoruba* (Yoruba News), a bilingual language newspaper, described two prevailing features of the Yoruba financial system. These were the 'credit system', where traders received goods from merchants and made payments at later dates, and the 'ready money system', by which traders paid cash at each transaction.[5] The article further noted that credit allowed people to trade without any capital as payment was due in future, and that it was therefore risky and could be usurious. It involved speculation since the risk of late payment, and we must add payment default, induced traders to charge higher prices than when the buyers paid on the spot.[6] In spite of the risks involved, trade 'trust' helped traders edge out rivals as merchants attracted allies and created wide networks by granting generous credit in cash and goods.

During the Atlantic slave trade, European merchants supplied the bulk of trade credit. Before Lagos became Yoruba's major trade port, credit in the form of goods and cash came from adjacent ports in the Gold Coast and the Slave Coast. Credit networks extended across West Africa linking one port to another. In 1777, King Ologunkutere of Lagos, where the Atlantic slave trade was slowly taking off, sent his representatives to Richard Miles, head of the British Royal African Company at Cape Coast, demanding credit in 'Good goods and

Tobacco' in exchange for 'Good Trade'.[7] Although Miles's response is unknown, British traders were involved in extensive 'trust' transactions with Lagos by the 1790s. A contemporary trader, John Adams described Lagosians as 'expert traders [who] obtain from ... vessels very extensive credit'.[8] Large European firms supplied goods and cash for European traders in Africa involved in the Atlantic slave traffic, so commercial credit produced an interdependent Atlantic world market.

Data from later decades show continuations of the old credit system. In the 1840s and 1850s, Portuguese/Brazilian merchants advanced goods to Yoruba traders in exchange for mostly slaves, cotton, palm oil and textiles. At appointed times, creditors returned to collect their goods or cash. Often payment was not expected for several months.[9] Demands for debt repayment show up in letters between Lagosians and Bahian traders from the period 1845 to 1850. One Brazilian trader listed four Lagos debtors; another wanted payment for a ship commissioned by King Kosoko in 1847; and a third demanded payment for cloths and knives sold by a third trader, also to Kosoko.[10]

The pattern of credit continued into the later years of the 'legitimate' trade in agricultural goods. Credit received in coastal towns was distributed towards the Yoruba hinterland. A writer noted that credit extension in the 'legitimate' trade only enabled 'the old slave traders, to obtain larger quantities of goods than they ever meant to pay for in [palm] oil. They took goods whenever they could get them.' In short some merchants were trading with other people's capital.[11] Put differently, commercial expansion encouraged speculation by traders hoping for quick profit. For example, in 1854, Tinubu, a Brazilian merchant who already owed an enormous sum of about £5,000, 'bought' on credit from compatriot Joaquim Pereira Machado, a further 2,000 rolls (apa) (80 lbs each) of tobacco and casks of rum.[12] Kristin Mann writes that during the 1870s following decade Lagosians owing huge amounts of debt to European firms from transactions in palm oil and cotton trade included Daniel Conrad Taiwo (alias Taiwo Olowo) to whom the French firm, Régis Aîné, annually credited with about £3,333 (valued at about 40,000 gallons of oil). Another Lagos merchant, James Pinson Labulo Davies, owed to his European partners about £11,000 in 1873.[13]

Nonetheless it is misleading to associate credit transactions only with big traders. Saro (Yoruba returnees from Sierra Leone) merchants in Lagos usually supplied goods on credit to traders in the Yoruba hinterland. Often times, receivers of these goods did not pay their suppliers until several months later.[14] Among such creditors were brokers such as Fagbemi Daodu, who granted small loans ranging from £18 to £1,000 – although only two traders received more than £100. Another merchant, Olowo, also distributed credit to the amounts of between £18 and £101. Again, in the 1880s, brokers Richard Blaize and B. C. Dawodu, made loans of between £200 and £2,500 to a number of traders in and around Lagos.[15] Troubles related to debts partly underscored the general disturbances in Yorubaland during the period under study.

From Borrowers to Debtors

Bad investments and unforeseen economic forces led many people into indebtedness. Losses associated with British naval disruption of slave trafficking were substantial. Of the 178 ships that loaded slaves principally from Lagos between 1801 and 1851, fifty-five (31 per cent) were seized by the British navy. Of that number, ten were seized during the years 1801 to 1825, forty-four from 1826 to 1850 and one in 1851. Seizure meant a great loss for slave merchants and ultimately drove slave ship captains away. By 1830, the maritime slave trade had been so reduced that Egbado traders wanted to know 'why the Portuguese do not purchase as many slaves as formerly; and make very sad complaints of the stagnation in this branch of traffic'.[16] In 1849, King Kosoko of Lagos, a leading slave trader, blamed the British patrol which seized many slaves he had sent to Brazil for his inability to pay some old debts to his Brazilian allies. In his words, 'the English have made several captures, in which I have had my share'.[17]

In coastal Yorubaland, abolitionism depressed the slave market, with prices falling by 25–50 per cent, from about £30–£32 per slave in 1805/6 to £12–£20 in 1807/8; £10 in 1827; £6–£7 in 1849 and under £5 in 1850 when the Brazilian abolition of the slave trade precipitated a collapse in the external slave trade.[18] Subsequently, the bulk of slaves reaching the coast were sent back to the interior for lack of buyers.[19] While low prices enabled local producers to buy, own and use slaves, market profitability appeared too marginal to pay for goods previously bought on credit when slaves were sold at high prices. One immediate effect of the slump in slave prices was the inability of slave traders to fulfil their credit obligations.[20]

Shifts in the slave trade and falling profits are evident in correspondence between Bahian traders and their partners in Yorubaland. One trader wrote in 1849: 'business is not going well here, and for this reason ... if you are to send me some new shipments they should be ... goods that can be quickly sold, for any ordinary one cannot be sold easily even when long term credit is given'.[21] Another trader informed King Kosoko he would no longer buy slaves even 'if they could be had at 5 or 6 reis each'.[22]

How did borrowing affect nineteenth-century Yoruba politics and economy? From the outbreak of the Owu war in 1817, Yorubaland was engulfed in violent conflict for most of the century. These, in turn, caused high rates of mortality, disease, famine, robbery, road closures, large scale population dislocation and trade disruption. Incessant conflict also resulted in high demand for arms, which increased the cost of munitions and borrowing among soldiers. In 1861 the *Dane* gun, although outdated in Europe, cost the equivalent of 10 per cent of the value of a prime slave (£10.15*s*) at Abeokuta; while some £23,000 worth of arms was imported into Yorubaland (mostly Ibadan), between July 1862 and the end of 1864 . By 1881, the cost of a rifle had risen to between £10 and £15.[23] Poor soldiers mostly bought on credit, hoping to offset their expenses from the sale of booty while army officers were largely obliged to supply their fighters. Some officers took loans to meet this obligation. In 1883, after six years of guarding Ijebu Ode against Ibadan Balogun (an army chief), Onafowokan was reported to have 'spent his money and used up his stocks of equipment' and by this become 'impoverished'.[24] At Ijebu Igbo in 1884, Balogun Ogunsigun owed about 2,000 bags of cowries borrowed in order to maintain a home defence army.[25]

We should view the cost of weapons in relation to other commodities. Apart from the trade in slaves, the Yoruba also sold palm oil, cotton, kolanut and food crops. In 1861, the *Iwe Irohin* (Yoruba News) put the price of ten gallons of palm oil at around a bag (20–22,000) of cowries, and palm-nut oil and cotton at respectively 1,000 and 900 cowries per pound weight.[26] A prime slave at Abeokuta at the time cost about 100 imperial gallons of oil. Twenty-two years later, a woman working an average of five hours to produce a pot of oil and ten hours to weave a roll of local textile needed 80 to 160 pots of palm oil, or 40 to 80 rolls of 'country cloth', to earn the equivalent of the sum needed to purchase a prime slave.[27]

Another reason why people became indebted was the withdrawal of the cowry currency from circulation and its replacement with British money. The shift created monetary instability. Anthony Hopkins traces cowry instability in the Bight of Benin in the nineteenth century to first excess supply and later to the withdrawal of cowries as money starting in the 1850s by British colonialists. In the nineteenth century, the value of a bag of cowries in British shillings fell precipitously from 100*s* in 1808 to 48*s* in 1830, 40*s* in 1851, to 18*s* by the 1890s.[28] The high cost of transportation, violence along trade routes and road closures, often resulted both in a relative scarcity of cowries in the interior as well as higher exchange rate. In 1860, Robert Campbell of the American Colonization Society, on tour of the Yoruba interior, observed that very few wealthy Yoruba could raise ten bags of cowries (worth £5) in ready cash in an emergency.[29] Campbell might have exaggerated cowry scarcity by not factoring in the impact on currency supply of the contemporaneous Ijaye war (1860–2), but his observations captured some of the economic pain experienced by people in the interior. The scarcity of money forced the Yoruba to resort to borrowing but also to default in their payment obligations. As Anna Hinderer, the wife of a CMS pastor, noted in 1860, at Ibadan: 'if we do get a few people to go down [to Lagos], they will not bring even half a load, because they may have to run from kidnappers'.[30] The lack of access to physical cash increased the rate of borrowing and difficulties to make payment.

One means of credit mobilization for cash-strapped traders was the *ele* (extra, interest), where the interest and/or principal had to be paid in a lump sum on a given date. A variant on this was the *ǫda* (ǫ + da, to gather), which provided for periodic payment of the interest. When the interest was paid in full, payment of the principal could be renegotiated with new interest calculations. Interest on loans varied over time and space. Around 1851, the interest rate paid by an Egba woman, Lubake was fixed at 5*d* or 2.5 per cent every ninth day on 16*s* 8*d* owed to one of her suppliers.[31] Four years later, in 1856, Rev. Crowther noted a case where debtors paid a flat rate of 200 cowries interest every fifth day on a loan of 20,000 cowries.[32] In the interior in the 1870s, interest rates per bag of cowries averaged about 1,000 cowries or 6*d* per pound (£), payable every seventeen days. In Lagos the rate rose from between 5 and 10 per cent to 30 to 60 per cent in the 1870s and 1880s. By the 1890s, the interest rate at Ijebu on the coast stood at between 300 and 400 per cent.[33] And sometimes the interest had to be paid upfront in lump sum; borrowers agreed to usurious credit contracts because they had no better access to credit.

To ensure that borrowers did not default on their credit obligations lenders took measures to secure their investments. One of the tools with which lenders secured their loans was by demanding and receiving from debtors pawns (iwofa) as collaterals. Pawnship had multiple functions: it was a reminder of an unpaid debt; a proof that the debtor would pay back; and interest paid on loans through the exploitation of the pawn. As we shall see below, the pawn was also a form of collateral laid aside to cushion losses to creditors should default occur.

On the duties of a pawn called Anna Hinderer, the 'pawn has to work so many days for *his master* ... and the remaining days, according to *master's* generosity, for *himself*, to earn enough for his entire food and clothing', and, one must add, to raise money to pay off his debt.[34] Further on the popularity of pawnship in Yorubaland, Rev. Daniel Olubi of the Church Missionary Society (CMS) at Ibadan reported in 1876, on the eve of the sixteen-year Yoruba war (1877–93), that the 'general cry among the people [of Ibadan] [was] for want of cowries'. Food, he noted was 'cheap but no money to purchase them. A man can be pawned for [20,000 cowries] or ten shillings'.[35] In normal times an adult could be pawned for not less than double this amount. That is, the scarcity of money cheapened the value of pawns.

Most pawns were freeborn women and children. In fact, many so-called slaves in nineteenth-century Yorubaland were pawns. In 1854, Anna Hinderer, a CMS agent, noted that many slaves at Ibadan were in fact children pawned by their parents as security for debts.[36] Twelve years later Andrew Wilhelm, another CMS missionary, also wrote that most people at Oyo 'are in pawn and debt'.[37] Pawnship reminded people of an existing credit and security that the debtor would pay. The reluctance to pawn slaves might be associated with the differential status of slaves and pawns. Slaves were essentially property. Even though the creditor liter-ally 'owns' the pawn, the real control was over the latter's labour. Pawnship was a contract, slavery was not. Pawns belonged to kin groups who cared about their welfare, but most slaves were generally 'kinless'. To the degree that most slaves looked forward to the freedom through redemption, emancipation of flight lend-ers considered it a great risk to accept as pawn someone who might flee at the earliest opportunity. Evidently pawnship signified indebtedness; and its popular-ity in Yorubaland signalled extensive credit transactions. No later than the 1850s, an Oyo farm was named *Majewofaku* (do not let the pawn die).[38]

So far we have shown how the availability of credit fuelled market transac-tions in food, weapons and slaves just as hunger and the quest to free people in captivity and prevent their enslavement promoted credit financing. Defi-cit financing is noted in the proverb *olowo a wa; alawin a wa; ilu ti a gbe ni a ngbawin, ara-isan ni ko sunwon* (the rich will come, and borrowers will come; it is in one's town that one buys on credit; but credit default is bad). That is, there is nothing bad about borrowing as long as one maintains a good credit history. The fact that very few people had adequate money to meet their needs there developed a booming credit market. Credit operations became so expansive and popular that in spite of the dangers of pawnship, as we shall see below, a num-ber of Yoruba people began to stress only the positive aspects. Drawing on his own family history, Bishop Samuel Ajayi Crowther, a Yoruba slave boy turned first black Anglican Bishop, described how pawnship saved many people from enslavement – including his relations. In 1821, a combined Oyo and Sokoto Muslim army captured members of Ajayi's family. Shortly thereafter, Ajayi was separated from his mother and siblings. An uncle managed to free his mother and sister by bribing some of the captors with 5 heads of cowries (about 25*s*). Another sister was ransomed for 24 heads of cowries (£6) taken as loan for which she was later pawned.[39] The ability to thus raise emergency funds through pawnship caused Crowther and other Yoruba Christians to criticize efforts to ban the institution. In 1856, Crowther wrote:

> The system of pawns as it is practiced in this country has proved beneficial to thou-sands of families since slave wars broke out with unbounded fury. It is very often the case that after war has destroyed a town ... not only the property is lost, but a large portion of a family is also taken captive to be sold into foreign slavery. Those who fortunately escaped being caught have no other resource to ransom their captured relatives, but this expedient, – to pawn a certain number of the family for as many cowries as they need, to ransom their captured relative from going into foreign slavery thus thousands have been kept back from being removed out of the country.[40]

The danger lies in a debtor defaulting in his/her credit obligations leaving open the door to debt enslavement. The Yoruba proverb '*afotele ko je ki a pe iwofa li eru*' ('an agreement prevents the confusion of pawns with slaves') is a warning to borrowers to pay their debts to avoid the enslavement of pawns.[41] During the eighteenth century, authorities in Benin, Bonny and Dahomey banned pawnship so as to prevent the enslavement of pawns. On the contrary, in Sierra Leone, the Gold Coast and Old Calabar, pawnship largely underpinned the funding of the Atlantic slave trade and it was no surprise a number of people, including members of ruling houses, who were pawned to European traders, were enslaved for debt.[42] The prevalence of women and children in debt bondage greatly made them very vulnerable to enslavement.

Enslavement for Debt

At the peak of Kosoko's financial troubles in 1848–50, his Brazilian trading partners put pressure on him to pay them. In 1848, Joaquim d'Almeida, a Bahian merchant threatened to seize a ship belonging to Kosoko in lieu of his debt. During the following year, and still in huge debt, Kosoko withdrew his two sons from Brazilian schools though they had not completed their education.[43] Perhaps Kosoko feared his creditors might seize the boys because of his debts and sell them into slavery. This thinking finds support also in the unwillingness of Lagos chiefs, including Kosoko to send their agents to the neighbouring port town of Porto Novo on account they could be enslaved for debt. To douse this fear the leading slave trade in Porto Novo, Domingo Martinez, enjoined the chiefs to send their agent vowing that no harm would befall him: 'you ... should send a ... man here ... [to] know what I have to propose ... do not be afraid your ... young man [and] those of the headmen for I give you my word that nothing shall happen.'[44] It is plausible that the sudden recall of the children from school and fear to send agents to trade allies reflect the fear of debt enslavement on the part of Yoruba traders involved in the Atlantic slave trade. The fear persisted after the trade ended.

In 1860, Richard Burton identified debt as one mode of enslavement in Yorubaland.[45] Later in 1874, Chief Fabiyi of Abeokuta indicated a Yoruba idea of 'legal' and 'illegal' enslavement – with the former involving people 'bought', 'captured in wars' or taken as 'gifts from friends in a far away country'. By contrast, being 'waylaid' and 'kidnapped' by 'wicked people of our own tribe' was illegal and constituted unjust enslavement. In summary, the Yoruba viewed slaves as outsiders 'belong[ing] to tribes other than the [slaveholders]'[46] except in cases of criminals when enslavement was a metaphor for banishment.[47] Indebtedness was one such avenue for enslaving an 'insider'. Fabiyi delineates two modes of enslavement for debt. First, 'a man may be sold for debt, and so become a slave'.[48] The second was a credit agreement that involved human pawning.

The literature on human pawning in Yorubaland is extensive but little attention has been paid to the enslavement of pawns or the link between debt and enslavement. Instead emphasis has focused more on the benign aspects of the institution.[49] However, it is incontrovertible that some pawns, perhaps many, ended up as slaves. As we will see below, if kinship safeguarded pawns from abuse, pawns who had been separated from their relatives, whether because they were removed from their communities or had lost their parents/guardians, had no such protection and faced the risk of enslavement. In Central and East Africa pawnship served the dual purpose of debt security and exchange for debt or a means of paying off debts.[50] In parts of West Africa including Yorubaland we also have instances whereby an implicit awareness that some pawns might not be redeemed and would instead be forfeited to the creditor was present from the onset. This was why women and children – usually drawn from among slave wives and their children and other marginalized individuals were more likely to be pawned than a freeborn wife and her children. Where the labour extracted from a pawn did not pay off the interest, the balance was added to the principal, and when this was too big to repay the pawn could end up being sold into slavery.[51] Fabiyi's statement complicates evidence on slaving operations in Yorubaland. Existing studies have shown that most pawns were held by members of their own community or foreigners known to them. Hence, enslavement for debt provided a nuanced justification of how people of the same community could legally enslave each other. I would now like to address the question of how and how many female and child pawns later became slaves in Yorubaland.

Although the expansion of pawnship derived from commercial activities, credit default on pawnship payments could result in enslavement. Long overdue debts meant lengthy service in pawnship, making the status of slaves and pawns indistinguishable to most people. Certainly, creditors often treated pawns who had worked for them for many years as if they were slaves. Indeed, they sometimes enslaved them (as we will see below) so that pawns and slaves became largely inseparable.[52] The fact that both slaves and pawns were concentrated in the hands of traders and members of the upper class led to frequent confusion between the two institutions. To the degree creditors had claim to a pawn's labour and the inseparability of pawns from their labour, creditors had similar rights over pawns and slaves. The subjection of a pawn to the creditor derived partly from pressure from the pawn's family to obey.

Women and child pawns were sold into slavery for overdue debts, especially when the creditor began to fear default. Whether creditors could enslave pawns without the permission of the debtor was the basis of a dispute between Madam Tinubu of Lagos later Abeokuta and J. G. Sandeman, a British trader in 1853. Two years earlier, when both lived in Badagry, Tinubu had sent a twelve-year-old slave girl, Rosa Alabon, as maid to the Sandemans as a 'country fashion' 'present'. Tinubu disputed the girl was a gift and Vice Consul Louis Fraser of Badagry testified that the Sandemans 'hire[d]' Alabon from Tinubu.[53] Perhaps the Sandemans claimed the girl as payment (or part payment) for Tinubu's debt at a time when her creditors had given up hope of obtaining payment. To this extent, we should see Alabon's detention as a form of enslavement for debt as is suggested by Fraser who asserted that the Sandemans had reluctantly written off Tinubu's debt.[54] Moreover, at the time in Lagos a number of European traders willingly accepted pawns and slaves as currency and debt payments under the guise of receiving 'gifts'. Before his appointment as consul, Frazer had three boys and a girl 'given to him as presents'. In July 1853, to end the exchange of slaves as gifts, payment of debt in slaves and the enslavement of pawns, the new consul, Benjamin Camp-bell, banned the practice of receiving young children as gifts.[55]

Another means by which pawned women and children became slaves was when the debtor died and there was no one to pay the debt and redeem the pawns. Whenever this happened the Yoruba people took it as automatic credit default and foreclosure of the pawn that the creditor could claim legitimately as a slave. This was the fate of an Oyo boy, Sangolowomu, who the creditor, a *babalawo*, later sold into slavery in 1858. The boy's family members had pawned him for five heads of cowries (10,000 shells) to pay for the funeral expenses of his father who died some years before 1858. At the time, the parents were divorced and the mother lived in Ilorin, many miles from Oyo. So she was not around to redeem the boy and the family did not redeem him either. With no one to pay the debt and redeem Sangolowomu the creditor enslaved him. After some time Sangolowomu joined the local CMS congregation perhaps hoping the church could facilitate his redemption. Because he was afraid that the CMS might be able to aid Sangolowomu's escape the *babalawo* sold him to Abeokuta. The boy's return to freedom was facilitated by the CMS in 1859.[56]

At Ibadan, when an army chief supplied firearms on credit to his soldiers, he was entitled to between 65 and 100 per cent of any booty they might obtain.[57] Yoruba soldiers were often captured by enemies or died in battle. And of those who did return, some soldiers did so with no booty and no means of liquidating their debts or redeeming pawns held by creditors. Through this process Ibadan traders and army officers amassed pawns resulting in the concentration of slaves and pawns in the same hands.[58] It is not fortuitous that the 1850s and 1860s, the most successful years of Ibadan military adventures, also witnessed the accumu-lation of pawns, mostly children. Many of the pawns were not redeemed hence taken as slaves by the creditors. Certainly during the Ijaye war (1860–2), a num-ber of Ibadan chiefs treated hundreds of young male pawns as if they were slaves by assigning them to 'suicide' posts in battle. Indeed, all child pawns forced into the military ('*baba ni n'ma sa*' – 'father asks me to be steady') were obligated 'to fight alongside their masters whatever may be the condition of the fight, and expected to fight until death'.[59]

The enslavement of women and child pawns during periods of war also occurred at Abeokuta about 80 km south-west of Ibadan. Like the enslavement of pawns by Ibadan army officers during the Ijaye war, Egba chiefs also enslaved Ijaye pawns who fell into their hands and were not redeemed. During the war, Egba had supported Ijaye against Ibadan. When food and munitions became very scarce in the besieged town of Ijaye its people pawned their children and wives to Egba soldiers, farmers and traders in exchange for firearms and food. More than seventy children were pawned to Christian missionaries mostly for food.[60] When Ijaye fell in 1862 the town was destroyed, many of the residents were killed or enslaved and those who escaped death took refuge in other Yoruba towns. This left no one to redeem many of the people pawned during the war. In turn Egba creditors sold many of the pawns claiming they 'had authority to catch and sell all such Ijaye people as fall within their power' in order to buy ammunition.[61] The victims were sold towards Ijebu, Lagos and Porto Novo.

The relative ease with which child and female pawns became slaves or were treated as such was the topic of discussion at the CMS conference on slavery held at Lagos in March 1880. Prior to the conference, agents of the CMS habitually hired pawns for various household and evangelical works. Soon it was revealed that some agents owned slaves, some of whom had originally entered service under a seemingly pawnship contract. That is, agents redeemed slaves hoping the freed slave would pay back the cost by working for the mission agent but with no fixed scale for calculating payment. In one case, a Mrs George, wife of a class teacher at Abeokuta received one such 'pawn' whose conduct she later found to be unsatisfactory. She transferred the young female pawn to her brother, Joseph Davis, who sold the girl, though it is unclear if Mrs George approved of the sale.[62] Evidently the girl was sold to recoup what she owed Mrs George – money spent on redeeming her.

Whenever pawnship did not provide adequate security for credit, lenders used additional coercive strategies to enforce payment. For instance, if a pawn ran away the debtor must find and return him/her or send a replacement to the creditor. The pressure to service or pay back debts was great on the borrower, so much so that parents of child pawns sometimes sold their own children for disobeying their creditors out of fear that refusal to obey a creditor could anger him and put entire families at risk should the he decide to adopt more punitive measures. In 1856, in the Yoruba town of Ijaye, a man sold his son into slavery because the boy refused to remain in pawnship. While this is an unusual incident, it could be that the father paid off his debt from the sale to obviate violent payment enforcement tactics by his creditor.[63] In a society organized around kinship ties and governed by the principle of joint responsibility, debt was troubling for borrowers and members of their communities. The proverb *dandan ni owo ori sisan* (payment of head money [tax] is compulsory) captures the popular attitude toward credit obligations. Moreover, as the Yoruba believed that debts were immortal, the death of a creditor or debtor did not annul a debt. Additionally, there was no concept of insolvency. In case of death or flight, the next of kin to the parties involved, no matter how remote, must inherit and complete the contract. Should the debtor have no kin, the burden of his debt would fall upon the head of the house in which he was living. This system was alien to foreign observers. In 1859, Robert H. Stone, an American Baptist clergyman, wondered why a Yoruba landlord should be responsible for the debts of his insolvent tenant. To avoid inheriting the burden of a tenant's debt, landlords, particularly those who could not locate their tenants' kin, evicted critically sick debtors to escape the troubles associated with kinship and debt burdens.[64]

The most violent form of credit enforcement was *panyarring* (*emu* or *amuya*), a system empowering creditors to seize a debtor or members of his/her community or their property to enforce debt payment. If pawnship marked the beginning of a credit contract, panyarring signalled its collapse. Pawning provided security to ensure that debts would be paid without resort to violence, while panyarring forced payment when debts were not secured. Violence and coercion were essential to slaving and panyarring operations.[65] Panyarring increased the bargaining power of the creditor who could demand more than the original debt. The creditor, for instance, could charge for the cost of seizure and accumulated interest on loans. Victims of panyarring were treated like newly-acquired slaves and locked up by the creditor to prevent their escape. To avoid feeding debt detainees the captor-creditor sometimes sold them into slavery and recovered their loans.

Creditors purposely targeted women and children for seizure for debt because they were less capable of defending themselves. At the time of her death in 1874, Madam Efunsetan Aniwura, the Iyalode of Ibadan, left about 2,000 slaves and some unpaid debts. Whereas generally the liabilities of a deceased woman passed on to her children or husband,[66] Efunsetan had died childless, predeceased by the husband, and no relative came forward to claim her debts. In July 1884, agents of Alantakun, an Ijebu chief and trader, also deceased, seized one of Efunsetan's female slaves to enforce payment of her debt. Four weeks later another batch of creditors seized and sold another sixty-four slaves to offset what Efunsetan owed them.[67]

If Efunsetan's slaves were enslaved for their mistress's debt, the seizure of women and children for debts incurred by fictive relatives also contributed to debt enslavement. Due to the Kiriji war (1877–93) in Ibadan, many Oyo soldiers became indebted to Ijebu traders who sold them weapons at exorbitant prices. When these debts were not paid, the Ijebu seized Oyo women who, if not ransomed, were sold into slavery or taken in payment for debt and kept as wives.[68] Chief Kuku, a senior Ijebu chief and trader gained notoriety for refusing to free women seized for debt even when relatives agreed to ransom them. Again, in 1887 Johnson noted charges against Lagos-Epe traders like Edu and Asani for panyarring and enslaving about 6,000 Ijebu women for alleged debt.[69] In the following year Ekiti traders at Imesi-

Ipole also seized and sold into slavery forty-eight Ibadan traders, mostly female on account of debt. The slaves were sold to Ondo.[70]

Sometimes a woman was sold into slavery by her legitimate husband to pay off debts. During the Kiriji war (1877–1893) Ibadan chiefs imposed war levies on soldiers and households, drafted young men into the military and women into the war economy. Every compound was taxed the value of a slave. Defaulters had their houses and properties ransacked and occupants taken captive and sold. To prevent attack on their families, many poor soldiers raised the war tax by selling their slave wives in violation of social norms that regarded such women as 'free'. Samuel Johnson described the sale of these women as a 'matter of pain and grief to [Ibadan people], as altogether contrary to their custom, but the body politic must be preserved at all costs'.[71] In order to prevent attacks on their households poor Ibadan families resorted to loans under pawnship contracts. In 1879, in a memo to the CMS conference on the manumission of slaves held in Lagos in 1880 Rev. Daniel Olubi, head of the CMS at Ibadan wrote with reference to the popularity of pawnship: 'if monies are not lent, a debtor's house is confiscated and people therein are all sold into slavery'.[72]

Yet not all cases of debt enslavement derived from commercial transactions. Others had social underpinning. From eastern Yorubaland came a report around 1890 that a man, Obe, had paid over a period of time 25 bags of cowries to Harowo whose daughter he wanted to marry. Sadly the girl died before she could be married to Obe. In turn Obe demanded 40 bags (£3) rather than 25 bags of cowries as refund of his expenses and losses from currency depreciation. Failing to receive the money he seized and sold two of Harowo's children into slavery. When told that slavery was illegal and that he could be charged with slave dealing, he retrieved the children and seized goods worth £3.[73]

Old women enslaved for debt sometimes suffered the worst as the Yoruba were fond of using old (and thus cheap) slaves for funerary sacrifices. In 1882, an old female pawn was killed at the funeral of the Odofinlobun, a senior Ondo woman. Sindo, the public executioner had pawned the woman, his slave, in lieu of debt, to Abigail Najo, a niece of the deceased.[74] This story is significant in various ways. It suggests that the woman was more than a pawn. Najo possibly accepted her not as security but as 'money' or a 'good' to settle the original debt.[75] The pawning of slaves implies a degree of assimilation into the owner's household such that creditors treated pawns as a debtor's kin. In this case however, upon her transfer to another master, the old woman lost her status as a long serving slave.

Enslavement for debt probably did not disappear until the end of World War I. In a 1917 civil case brought before the Grade 'A' customary court Ake, Abeokuta, the defendant, Alhaji of Ikereku-Abeokuta declared his father was a slave (Alhaji's name indicates that his father could have been a Hausa) who, although he had redeemed himself, chose to remain with his master until the latter attempted to sell him to pay off his debts. This case is important as it demonstrates that some masters did not demarcate between serving and freed slaves.[76] As Ajayi Ajisafe noted, there was limit to which slaves or their descendants or foreigners could advance in Yoruba society.[77]

Conclusion

Testifying before the British Parliamentary Select Committee on the Atlantic Slave Trade in 1789, two British slave traders, Richard Miles and John Fountain, both drawing on their experiences in West Africa from the 1760s to the 1780s, noted linkages between debt and enslavement. About the Gold Coast, Miles observed that 'thousands of debtors' were 'sold for the benefit of creditors'.[78] Another witness, James Frazier of Bristol, described how 'debts of long standing have by order of the magistrate been adjudged to be paid seven fold, agreeable to custom'. If unable to pay the huge sum, debtors or their slaves, children and wives could be seized and enslaved.[79] Reports about enslavement for debt also came from the Senegambia, the Windward Coast and the Bights of Benin and Biafra all manifesting close interface between European and African financial systems and where credit default led to enslavement and the transfer of debtors and pawns to the Americas as slaves.[80] It is unclear how much the financing of the Atlantic slave trade in Yorubaland resembled others parts of West Africa. We should, therefore, be careful about broad generalizations. However, if not in the eighteenth century, certainly during the nineteenth-century enslavement for debt was a feature of the Yoruba economy. The growth of the Atlantic slave trade and the subsequent trade in slaves largely underpinned the violence which pervaded Yorubaland throughout the nineteenth century resulting in a huge credit industry to fund warfare and ameliorate its consequences. The interface between warfare, the slave trade and credit operations is evident in surges in the incidence of enslavement for debt during war years. This was certainly the case during the Ijaye and Kiriji wars. Although most accounts on enslavement tactics in Yorubaland have focused on warfare and kidnapping, many also owed their enslavement to debts. There is a second message in the cases examined above. Whereas adult males who predominated in the military were more likely to be taken in combat women and children often fell victim to enslavement through non-violent means such as credit default. Male debtors pawned their children and wives. However, payment default was common so creditors kept many pawns or victims of panyarring for so long that pawns, debt prisoners and slaves became indistinguishable. On more than a few occasions creditors sold pawns into slavery or kept them as personal property. The most vulnerable women and children enslaved for debt were 'outsiders' – slaves and strangers as well as orphans – with few or no local allies to prevent them from been given away as pawns or seized for debt or to force the debtor to seek their release from debt bondage. The prevalence of Yoruba women among the worshippers of Orisa Oko is usually attributed to the Orisa's function as the god of agriculture and fertility. These women wore a small, flat, piece of white and red clay on their forehead as symbols of ritual affiliation. One would think that another reason why women chose Orisa Oko was because it protected its followers against enslavement and panyarring.[81]

6 THE AFRICANIZATION OF THE WORKFORCE IN ENGLISH AMERICA

Russell R. Menard

One of the most important developments in the English colonies in America during the seventeenth century was the emergence of African slaves as a major component of the labour force. Population figures tell the story. As late as 1650, there were only 17,000 Africans in English America, just 2.5 per cent of the total population. Most Africans lived on the Caribbean islands. On the mainland, there were only 2,000 Africans in 1650, a mere 4 per cent of the total. By 1700, however, the African population approached 150,000, more than a third of the population of the English colonies as a whole, while on the mainland, the African population approached 31,000, 12 per cent of the total. There has been considerable debate over how to explain this development.[1]

On Barbados, the growth of African slavery occurred quickly in the 1650s and blacks were a majority of the island's population by 1660. In the Chesapeake colonies, by contrast, the process was more gradual, and Africans did not form a majority of the unfree labour force until the 1690s. As a consequence of Chesapeake gradualism, the debate has focused on the Tobacco Coast. Why, historians have wondered, did they take so long?[2] In its early stages, the debate focused on the legal status of the first Africans in the region and on the relationship between slavery and racism, but more recently it has concentrated towards the shift from a work force dominated by British indentured servants to one dominated by African slaves.[3]

Since indentured servitude was the major alternative to African slavery, and one of the ways debt shaped the Chesapeake labour system, as servants borrowed funds to finance their passage across the Atlantic and repaid the loan by agreeing to serve the creditor or his assigns for a term of years, it deserves close attention. Although the principle behind it was articulated as early as the 1680s, the Virginia Company devised indentured servitude in the late 1710s to finance the recruitment and transportation of workers to the colony. There is uncertainty regarding this institution's antecedents. While some historians view it as an entirely new development, most view it as an adaptation of apprenticeship to new circumstances.

There are broad similarities between servitude and apprenticeship, but there are also major differences. Servitude was largely an agricultural institution designed to move people into fieldwork, while apprenticeship was urban, aimed towards trade, crafts and the professions. Servitude attracted those too poor to purchase passage across the Atlantic, while apprenticeship was for those able to pay an entry fee in exchange for training. Servants could be sold from one master to another without consent or even consultation, while apprentices could not be sold. And despite occasional promises that servants would be instructed in 'the mystery, art, and occupation of a planter', servitude was a labour system, not an educational institution.[4]

These considerations led David Galenson to suggest another antecedent for indentured servitude: 'service in husbandry'. Farm servants were numerous in Stuart England, accounting for perhaps 10 to15 per cent of the labour force, appearing in about a third of all rural households and making up about half of all hired full-time agricultural workers. Typically they were boys and girls from poor families who left home in their early teens to work for more prosperous farmers until they could marry and set up on their own. They usually lived in their master's household, agreed to annual contracts for wages, food, and lodging and changed places frequently, often every year. Given the pervasiveness of this form of life-cycle service, it was likely an antecedent for indentured servitude and a major source of recruits for American plantations.[5]

There were important differences between indentured servitude and service in husbandry. The major differences followed from the distance servants travelled on leaving home and the length of term needed to repay the debt incurred to cover the cost of trans-Atlantic passage. This 'proved a sufficiently important economic difference to necessitate several modifications in the institution', all of which made the indenture system more rigid and formal than its English counterpart.[6] The major changes concerned length of term, the sale of contracts and discipline. Servants in husbandry served short terms seldom remaining with a master for more than a year or two, and usually renegotiating contracts annually. Indentured servants served longer periods under fixed terms negotiated at departure. While four years was the normal term for mature servants, the length of contract varied with an estimate of the time needed to repay the borrowed passage fare. Longer terms led to transferable contracts. Planters would have been less willing to pay the substantial sum to purchase a servant if they had to commit to the full term without the possibility of sale. The servant trade could not have functioned had ship captains, merchants and recruiters been unable to transfer contracts to colonial masters. To sell an English man or woman 'like a dammed slave' was shocking to some, but it was essential to the success of the indenture system.[7]

These changes, Galenson notes, introduced 'a new adversary status into the relationship between master and servant'. Longer terms joined with the inability to renegotiate contracts and change masters to produce tension and conflict evident in the frequency with which servants ran away and were hauled before magistrates.[8] There were at least four distinct forms of indentured servitude in British America, three of them voluntary. Under the most common, servants signed a contract or indenture in Britain before departure, which specified the length of term and conditions of service and which was sold to a master when the servant reached the colonies. Many, perhaps 40 per cent of those who migrated to seventeenth-century Chesapeake, arrived without written contracts, to serve according to 'the custom of the country', customs being gradually specified in colonial legislation. There were systematic differences between the two groups. Customary servants were usually younger: sixteen on average when they emigrated, in contrast to servants who arrived with contracts, who were usually in their early twenties. They also served longer terms than those who arrived with contracts even if age is held constant, perhaps reflecting that from the planter's perspective they were less productive than those with written contracts and thus would need to serve longer to work off their debt. They may also have been less skilled, more likely to be illiterate, without prior work experience, of lower social origins, more often without living parents or guardians to look out for their interests, easier marks for an unscrupulous 'crimp' and generally less sophisticated about labour relations and opportunities in the New World.[9]

The third form of voluntary servitude appeared in the eighteenth-century German migration to the Middle colonies. German redemptioners promised to pay passage fare upon arriving in the colonies, which they usually did by arranging a service contract with a farmer. If they proved unable to do so, they were sold as servants by the ship captain to satisfy their debt. In addition to these voluntary systems, penal servitude, a minor institution in the seventeenth century, became an important source of labour later in the colonial era.[10]

Indentured servants played a central role in the development of British America. During the seventeenth century, roughly 360,000 indentured migrants reached the colonies, the majority going to the Tobacco Coast and the West Indies. Servants were especially important in the plantation colonies. Roughly 70 to 85 per cent of European migrants to the Chesapeake in the seventeenth century arrived as servants and the share to the Caribbean was probably higher.[11]

Some historians object to my characterization of servants as voluntary migrants, especially to the implication that servants were able to choose among the several available destinations. Gary Nash, for example, maintains that servants 'were not making the choices. For power in the commercial connections transactions that brought labor across the Atlantic resided in the hands of the supplier and the buyer.'[12] Similarly, James Horn contends that the servant's individual desires played little part in determining where he ended up. Instead, it was the trading community that was responsible for directing and regulating the migration in response to the needs of the colonies.[13] While there were doubtless instances of outright coercion, and uneducated rural youths must have been at a disadvantage in negotiations with shrewd experienced merchants, servants were not simply passive victims of a process beyond their control. The best evidence on the issue is David Galenson's analysis of indenture contracts. Older servants with skills and work experience who could read and write served shorter terms than younger, inexperienced unskilled and illiterate ones. Furthermore, servants clearly discriminated among destinations. Those who went to Barbados, where death rates were high, opportunities slender and work regimes harsh, served shorter terms than those who went to the mainland.[14] The variations in length of term were not trivial. Among servants who left London in the 1680s, for example, those who could write their names signed on for a term seven months shorter on average than those who could not, while those who went to Maryland served nine months more than those in Barbados. Given an average term of five or six years, these are substantial differences. The patterns only make sense if it is assumed that migration was voluntary and that servants struck bargains and made choices among competing destinations.[15]

There is evidence of another type that helps evaluate the proposition that the choices servants made helped shape the pattern of migration to the colonies. If servants made the decision, one would expect that they would pay close attention to opportunities at home and that the size of the migrant stream would be inversely related to English real wages. If, on the other hand, the choices of merchants and planters controlled the migration, there should be little relation between real wages and the volume of migration. A comparison of annual fluctuations in the number of migrants who left Bristol in the seventeenth century with an English real wage index shows a strong inverse relationship, strong evidence that servants were participating in the decision to move. Servants left when wages were low. A comparison of the volume of servants arriving in several Chesapeake counties with real wages shows the same pattern, indicating that even servants who came without contracts, and who one might assume were least likely to be in control of the situation, made decisions informed by an assessment of their prospects at home.[16]

Most recent participants in the debate over the shift from servants to slaves can be grouped into two broad categories. One, which can be labelled the labour supply school represented by myself, Gloria Main, Paul Clemons, David Galenson, Allan Kulliкоff and others, views the transition as an economic process, maintains that servants and slaves were close substitutes and contends that the transition can be understood by attending to labour markets, especially to changes in the supply of servants and slaves. The argument of the labour supply school can be summarized briefly. Planters did not shift from servants to slaves because they preferred slaves, but because of changes in the supply and price of the two groups. During the first half of the seventeenth century, Chesapeake planters found an adequate supply of labour in British indentured servants. However, around 1660, the supply of servants began to decline as England's population fell while real wages rose leading to improved opportunities at home. As a consequence, after mid-century migration from Britain to America fell, for a time, Chesapeake planters did not feel the full impact of the decline as the migrant stream, initially divided between three destinations – New England, the Upper South and the Caribbean – concentrated on the Chesapeake, the one remaining region in English America where demand for labour remained high and opportunities for newly freed servants abundant. By the 1680s, however, continued decline in the size of the British–American migrant stream joined with falling opportunities and growing demand for labour along the Tobacco Coast and the opening of new American regions to settlement soon led to a labour shortage in the Chesapeake. Simultaneous with the contraction in the supply of servants, the supply of slaves exploded. The number of slaves brought to America in British ships rose three-fold from the mid-seventeenth century to the beginning of the eighteenth century: 47,900 such slaves arrived in the 1660s and 100,500 arrived between 1700 and1709. These shifts in supply led to a rise in the price of servants relative to slaves. Planters responded to the new conditions by buying Africans, and by the 1690s, slaves outnumbered servants in most regions of the Chesapeake.[17]

The increase in the slave population transformed the region, making it what has been called an 'elite slave society' in which 10 to 15 per cent of the population was enslaved, but only about 20 per cent of free households owned slaves and slave owning was largely confined to a small segment of the population: wealthy older men with political power, who owned substantial amounts of land. The slave population of the Chesapeake colonies grew dramatically over the eighteenth century, from 14,000 in 1700 to 252,000 in 1770; as it did so, slavery sunk its roots deeper and more firmly into the Tobacco Coast, gradually transforming the elite slave society of the early eighteenth century into what can be labelled a popular or pervasive slave society by the 1770s. In such a society, slaves accounted for a third of the total population and slave ownership was much more widespread as slave-owning was no longer confined to the elite. 60 per cent of the free households contained slaves, while younger men of middling wealth who rented rather than owned their farms and were without positions of power were often found among the ranks of those owning slaves.[18]

The other school, which might be labelled the planter preference group, represented by Edmund Morgan, T. H. Breen, Kathleen Brown, Theodore Allen, Anthony Parent and others, contends that the planters preferred slaves to servants for a variety of reasons and made the shift to achieve broader social, political, economic or cultural goals.[19] Unfortunately, the position of the planter preference group cannot be quickly summarized as different historians stress various attribute of Africans to explain why they were preferred. Of course, other than these to schools there are other arguments engaged in the current debate. For example, there is an emerging Atlanticist position which argues that the debate has tended to study the colonies in isolation, and thus missed the extent to which interactions between the several colonies shaped the development of slavery in English America.[20] Furthermore, it is sometimes difficult to decide to which of the two schools a particular historian belongs. Eric Williams, for example, who usually took clear, forcefully-expressed positions, straddles the fence on this issue, at one point emphasizing the differences between British servants and African slaves, and at another stressing the role of the demand for labour generated by plantation agriculture. Anthony S. Parent, Jr, to cite a second example, declares himself a critic of the labour supply school in the preface to his important *Capitalism and Slavery* (1944), but then goes on in his chapter on the labour switch to follow closely the labour supply-driven explanation of the transition from servants to slaves.[21]

Despite the variety of argument and focus among the planter preference group, their differences from the labour supply school can be efficiently summarized. Historians who stress the role of planter preferences reject the argument that the shift to slavery was, in Winthrop Jordan's phrase, an 'unthinking decision' on the part of many aspiring planters pursuing their own interests in response to shifting labour supplies. Those planters who had no preference for African slaves over British servants, but rather viewed servants and slaves as substitutes for each other, made the best deal possible without regard to long-term consequences. The planter preference group by contrast argues that planters purchased slaves because for various reasons they preferred them to servants.[22]

Despite their differences, most recent participants in the debate agree on several key points. Firstly, as John C. Coombs has noted, there is widespread agreement on chronology. Participants in the debate agree that slavery grew slowly and gradually in Virginia until the last third of the seventeenth century, when it surged before undergoing a second, more accelerated period of expansion in the first few decades of the eighteenth century. This consensus on chronology, Coombs continues, has led to 'virtually unanimous agreement' that developments in the second half of the seventeenth century triggered the shift to slavery. Historians now agree 'that the impetus behind the transformation of the colony's workforce stemmed from the precipitous decline in the availability of white servants after 1680, from systemic social instability that reached its apogee in Bacon's 1676 rebellion, or from some combination of the two'. Participants in the debate also agree that it is adequate to treat the Chesapeake as an aggregate, without distinguishing among regions along the tobacco coast or among planters of different wealth and status levels. Finally, there is general agreement that the process was completed by the early eighteenth century, by which time the region had been transformed, to use the terms of Keith Hopkins and Moses

Finley, from a slaveholding society or a society in which there were slaves into a 'slave society'. On the surface, this consensus looks promising, suggesting that we might be on the verge of constructing a broadly satisfying and widely accepted account of a major development in the history of English America. However, as we will see, the consensus is beginning to crumble, and all the points of agreement have been forcefully challenged in recent scholarship.[23]

In the mid-1970s, with the publication of Morgan's masterful book, one or another version of the planter preference approach to the transition from servants to slaves seems to have won the allegiance of many historians. By the mid-1980s, however, judging from textbooks and surveys, the labour supply explanation seems to have swept the field.[24] Recently, however, the planter preference school is making a strong recovery due to the work of Walsh and Coombs. Based on careful, painstaking empirical work, Walsh and Coombs have established that nearly all members of Virginia's elite were thoroughly committed to slavery well before either of the triggers that supposedly drove the transition. They infer from this evidence, correctly, I think, that members of the elite preferred slaves and that theirs was not an 'unthinking decision', but was rather driven by the expectation that slaves would prove more profitable than servants. The contribution of Walsh and Coombs goes well beyond reviving the planter preference school, however. In fact, they have thoroughly transformed the debate by shattering some key components of the emerging consensus detailed above. Most of Walsh and Coombs's new insights stem from their commitment to disaggregation. Previously, most students of the rise of slavery along the Chesapeake have treated planters as an undifferentiated mass and the Chesapeake as a seamless whole, distinguishing at most between Maryland and Virginia. Walsh and Coombs, by contrast, distinguishing first among planters, between elite office holders, divided between members of the Council of state and those who held high office at the county level. Indeed they leave the impression that they would like to discriminate further, but the data will not support further division. Furthermore, building on Walsh's seminal 1999 article, they have divided the Chesapeake into three subregions: Walsh argues that three distinctive agricultural subregions are identifiable around the Bay by the third quarter of the seventeenth century. Firstly, in the York basin and along parts of the Rappahannock, planters produced the sweet-scented strain of tobacco, which was much favoured in the English market and commanded relatively high prices. Secondly, on Maryland's lower Western and upper Eastern shores and on the Virginia side of the Potomac, planters raised the Oronoco strain of tobacco, which commanded lower prices and was increasingly re-exported to continental markets. Thirdly, in the lower James basin and the lower Eastern Shore there was what might be called a peripheral or provisioning region where planters were abandoning tobacco for wood products, naval stores and provisions for the West Indian market.[25]

Viewed through this disaggregated prism, the widely accepted chronology simply melts away, and along with it the triggers that supposedly drove the late seventeenth-century shift to African slavery. That simple if compelling story is replaced by 'a complex process, with multiple overlapping phases and significant subregional diversity in which the timing and extent of planters' investment in slave labour varied widely according to their wealth, location and economic need'.[26] Coombs identifies two phases in the shift to slavery (actually, he identifies four phases, which I have collapsed into two for reasons that will soon become apparent. I do not think the collapse distorts Coombs's argument).

During the first, which lasted into the 1670s, the Virginia elite, led by members of the Council of state, but in the last stages of the first phase followed by men who held positions of power at the county level, thoroughly committed to slavery. A second stage, lasting from the 1680s to the 1730s, was marked by an increase in the supply of slaves and the extension of slave holding to significant numbers of ordinary planters, initially to those in the sweetened tobacco regions, where planters were able to use their relationships with the great London merchants to acquire the credit and connections needed to purchase Africans. Their entry was followed by ordinary planters in the provisioning regions who were able to obtain slaves through their trade with the sugar islands. At first, planters in the Orinoco regions were left behind, but they were eventually by the 1730s able to join the ranks of slaveholders as the destruction of the Royal African Company's monopoly led to a sharp increase in the supply of African slaves.

The notion that the late seventeenth century surge in slavery transformed the Chesapeake from, in the language of Keith Hopkins and Moses Finley, a society in which there were slaves into a slave society has also come in for some recent criticism.[27]

Before concluding, I want to return to the question of the rise of slavery in Barbados, because events there proved so critical to developments elsewhere in the Empire, and because there are signs that a debate on the process on the island is about to emerge.

To date there has been little controversy about the rise of slavery on Barbados because it happened so fast and the explanation seemed so clear. One reason there has been relatively little debate about the rise of slavery on Barbados is that it happened quickly, without any evidence of doubt or hesitation on the part of planters. People of African descent were a majority in Barbados as early as 1660, at which time they were only 4 per cent of the inhabitants of the Chesapeake colonies.

Furthermore, there was a pervasive and compelling explanation for the rise of slavery in the concept of the sugar revolution. The Barbadian sugar revolution transformed the island in the decades surrounding mid-century. With the rise of sugar, monoculture replaced diversified farming, large plantations consumed small farms, blacks arrived by the thousands while whites left, destructive demographic patterns took hold, the island began to import food and fuel and the great planters rose to wealth and power. The central changes were the shift from English indentured servants to African slaves and the rise of the great plantations, and the explanation seems straightforward. Sugar, because of its substantial scale economies and large profits, was most efficiently grown on big units, greatly increasing demand for labor. Growing demand pushed indenture prices up, stretched the servant trade to capacity and forced planters to look elsewhere for workers. African slaves, available in large numbers in the century-old Atlantic slave trade, were the most attractive option.[28]

Yet while the sugar revolution is still widely accepted in current scholarship, it has come in for some recent criticism. Although it is clear that Barbados was changed profoundly in the middle of the seventeenth century, it is an error to attribute those changes entirely to sugar. Barbados was on its way to becoming a plantation colony and a slave society in response to the decisions of planters who grew tobacco, cotton and indigo well before sugar emerged as the island's dominant crop. Sugar did not transform Barbados by itself, but rather sped up and intensified a process already underway. The point of the critique is not only that other crops started Barbados along the road to slavery and plantation agriculture, and that sugar then arrived to finish the task, but that the success with tobacco, cotton, sugar and indigo was central to the rise of sugar. Those successes allowed planters to generate incomes and build estates that would help finance the rise of sugar. The successes with other crops permitted planters to establish their competence and create reputations as men who could be trusted with loans of the size needed to build sugar plantations.[29]

No matter how the emerging debate over the Barbadian sugar revolution is finally resolved, it is clear that the rise of African slavery in Barbados was critical to the spread of slavery throughout English America. Once they committed to slavery, Barbadians created a dense network of connections throughout British America that quickly spread slavery through the entire British Atlantic World. We can begin to penetrate that network by examining the exodus from Barbados that followed the island's commitment to African slavery, plantation agriculture and sugar monoculture. Although it is sometimes described as the most consequential inter-colonial migration in British America, historians have been unable to get a firm fix on the size of the exodus. Between the years 1650 and 1680, estimates place the numbers leaving Barbados at between 10,000 and 30,000. While the range is large, the conclusion is robust. Following the sugar boom, Barbadians scattered throughout English America, bringing with them ideas, institutions, ideologies and aspirations developed on the island, in the process making Barbados a major cultural hearth for the British Empire in America.[30]

Barbadian emigrants played an important role in spreading African slavery around the Empire, often serving as innovators, those who introduce a new idea or institution into a society or early adapters, who 'decrease uncertainty about an idea by adopting it and then conveying their evaluation to near peers'.[31] Once in their new homes, many of these Barbadian émigrés were able to establish commercial connections with the island. Very quickly, slaves began to move through these connections. Over the years 1619 to 1810, more than 70,000 slaves reached the mainland colonies by way of the Caribbean, most travelling to the plantation colonies around the Chesapeake and in the Lower South, while smaller but not insignificant numbers went to New England and the Middle Colonies. This trade has often been misinterpreted by historians, who describe such slaves as partly acculturated with some knowledge of English and planta-tion work routines, the implication being that this allowed mainland planters to ease into slavery as slaves from the islands would have seemed less strange and frightening than those directly from Africa. This is not the case, as slaves who reached the mainland by way of the Caribbean had seldom spent much time on the islands. Instead, they were simply transshipped, often purchased immedi-ately at the end of the middle passage by ship captains in the Caribbean to work the commercial connections established by Barbadian migrants.[32]

In order to make slavery work, the Empire had to guarantee property rights in slaves and create the institutional structures needed to enforce those rights. Metropolitan officials accomplished this by leaving the particulars up to the colonies, which meant putting the issue in the hands of planters; this allowed them to maintain the fiction that slavery was incompatible with English law while they went about the business of building an empire with the early modern world's largest slave population. This offered Barbadians one further opportu-nity to shape slavery throughout British America. In 1661, one year after persons of African descent became a majority of the island's population, the Barbados legislature enacted British America's first comprehensive slave code, perhaps the most influential piece of legislation ever created in British America. Four colo-nies, Antigua, Jamaica, South Carolina and Georgia adopted the entire code, while portions of it appear in other colonies, even those without plantation agri-culture or large slave populations. At the most fundamental level, the Bravados code told planters they could use slaves as they saw fit, punish them as necessary and promised that their right to control and discipline their slaves would be sup-ported by the state in Britain's rapidly developing American Empire.[33]

One key feature of the Barbadian code universally followed in British Amer-ica was the decision to classify slaves as 'goods and Chattels'. The alternative, which Jacob Price calls the Latin Rule, followed in Brazil and much of Span-ish America, was to provide slave property with special protection by classifying slaves as real estate attached to a particular plantation. Under English law at the time, this would have prevented creditors from dismantling plantations by seiz-ing their work force in debt cases. This decision was not inevitable, and it was crucial to the rise of slavery and plantation agriculture. Several colonies experimented with classifying slaves as real estate, but eventually the experiments were abandoned and all the English colonies followed the Barbadian example. This was critical to the rapid growth of slavery in British America.[34]

Slaves were expensive and planters often needed outside capital supplied by merchants on the plantation trades to build workforces. As Gavin Wright has shown, slaves were low risk investments as their mobility and liquidity made them especially good collateral, so merchants were willing to extend credit to planters to purchase slaves. Slaves were only good collateral, however, if the legal system would permit creditors to seize them to collect a debt.[35] Differences in the law may explain some of the differences between slavery and plantation agriculture in British America and places where the Latin Rule prevailed. Other things being equal (they seldom were), one would expect that in places where slaves were goods and chattels, credit would be more readily available, slavery would expand more rapidly, work forces would be larger and planters more heavily indebted than in places where slaves were real property.[36]

In conclusion, I want to suggest a way of thinking about the transition to African slavery that integrates the leading contending interpretations, including the emphasis on elites from Coombs and Walsh, the labour supply school and the emerging Atlanticist perspective, into a coherent whole. We can begin by thinking of the transition to slavery as occurring in two stages. During the first, many of the early investors in slavery migrated to the Chesapeake from Barbados, bringing with them a commitment to African slavery and plantation agriculture. Chesapeake's elite planters can be divided into those innovators who introduced slavery to the Bay and early adopters, who picked up the institution from the innovators.[37] The activities of these first investors were sufficient to produce a significant African presence in the region and to transform the Bay colonies into an elite slave society. In 1680, there were just over 4,000 persons of African descent in the Chesapeake region, about 1 per cent of the total population. These elite slave owners demonstrated that slaves could be used profitably in the Chesapeake system of husbandry, and they used their political influence to create the legal structure needed to guarantee property rights in slaves. During the second stage, ordinary planters, faced with evidence that slaves could be profitable and secure in the knowledge that the law would protect their investments, responded to shifting labour supplies and prices by investing in slaves. As ordinary planters bought slaves, the slave population grew and slavery sunk its roots deeper and deeper into the region, gradually transforming the Chesapeake into a popular or pervasive slave society in which nothing escaped slavery's impact, 'nothing and no one'. By 1740, there were more than 80,000 persons of African descent in the region, and slave owning was no longer confined to older wealthy men with political power, but had become common among younger men of middling wealth who did not hold office.[38]

7 CREDIT, CAPTIVES, COLLATERAL AND CURRENCIES: DEBT, SLAVERY AND THE FINANCING OF THE ATLANTIC WORLD

Joseph C. Miller

This essay embeds the more-than-welcome focus of this volume on debt and slavery in an explicit consideration of 'the history of a process', or rather of the many historical processes that combined to gain overwhelming momentum in the seventeenth and eighteenth centuries in the particular case of the Atlantic world.[1] The compound 'process' I will present was a culmination of long-term growth in the commercialized resources of world history, with emphasis on the significance of slaving in acquiring and building them that eventually led to the creation of the modern capitalist world. However, the process was not spontaneous; it had to be built, by concentrating and deploying the financial capital that has always been a principal means of creating historical change.

Readers familiar with my previous contributions to the series of innovative conferences in Avignon and Montréal[2] will recognize my emphasis on history as an analytical mode of understanding. With respect to the specific focus of this volume on debt and slavery, I make a distinction between 'slavery' (as a modern institution) and the historical strategies of 'slaving' that prevailed earlier and elsewhere around the world. People, the vast majority of them women and children, were enslaved in uncounted numbers, though without recourse to the public institution elaborated in the eighteenth-century Atlantic, in no small part because of the key contribution – which I devote this chapter to explicating – to funding the first fully commercialized economy in the world. 'Slavery' treated as an institution centres on what I have called a 'master/slave dyad', abstracted in timeless isolation from the historical contexts in which the parties to these dynamic relationships in fact lived and strategized. This process of analytical elimination leaves only a general structural relationship of 'domination' or 'unfreedom', with all of the effective initiative on the side of the master. In contrast, viewing historical 'slaving' and debt as historical strategies systematically embeds both parties in the swirling worlds of competition and change in which they lived, as makers as well as reactors. Thus I elaborate here my long-festering fascination with *slaving* as a *historical process*, intelligible as a richly contextualized strategy of effecting change.

Financing the Atlantic on a Shoestring

Increasingly effective banking and lending strategies in Europe, initially by the Genoese, created the financial base that supported the initial ventures into the Atlantic of the Portuguese by multiplying returns from slaving. In the fifteenth century Italian traders had sold captive Slavic women for cash in the wealthier cities of Christian Iberia. Slaving thereby gave them access to the emerging military rulers of maritime Europe, as they integrated firearms into a costly new range of military capacities. Genoese thus became merchant-bankers to the obscure house of Avis on the remote Atlantic coast of the peninsula, as its leaders struggled to impose monarchical authority on the scattered ruins of the preceding Moorish era.

The ensuing story in the Atlantic, usually told in terms of unproblematized, and implicitly highly teleological 'European expansion' or 'Portuguese discoveries', leading with tragic rapidity to 'the slave trade', I gloss less in terms of these outcomes and more – and more historically – in terms of the unprecedented challenges of financing an enterprise so costly as extending the range of intra-European commerce to the vast proportions of two (arguably three) oceans and – more significantly – extending commercial investments in the Americas definitively into production and then generating the funds to pay for the escalating military costs of protecting these remote and vulnerable investments. The financial challenge of the Atlantic was enormous relative to the limited resources of merchants in Europe, and far beyond the already strained military capacities of then-only-nascent monarchical regimes on Europe's maritime margin.

The sequence of incremental historical strategies through which Europeans invested in the Atlantic economy and made lucrative purchases from the highly productive Asian economies of the Indian Ocean, were all based on credit. The previous two thousand years had demonstrated the efficacy of debt, or borrowing against the future, as a key historical strategy of initiation in the present, an efficacious means of making changes. Credit was – unsurprisingly – central to financing the extraordinarily rapid growth of the Atlantic commercial economy from the fifteenth to nineteenth century. Since commercial debtors borrow cash, or liquidity, they therefore repay what they owe by cutting expenditures of cash and running their operations to maximize returns in currencies, or in near-equivalent similarly liquid forms. Whenever they can, they therefore appropriate resources, or factors of production – land, labour, raw materials – from outside the commercial sphere, that is from the great majority of the economies of the world, from domestic communities that did not use cash.

The European commercial economy in the era of Atlantic slaving was thus initially a small part of a much larger non-commercial world, significantly so still in Europe, and in the Americas and in Africa almost entirely so. Other general forms of non-cash subsidies include windfall or fortuitous discoveries, depleting unclaimed 'natural' resources, and coercion; the future, accessed through credit, may be the greatest of these subsidies, as it lies in the inexhaustible non-cash domain of the human imagination. The large amounts of free land and low-cash-cost labour available around Atlantic shores multiplied the cash returns on commercial investments enormously. Family farms in temperate latitudes, peasants in Europe and the populous parts of the Americas, and captives seized in Africa and put to work on the highly capitalized plantations of the American tropical lowlands thus reduced the entry costs of commercial investment in production, accelerated the resulting process of growth and concentrated its liquid returns in Europe.

The challenge, first, of financing remote outposts on African shores, and then in establishing commercial beachheads on the coasts of the vast depopulated lands of the Americas, created a long-term deficit of capital to repay the debt, first for the commercial networks that could tap extracted resources at low entry costs and then, only later, for better-financed successors able to make much more costly investments in commodity production. The financial challenges of consolidating the Atlantic increased further with the military costs of defending these commercial ventures with fortified government positions and then royal navies to defend these against attack from rival monarchies. The general shortage of capital in relation to the vast lands of the Americas and – perhaps surprisingly – also labour in Africa in turn gave advantages to opportunists who took advantage of largely fortuitous reductions in the costs of entering the race. The significant early accelerations in the process thus resulted from indirect subsidies of many sorts,[3] and the innovations of the first two centuries of consolidating the Atlantic economy – to roughly the middle third of the eighteenth century – drew their principal funding not from Europe but rather from the tapping the internal historical dynamics of Africa and the Americas.[4]

In other words, European investment in transportation and military defence of trans-shipment points was modest, or even small, in relation to the contributions of the debt-based Asian artisanry, the bullion and woodland and forest resources of the Americas, and Africans' investments in the people whom they gathered in the collectivities (local groups calculated by descent and patrons' retinues of clients, larger ethnicized regional and occupational groupings) and slaving, through which they reacted to, and initiated, historical change.[5] Rephrasing these dynamics of financing Atlantic integration in historical terms of human strategies, it could be said that the energies that allowed European seaborne merchants to prosper before the early 1700s came from the domestic and semi-commercialized economies they tapped in Africa, the Americas and Asia.

Minimalist strategies of investment also financed the fifteenth- and sixteenth-century military occupation of the eastern Atlantic archipelagos. Portuguese mariners, searching for western Africa's legendary gold, established provisioning points on uninhabited islands off desolate Saharan coasts by releasing domestic livestock to forage and returning later to hunt their feral descendants for meat for the crews of their ships. They also extracted these islands' natural resources – such as salt, wood and dyestuffs[6] – at very low costs, using short-term working funds but investing no significant fixed capital. When timber extraction left clearings, they settled small farmers from the dregs of Iberian society, leaving them to survive – or sometimes not – by making initial, though still minimal, investments in land improvements from their own and, in more successful instances, also their families' labour.

Mercantile appropriation of the plundered trophies of the military on the uninhabited islands of the eastern Atlantic met with unique success. Investment in these empty, manageably small spaces required far fewer funds than attempting to intrude on production in the populated regions in Europe (or Africa or Asia). For funding, the Portuguese military monarchy turned to the Genoese, whom they excluded from access to the gold dust from Senegambia and from Elmina on the Gold Coast – the principal returns of these Atlantic ventures. In compensation, they allowed the Italians to invest in production on the island staging posts necessary to secure return of the precious metal to Lisbon. Production of sugar appealed to the Italians. Others had been growing cane in the Christian Mediterranean for some two centuries in characteristically incremental extensions of the agricultural systems of medieval manors. They grew cane in small quantities, drawing on the improvements in land and other investments focused primarily on producing grain. They had not brought in field labourers through slaving. Crete, Cyprus and Sicily, and eventually southern Spain, were amply populated, and the numerous slaves circulating in the cities on both the Muslim and Christian shores of the Mediterranean were too skilled and costly to make them affordable for agriculture; in any event, most of them were women sought for domestic services. In terms of financing, sugar was an incremental, small-scale, low-investment, secondary add-on of the landed aristocracy rather than a primary outlay of commercial capital.

On the islands of the eastern Atlantic Italian investors faced no landed, ecclesiastical or military competition for local productive labourers. The minor aristocrats to whom the Portuguese monarchy formally granted the islands as military fiefs had few or no resources of their own to develop them. But cultivating a tropical grass, domesticated in monsoon Asia, on offshore extensions of the arid climate of the Sahara Desert, required significant water to produce the sweet juice for which cane was valued. Irrigation in turn required large amounts of capital invested in channels and equipment. Such significant, long-term investment in locations so far from both Lisbon and Genoa, and subject to maritime assault from the agents of rival European monarchies, required liquid collateral, that is, transportable, fungible, personal property capable of being seized and sold in satisfaction of unpaid debt. The land and fixed improvements, typically entailed in Europe as heritable productive combinations of land and its occupants, did not meet the liquidity requirements of commercial investors. But enslaved Africans, acquired on the mainland through commercial exchanges and held as personal property, sufficed. By extending the limited proprietorial aspects of commercial transactions in human beings in the Mediterranean legal tradition from transactional moments en route to the domestic privacy of large aristocratic or merchant households to a primary quality of fungibility, captives could be rendered collateral for the debt necessary to fund expensive equipment to irrigate the fields, crush the cane and boil its juices.[7] The definitive financial outlays came with Italian (or German, in the case of Spain's parallel strategy in the Canaries) investment in a productive labouring population acquired through slaving, itself largely an extension of the well-developed markets for captives on the adjacent African mainland. The Iberian monarchies had no direct dependence on the services of these people and no political commitment to quite alien populations, idolaters or Muslims, consigned to private interests as property. Commercialization of labour as personal property in the eastern Atlantic thus established slaving as a key strategy of financing mercantile investments, for the first time, in production.

Financing the Americas

Though the initial engine of economic consolidation of the Atlantic economy was bullion, slaving enabled merchants to supplement, then challenge and finally assert control over the key historical process of commercialized production, first in the Americas and then in Europe. It was the side entrance through which private merchants gained the initiative over military-monarchical plundering for treasure. Since enslaved Africans produced commercially valuable commodities in the Americas without substantial maintenance expenditures in cash, they contributed significantly to concentrating the specie in the system in Europe. Industrial investment, with workers paid cash wages, followed.

A fortuitous abundance of precious metals from the Americas supplemented the initial introduction of Akan gold from Africa at the core of commercial liquidity in the Atlantic. This cornucopia of gold and silver financed Spain's military seizures of the Americas in the early sixteenth century. Caribbean gold secured Columbus's first insular foothold. Plundering the treasures of the mainland Aztec, Maya and Inca extended the Old World pattern of Asian and European militarists supporting themselves by pillaging distant populations.

The English and Dutch joined the race for bullion with maritime strategies that exploited the vulnerability of Spain's silver fleets in the Atlantic.[8] Their largely self-financed privateers thus laid the groundwork for the eventual unprecedented costs of developing monarchical navies.

African and American specie also financed the three initial phases in European maritime slaving.[9] The first wave of captives in the fifteenth century, from the Upper Guinea Coast regions, filled the otherwise empty holds of ships carrying gold on the relatively short voyage back to Portugal. The second developed in the late 1400s in the Gulf of Guinea to carry captive Africans from suppliers inland from the Bight of Benin to expand the Akan mines behind the Gold Coast (Elmina) to meet Portuguese demand for the precious metal. When Benin authorities terminated these supplies in 1516, other Portuguese present for unrelated reasons in the vicinity of the mouth of the Congo/Zaire River in central Africa took up the slack. But on the challengingly longer sea route from western central Africa to the Gold Coast boats loaded with captives stopped to refresh their cargos of humans at the uninhabited island of São Tomé. The incidental, temporary presence of captives on this well-watered, heavily-wooded equatorial island invited Italian merchant investments in producing sugar there at much lower cost than on the dry islands off the Saharan shores of western Africa. By the mid-sixteenth century they had built São Tomé into the world's largest producer of sugar.

The island's Portuguese- and Kongo-linked planters demanded more enslaved Africans than they could obtain in the vicinity of the mouth of the Congo River by the 1550s and 1560s, and so they began, at little to no investment of currencies, to exploit militarism then flaring in the regions along the Kwanza River to the south. The mountains of silver rumoured to be found there also led the Portuguese monarchy to dispatch a contingent of troops, who were present in the 1580s when drought and wars and banditry overspread the area.[10] This 'perfect storm' of converging independent initiatives – São Tomé planters seeking African captives on the cheap, a Portuguese dynasty desperately hoping to emulate Spain's windfall of American silver, and climatic catastrophe enhanced by disruptions in the politics of western central Africa – financed the wave of virtually costless refugees and captives whom Portuguese merchants carried to the New World under Spain's *asiento* contracts in the 1590s. The further effective subsidy of selling them for direct payment in American specie covered the significant start-up costs – including high mortality – of learning to carry large numbers of war-torn and starving people on the lengthy trans-oceanic course from Angola to the Gulf of Mexico.

Specie – Spanish silver, supplemented by African gold – provided the liquid asset that underwrote, and ultimately repaid, European investment in the Atlantic, including Africa. Slaves were the strategy of choice primarily for merchant interests marginal to the primary flows of specie to European financial capitals. The most marginal were the Sephardic Jews, expelled from Portugal in 1580, who had congregated in the maritime, commercially open and religiously tolerant Netherlands. The Sephardic merchant networks, through connections to Portuguese Brazil, introduced the foreign capital to inaugurate Brazil-based slaving ventures to the declining Portuguese posts in the Upper Guinea region.[11] Aside from opening the sugar business for the first time to eager Dutch capital and launching a significant refining industry in the Netherlands, thus priming their major Atlantic initiatives throughout the seventeenth century, this initial introduction of European commercial investment into the Americas also set the persisting position of slaving in Africa on the periphery of the Atlantic economy.

English investments in West Indian sugar followed the prevailing incremental course. They developed first in Barbados. Until the 1640s this small island in the eastern Caribbean, settled in 1627, moved through typical slow initiatory steps centred on small farmers supported by relatively low-investment indentured servants and prisoners of war from England.[12] Dutch-related interests driven out of Brazil in the 1640s and an initial burst of English capital during the Commonwealth (1649–60) financed the conversion of the island to large, costly, slave-worked sugar estates that dominated by the 1680s. The start-up costs of this extraordinarily rapid consolidation and growth required investment well beyond the ability of the first-generation plantations to finance from operating profits.

The enabling financial credit came, again as a by-product of the quest for specie underlying the seventeenth-century development of the Atlantic, through the Royal African Company, chartered in 1672 to establish an English commercial presence on Africa's Gold Coast. The restored English monarchy (Charles II, 1660) had looked to Africa for the bullion needed to develop a navy.[13] After failure of an initial Company of Royal Adventurers Trading to Africa (1660–72), the crown chartered a Royal African Company. This Company is usually examined in relation to buying and transporting captive Africans to Barbados's burgeoning sugar plantations. It has only recently been considered in relation to the broader financial strategies of the restored English monarchy. Charles II simultaneously seized Jamaica from Spain, initially as a base to buy silver by smuggling English goods into the nearby Spanish cities of northern mainland South America. The English monarchy was strategizing still in the seventeenth-century mode of financing primarily (particularly initially, as in this instance) through plunder or otherwise seizing bullion directly.

The Royal African Company was similarly designed with specie in mind, specifically to acquire gold in Africa. It was not an integrated financial corporation but rather a company of investors connected to the monarchy and seeking quick returns for themselves, without particular concern for the long-run liquidity of the corporate entity they created to absorb the costs. The shareholders skimmed the liquid returns in specie for themselves and sold the Africans they bought to the cash-short planters in Barbados and Jamaica, on credit underwritten by the values of their enslaved captives as property. Under the circumstances of capital scarcity, the personal and other notes of debt that they accepted, and recorded in the company's books as assets, proved fatally illiquid. By the 1690s, whatever the gains to London shareholders in African gold guineas channelled through the Company's activities in Africa, the Company as an entity was holding mostly worthless paper of uncollectable debt in Barbados.[14] To relieve the ensuing liquidity crisis, the Company relinquished its monopoly on English trade along the African coast in 1698, and private traders flocked in to reap the cash beginning to flow from the maturing operations of the plantations that the Royal African Company had financed.[15]

Europeans thus paid for their principal Atlantic initiatives to the end of the seventeenth century with minimal investments of financial capital – from the islands off western Africa to the Caribbean and continental northern and southern America. The extractive strategies that their American and African suppliers adopted required similarly minimal diversions of time or resources. Although these extractive strategies were capable of sustaining the limited volumes of trade in the sixteenth century, their small and manageable scales were not capable of meeting the growing demand for further financial resources as subsequent generations of merchants extended their investments in the Americas from trade into the much more demanding requirements of establishing production. Radical extensions of merchant (and merchant-banker) investment from products into people significantly subsidized commercial production in the Americas, and hence slaving contributed to financing the initiation of the Atlantic world as a whole.

From Bullion to Banknotes: The Eighteenth Century

In contrast to these local non-cash strategies of extraction-tending-towards-violence, commercial slaving in Africa was not cheap. Rather it required significant reallocations of personnel into violence, moving captive people against their wills and defence against capture. Such investment could be undertaken only in the eighteenth century when it first became possible to borrow significant working capital from the much greater commercial and financial resources that Europeans were then able to bring to Africa. It is well known that Europeans spent more in Africa to acquire gold alone than to buy slaves until after 1700.[16] The subsequent turn to widespread slaving was also the moment at which private English traders began to lend start-up working capital to African suppliers of captives for the sugar plantations in Barbados and Jamaica.

With the Portuguese in southern Brazil burdened after *c.* 1700 by a massive infusion of gold from Minas Gerais, a not-entirely coincidental[17] 'financial revolution', centred in the City of London, multiplied by orders of magnitude the financial leverage that British investors could build on the bullion they had acquired, positioning them to lead a vast expansion of European investment around the eighteenth-century Atlantic. This asset base underwrote a Bank of England that could issue its own circulating paper, guaranteed by the English (and then British) government, and – more importantly – backing up the commercial notes of private merchants.[18] In addition, the British South Sea Company (est. 1711) secured Spain's *asiento*[19] to gain entry to the ports, and silver, of the Spanish Main; it accordingly functioned significantly, if not primarily, as a bank.[20] At the same time, the 'bills of exchange' that underwrote expanding sugar production in Barbados and Jamaica allowed European suppliers of the plantations, including slavers, to realize their returns from West Indian and African ventures in currency in Britain, and thus to reinvest in further commerce. The French monarchy, lacking similar financial infrastructure, joined the competition by subsidizing its own merchants' slaving to expand sugar production in Saint Domingue at a breakneck pace that brought enslaved Africans to the island in numbers that ultimately proved spectacularly risky.

The American and African regional economies marginalized by this growing European investment in Atlantic production were correspondingly depleted of cash resources. The familiar American examples include Chesapeake planters operating their tobacco economy in terms of private notes conveying title to bales of leaf. Traders in Luanda, Angola, developed a similar system of local private merchant notes backed by claims to the trade goods imported there to buy slaves.[21] Cash-short shippers in European outports such as Bristol, Liverpool and Nantes, but not the financial centres of London, Paris, Rouen or Bordeaux, used African markets as a round-about route to accessing first European merchant resources, and then the much greater credit developed in the eighteenth century in financial institutions. They sent second-rate and second-hand goods and guns to Africa, where they assorted them with Asian textiles and shells and American rum to buy captive Africans. These captives they sold in the Americas for specie, if possible, for commodities saleable for specie where they could, and for merchant bills of exchange redeemable for cash (even if discounted) when they had to. These circuitous investments in captives as commodities yielding cash tended to flood American labour markets, to increase production of American agriculture, sugar in particular, beyond the ability of European markets to absorb their output, and to burden the plantation sectors with debt.

Planters accordingly sought to reduce their currency operating costs by acquiring enslaved Africans with as little expenditure of cash as possible. The best-known examples include Bahian planters, in north-eastern Brazil, who bought captives with an ingenious combination of by-products of their primary cash crops, sugar and tobacco. They loaded ships with molasses-sweetened rolls of third-grade tobacco, which they sold at Ouidah and elsewhere on the Mina (or Slave) Coast in western Africa, for slaves, or to European slavers lacking these key components of the trade.[22] The Bahians sent a significant portion of the captives brought back to Brazil to Minas Gerais to sell for gold, which they smuggled down the San Francisco River and sent to Africa. There they used it to pay for Dutch, French and British goods, needed to assort the bundles of diverse imports in which transactions all along Africa's coasts were calculated, adding Brazilian to African gold and American silver for northern European slavers seeking to reduce their risks of realizing returns in specie from their otherwise circuitous exchanges of captives for commodities and credit notes in the Americas.

Gold from Minas Gerais backed a larger, parallel slaving-centred bypass of specie inflows to Europe based in Rio de Janeiro, the primary port serving the mining district hinterland. In the first half of the eighteenth century, merchant investors in Lisbon, backed by British merchants, dominated the trade to Minas Gerais that supported the city's growth from a small southern backwater to the eventual (1763) administrative capital of Portuguese viceroyalty of Brazil. In Rio de Janeiro local merchants, linked with sugar planters in the vicinity of the city and its capacious bay found themselves side-lined by Royal monopolies and a carefully controlled fleet system based in Lisbon. However, they gained a strong secondary position in the gold trade by sending a high-proof rum, a by-product distilled from the molasses left from boiling the cane juice down to raw brown sugar, to Angola, taking their returns in captive Africans, and selling them for the gold extracted from the mining district.[23]

Others, particularly in Brazil's older and less competitive north-eastern sugar plantations, kept themselves financially afloat by cashing out their proprietorial interests in slaves. Until Brazil ended African slave imports in the 1850s, the very low cash-cost strategies of Bahia and Rio de Janeiro merchants effectively subsidized the older, relatively remote, under-financed and inefficient sugar planters of Portuguese America. Gold from Minas Gerais made it cheaper for planters to acquire new hands from Africa than to attempt to control experienced, restless and skilled native-born Afro-Brazilian slaves who were fluent in Portuguese. The culture of slavery in Brazilian coastal cities had been established earlier than that in the Caribbean sugar islands and evidently carried a stronger heritage from the domestic slaveries of sixteenth- and seventeenth-century Iberia. In the general absence of legitimate wives of Portuguese background, the practice intensified whereby slave owners created local families with women of slave backgrounds and treated sons and daughters by these informal wives as clients whom they manumitted under contracts of self-purchase.[24] Restating these strategies in financial terms: masters of large cash-starved households filled with enslaved dependents, some of them their own children, released them into the streets to earn cash as hawkers or artisans, and in whatever other ways they could devise, to pay in installments for eventual legal recognition as manumitted people. In effect, their slaves were worth more to them than the prices other masters might have been willing to pay to buy them, given the ready availability of new and cheaper slaves from Africa, subsidized in the cash-saving ways sketched here. In these ways, too, the enslaved helped to pay for the financial drain on indebted American producers and for the slaving that replaced them.

Financing Commercialization in Africa

The exploding British-led commercial capacity that financed the rapid growth of indebted productive sectors of the American economies in the eighteenth century flowed no less momentously into Africa. There, commercial credit, the bundles of assorted goods offered on 'trust', stimulated and then underwrote the striking violence of slaving, as well as commercial sectors of African economies that – because they were backed by foreign capital rather than financed internally – grew into what later colonial-era economists criticized as twentieth-century 'enclave economies', independently of the local communal ethos. The Dutch, who seized control of Elmina in 1637, and the English adventurers trading to Africa after 1672, brought commercial resources to the table in significant amounts. These growing commercial credits from the Atlantic must have exceeded the capacity of Africans to repay through strategies of extracting commodities that hitherto had sufficed to meet modest European demand. More European merchants on the scene competed among themselves by offering more goods, in advance of receiving returns; they effectively were attempting to invest in 'futures' contracts on deliveries of gold and commodities, and as supplies of these were depleted, increasingly also captive people.

That is, European investors advanced, or 'entrusted', trade goods to anyone in the African communities with which they had opened relations through recognized authorities, of whatever standings. They also enabled ambitious representatives of the delicately balanced composite African political systems to obtain goods in quantities beyond what they could repay with the resources of the communities they represented. Some invested the credit they obtained from Europeans in personal clienteles of the sort that the communal ethos, based on internal resources, had previously managed to absorb back into communities. Over time, Africans financed by growing European credit were increasingly marginal people, starting from deficit positions in their local communities, and attempting to buy their ways into its networks of connections with credit from outsiders. European credit thus shifted the initiative in Africa's exchanges with the Atlantic from ongoing local dynamics to individuals who used assets borrowed from European creditors to stand apart from their communities. European commercial credit thus also financed indebted Africans' escalating turn to systematic violent slaving in the second half of the seventeenth century.

The independent initiatives that, successively, Dutch, British and French capital financed, appeared everywhere along Africa's Atlantic coasts. For example, 'Fante' coastal traders along the Gold Coast developed armed caravans to compete to sell Akan gold to the Dutch and others, and these provoked authorities inland to buy muskets for self-defence. Then warrior regimes had to meet the growing costs of militarization through the territorial expansion characteristic of military regimes anywhere in the world, but in Africa – owing to the European market for captives – raiding and removing people.[25] In the 1670s the escalating militarization, launched on credit from European merchants, increased African demand for muskets and gunpowder, and the English ability to meet this demand for arms had a great deal to do with establishing their strong position in the growing Atlantic trade in African captives. The wealthy and well-armed network of Akan chiefs controlling the sources of gold in the forests still further to the north then united in a military alliance that by the 1720s became the famed Asante warrior polity that subsequently dominated the region. The costly debt on which militarization was launched forced borrowers to pursue further violence to capture people to sell to maintain their sources of credit. The resulting escalation drove a tidal wave of violent expansion north towards the interior between *c.* 1600 and the end of the eighteenth century.

The efficiency of militarized violence, self-financing in its initial stages, as previously throughout Asia and Europe but in Africa amplified by the external debts that drove borrowers in danger of default to save themselves by stealing, explains why the pattern recurred so regularly throughout Atlantic Africa. But plundering – or in the African case, capturing people to sell as slaves – quickly reached the point of diminishing returns as the communities targeted built defences or retreated into inaccessible locations[26] and as the logistics of operations on increased scales became more costly.[27] This financial dynamic of initial successes followed by rising costs, based on borrowing, produced what I have called a moving 'frontier of slaving violence',[28] as raided community after raided community on the inland edge of the borrowing took goods on credit, drifted towards default, and took up raiding to save themselves. These longer-term failures of expansive violence also account for the pattern of its repetition. As this slaving frontier moved convulsively inland, the older military regimes in the regions nearer the coast covered their growing costs of sustaining military rule by borrowing from the brokering communities near the beaches or by developing regional trades in commodities to supplement their deficits to the Atlantic. The Asante were perhaps most successful in diversifying their economy into kola nuts for sale to the Muslim populations to their north.

To the east and south in the Niger Delta, the Cross River and the Cameroons River, riverine transport routes shifted the African competition from militarized raiding of territories and control of populations to much cheaper, mobile canoes staffed by armed paddlers and other personnel recruited through slaving. The famed 'kinglessness' of this region, considered in the context of monarchical or other political authorities' interests in protecting local populations against seizure and removal, may also have contributed to the seemingly limitless numbers of captives produced by the commercial credit of the British, the principal financiers of the trade in this region.[29] Among the many small communities competing for land and population east of the lower Niger and south of the Benue as far as the Cameroun Grassfields the pressures of taking on debt to get ahead of neighbours would seem to have been all but unavoidable. Semi-mercenary bands, using credit obtained from Europeans to distribute imports widely through the interior, operated outside the networks of its reproducing agricultural communities. Without diversion of scarce funds to support the costs of full-scale militarization, the volume of slaving in this region grew accordingly.

The traders offered goods to local communities on terms of credit that ultimately exceeded the ability of borrowers to repay in forms other than captives, and the creditors operating the legal institutions through debt ended in foreclosing on the debtors. Certainly one suspects collective debt underlying the 'enforcers' among Igbo populations who, by the late eighteenth century, operated the Aro Chukwu oracle as a 'court of no return'. The well-known anomalously high proportions of women among the captives eventually appearing at the coast in the Bight of Biafra for sale to Europeans would have been the product of whole communities condemned, women and children as well as men. Credit was more productive of captives than conquests.

In general, since Africans preferred to keep female captives for their reproductive abilities, and since European buyers of slaves in the Americas desired young males for heavy labour, the proportion of women in the Atlantic trade, about a third, was not low relative to the males crossing the Atlantic but instead high relative to both demand and supply. The anomaly can be explained by the degree to which debt in Africa, and in the Americas, financed slaving. Suppliers and buyers alike had too much invested in their business, and so African debtors sold females they would have preferred to keep, in effect liquidating their human assets, and the planters bought women (and eventually children) to protect their investments in the assets needed to produce sugar, even at lower levels of efficiency, so long as they covered their maintenance costs, thus allowing their enterprises to slip back into debt.

Financial Collapse and Colonial Conquests

Following British suppression of European maritime slaving in the nineteenth century, Africans extended from collecting extracted commodities – wild rubber, beeswax – towards processing them. In developing vegetable oils for export

Africans moved to production itself, largely in the form of personnel, most of it acquired through slaving. Palm products from wetter regions were transitional between extraction and production, and peanuts from the drier latitudes near the Sahara were fully agricultural. Both were cultivated by slaves. The parallel with European merchants' move into production in the Americas, also via slaving, was exact.[30] But, again, production was not cheap. Loans backed by European commercial credit forced foreclosures on African debtors and were often extended to entire communities by the communal ethos of collective responsibility to outsiders. Arguably, foreclosure on debts – backed by violence – became as important as a source of captives as systematic militarization. Financial techniques of obligating, then seizing debtors no doubt operated through many, if not all, of the networks built through the preceding phase of borrowing, from heirs to the military strategies of a century earlier to the caravans that ranged across central Africa, to Bobangi canoe traders of the Congo River basin and the Aro of the Niger Delta, to 'kings' in the grassfields of Cameroun, to owners of shrines in Senegambia. One can speculate further on the growing indebtedness, which – as Tony Hopkins famously pointed out almost half a century ago[31] – triggered requests for European government intervention by British merchants at Lagos and elsewhere in western Africa when global prices for vegetable oils collapsed after 1873;[32] even marginal, reluctant government moves in support of beleaguered marginal merchants set in motion diplomatic processes in Europe that culminated in the colonial partition of Africa in 1884–5 in Berlin. This era of pervading commercial debt generated the lingering sense of commercialization as a plague of witches,[33] eating away at the bonds of the communal ethos and converting a secure and mutual sense of belonging to the one-sided commercial sense of bondage. The consequences of unpaid commercial debt were binding as the personal proprietary control of commercial slavery.

With British suppression of trans-Atlantic slaving proceeding incrementally, slavery in the United States and in significant sectors of southern Brazil became self-financing through demographic reproduction of native-born populations of African descent retained in increasingly proprietorial conditions. Slaves became the fungible assets, from the sales of whom declining agricultural sectors on the Atlantic seaboard of North America, and also in north-eastern Brazil, preserved the aura of their former prosperity into the 1830s and 1840s. Surplus slaves sold into the booming labour markets of the Cotton South simultaneously became the instruments through whom planters in the Chesapeake shifted their investments from tidewater tobacco to wheat in the upcountry piedmont and into local infrastructure and industrialization.[34] Enslaved Africans and African-Americans were the collateral on whose commercial value new sugar and coffee estates in Cuba could be financed as well.

In these varied, infinitely flexible ways, assets held in human form may be said to have financed not only the beginning of slavery in the Americas but also the beginning of its demise, as they contributed their value as assets to the creation and early growth of productive sectors in the Americas, independent of European (principally British) investment that was otherwise moving on from direct interests in production of commodities to the infrastructure – railroads, canals – that connected inland agricultural producers with urban markets on the Atlantic coast and to the growing industrial processing capacities of Europe and New England. Burgeoning financial institutions in the north-eastern United States followed the path blazed more than a century earlier by the private successors to the Royal African Company in Barbados by underwriting the viable slave-based production that had advanced from initial phases of indebted investment to profitable returns.

Conclusion: Atlantic Commerce, Credit, Debt, and Slaving

The long-term strategies of financing the unprecedented, and eventually globalizing, commercial growth of the Atlantic from the fifteenth to nineteenth centuries represented a novel and definitive disturbance in an enduring tripartite balance that land-based militarists, merchants and agrarian peasants in Asia had maintained for two millennia. The mobility and relatively low costs of maritime transport and the vast liquidity leveraged on African gold, American silver and then also gold from Brazil enabled merchants for the first time to move beyond transporting, inventorying and distributing the products of others – landlords (military, ecclesiastical and the cultivating communities resident under their control), or master artisans and workshops filled with apprentices, and to invest in production itself in Atlantic plantations. Merchants in Eurasia had previously operated entirely without people, the human energy then at the base of all production. In maritime Europe in the sixteenth and seventeenth centuries, they made this move from positions marginal to the landed wealth, military power and sanctity of their Christian homelands. Their commercial economy in the Atlantic grew faster even than the specie entering it could finance, and slaving in Africa – the single region among all those involved not dependent on gold or silver for its productive systems and trading networks – effectively subsidized specie-based commercial growth in the European Atlantic by accepting goods, by-products of artisan industries in Europe and Asia, in return for human beings saleable for cash, whose labour in the Americas produced commodities worth the currencies they sought in Europe, or in specie itself.

The other novelty in the Atlantic was the unique backing given merchants by monarchies on the maritime fringe of Europe. They were similarly marginal on the pan-Eurasian scale. Unlike their counterparts in the immense and heavily populated territories open to conquerors in Asia, warlords in the confined spaces of fifteenth-century Europe had limited populations or land for the waves of conquests necessary for warlords to prevail by plundering. Although a Christian community of faith was difficult to reconcile with the acquisitive individualism of commerce and corresponding investments in debt, the Catholic Church and Christian kings, the military defenders of the faith, had benefited from growing commercial wealth by isolating merchants and bankers in independent cities or working with merchants of origins foreign to their terrestrial domains. It was therefore that the financial backers of Atlantic commerce emerged from regions in Europe unburdened by strong military rulers – led by the Italians associated with the Portuguese, but joined by German bankers working through Spanish monarchs, and then Jewish merchant communities working with the Protestant Dutch. On then did monarchs in late-starting England and France combine powerfully with merchants with bases in home ports. With military protection overseas they found fertile ground to invest significantly for the first time in production in the demographically and legally open spaces of the Atlantic, with their major initiatives resting on an accumulating pyramid of debt secured by the commercial value of enslaved Africans.

Merchants' resulting large-scale commercial ownership of productive lands in the Americas, not to mention also their enslaved occupants, was unprecedented in Europe, Asia and Africa. Financed by an extraordinary infusion of specie, by the end of the seventeenth century the financial demands of Asian trade, militarization and increasingly grandiose monarchies, and plantations staffed by expensive imported African workers nonetheless outgrew the capacity of Europe's bullion reserves to finance them. With the failure of the Royal African Company, and not yet transfused with Brazilian gold, England side-stepped the looming shortage of specie by shifting to paper instruments of credit and institutional methods of reducing the increasingly leveraged risks. This financial breakthrough, followed elsewhere only with significant delays owing to shortages of specie to support it, made the eighteenth-century Atlantic an era of a rich array of competing investors in indebted producers of plantation commodities in the Americas and in no-less indebted reproducers of people in Africa. Commercialized slaving had supplemented bullion in integrating the Atlantic economy, transcending local and regional senses of community and corroding enduring relationships of mutual responsibility in Africa, eliminating them in the Native Americas, and concentrating material wealth in Europe.

As merchants developed slavery in a proprietorial sense in the earliest phases of creating plantations dedicated to producing sugar, human capital became a significant means of creating the collateral that secured otherwise unlikely – or prohibitively higher-risk – commercial investments beyond what had started as an essentially military overseas venture. The Iberian monarchical sponsors of this first round of exploration and conquests, keyed on bullion, particularly Spain, spent their returns in armaments and further military campaigns in the Mediterranean. Later, more marginal monarchs in England turned to local merchants who invested in productive – and thus economically modernizing – ventures of lesser risks closer to home, technologies and cash wages in Europe, as well as armaments. Their concentration on a growing European economy left the Atlantic to other, less well funded interests to try to 'cash in' on the core bullionist financial strategies in the Atlantic, though only from the margins. Slaving thus helped to turn a commercial sector of a much larger economic system dominated by military and ecclesiastical interests into a thoroughly commercialized modern economy.

8 UNPAYABLE DEBTS: REINVENTING BONDED LABOUR THROUGH LEGAL FREEDOM IN NINETEENTH-CENTURY BRAZIL

Henrique Espada Lima

Many workers in contemporary Brazil experience conditions analogous to slavery. Usually bonded by debts related to the payment of alleged costs of transportation, tools or even food, many workers in very different circumstances are forced to perform harsh physical labour in order to fulfill obligations that were never part of any clear agreement or legal arrangement. These forms of labour bondage, often termed contemporary 'slavery',[1] are present in both remote rural zones, such as in the illegal timber extraction and charcoal burning areas of the northern states of Pará or Maranhão, and urban areas, such as the sewing sweat-shops of São Paulo that exploit illegal Bolivian immigrants.[2]

These forms of bonded and forced labour inhabit the fringes of the legal system, drifting sometimes into grey areas unforeseen by laws intended to protect workers. The usual attempt to read these forms of forced labour as 'survivals' of a slave past often miss the point about the profound differences between chattel slavery and forms of forced labour linked to indebtedness. Much contemporary bonded labour is found in economic sectors integrated into global market, such as the steel industry (for example, pig iron manufacture) and agri-business. However, the question of the connection between new and old forms of bonded and 'un-free' labour can be fruitful if reframed in a historical context that illuminates some of the ambivalent relations between chattel slavery, debt bondage and other forms of coercive labour. I argue that this historical nexus is less dependent on the survival of old practices of enslavement than on the creation of legal and socioeconomic conditions that allowed new forms of bondage to be reinvented – as occurred in nineteenth-century Brazil, even while the ideologies of free labour and voluntary contract increasingly became the rule.

This essay will address these questions by drawing on sources from nineteenth-century Brazil at a time when human property was a legal and intrinsic part of a broader system of labour management in the country. The time frame runs from the slow introduction of new legislation from the early 1830s that progressively limited the slave trade, to slavery's final abolition in 1888. This chapter examines two intertwined issues during that critical transition: First, these new laws' means of regulating free labour developed in tandem with legislation concerning slavery and the slave trade; and secondly, the range of different labour arrangements in which free workers engaged was related to the changing legal framework. Through an analysis of contracts made by ex-slaves to pay for their manumission – a practice regulated by laws aimed at the gradual extinction of slavery – this chapter will further demonstrate the centrality of debt in the creation of new forms of bonded labour.

Free Labour and the Law

For a long time, the conventional view was that abolition of slavery in 1888 marked the critical turning point for the development of a free labour market in Brazil. Over the past few decades, however, revisionist historians have argued that throughout the nineteenth century the boundaries between 'slavery' and 'freedom' were often unclear. They rather pointed to the 1871 'Free Womb' Law[3] as the decisive moment in the transition from slave to free labour, for it ruled that thereafter all children born to slave mothers would be considered free, and that masters accept self-manumission from slaves able to pay them their market value.[4] Revisionists have since also acknowledged that prior laws limiting slave imports had an impact not only on slaves but also on the concept of free labour.[5]

From 1815, due to British pressure, late colonial and early independent Brazil adopted progressively anti-slave trade legislation.[6] In 1831 it promulgated a law outlawing the importation of new African slaves. Although not enforced – at least 760,000 Africans slaves were illegally imported between 1830 and 1856[7] – this law served as a warning to plantation owners, especially those from the flourishing new areas of coffee cultivation in south-east Brazil, many of whom served in parliament, that future slave supplies were in jeopardy.

An important counterpoint (and complement) to anti-slave trade legislation was simultaneous, if gradual, introduction of 'free', mostly European immigrants. Among the various attempts to encourage organized immigration (including localized experiments with Chinese labourers in the 1830s and 1850s),[8] two main patterns emerged: first, the introduction of self-employed *colonizers*, settled in regions without large export-based plantations such as the southern states of Rio Grande do Sul and Santa Catarina (where a German colony was established as early as 1829). More important for the purposes of this chapter was the introduction of immigrant workers onto the larger coffee and sugar plantations in the south-east where the use of slave labour was widespread. Planters there established 'Colonization Societies' to recruit and transport poor (mostly Portuguese) European workers as part of an 'agrarian policy' designed to ensure a sustained labour supply.[9] Some leading planters were simultaneously involved in the illegal slave trade, the recruiting and importing of 'free' workers, and in the parliamentary discussions about the creation of a proper legislative environment to frame and regulate labour contracts with nationals and immigrants, and to protect their investments in labour.

It is important to note that slave-owning planters were the main architects of state policies in early independent Brazil. After the proclamation of the 1824 *Constitution of the Empire*,[10] which tried to combine centralized state power with expectations of political modernity, national sovereignty and liberal notions of citizenship, legislators sought to draft legislation to effectively enforce these ideals. Reflecting their awareness that slavery as an institution was under challenge, and with it the future supply of a reliable and disciplined workforce, their discussions centred around the future of slavery and the problem of how to encourage immigration of free labourers.[11] They sought to complement immigration policies advanced from the later 1820s with new legislation regulating free labour contracts.

Parliament passed the first such law on 13 September 1830. Proposed by Nicolau Pereira de Campos Vergueiro, the São Paulo senator, one of the most powerful politicians of the early Empire and an important coffee planter, the law provided the first general 'written contract for hiring the services of a Brazilian or foreigner [worker], inside or outside the Empire'.[12] It dealt essentially with the transfer of labour contracts made between workers and labour supply agents, and the obligations of hired workers. Specifically, it imposed heavy fines on workers who changed employers, and foresaw penalties, including imprisonment without trial, for failing to perform, or for evading, the duties for which workers had been hired.[13] While no safeguards were granted to labourers, the law aimed to ensure planters that their investment in workers (including transport and the administrative costs of contracts) would be protected against other employers who attempted to entice their workers away. A worker's ability to renegotiate the terms of the contract was therefore extremely restricted. In short, the 1830 law attempted to ensure the availability of a cheap workforce in a way that would not undermine traditional strategies of labour management.

A second law passed in 1837 stipulated the conditions whereby contracts involving foreign immigrants could be revoked by employers and, in the case of proven employer abuse, by workers. However, it chiefly represented the planters' interests. For example, workers (and any agents who attempted to entice them) who tried to leave one employer for another could be sentenced to imprisonment or forced labour in public works. Remarkably, the word 'debt' appears several times in the clause covering the original bond between the lessor (of a service) and lessee, making it clear these early labour contracts explicitly and intentionally entailed worker indebtedness to the employer.[14] This 1837 law stipulates onerous penalties for a worker who signs and then breaches a labour contract; the law's Article 9 states that the contracted worker – defined as the 'lessor of service' – who '*without just cause, quits or is [otherwise] absent before completing the time stipulated in the contract, will be arrested wherever he is found and will not be released until he has **not** paid double the amount that he owes to the lessee*,' minus the amount the worker had already earned in wages. Should he be unable to pay the debt, he would have to work it off.[15]

The contracts envisaged by the 1830 and 1837 laws were very similar to colonial *indentured* labour contracts. In his analysis of Portuguese *engajados* (contract labour) from the 1830s, historian Luiz Felipe Alencastro emphasizes that the circumstances of their transportation, and their sometimes illegal status (some immigration was clandestine),[16] often placed contracted workers in a highly precarious situation. Immigrant Portuguese workers probably provide the best example. From the 1830s, large numbers of people, mostly from northern Portugal and the Azores Islands, migrated to Brazil to escape pauperism and increasing land prices. Some found work as clerks and assistants in the retail trade businesses run by their countrymen in cities like Rio de Janeiro (where the Portuguese had a near monopoly on retail commerce), working for very small wages or simply in exchange for food, housing and the promise of future partnerships. Others engaged in public works like road building. However, most signed contracts with the captains of the ships on which they sailed to Brazil or with the 'Immigration Company' representatives who directed them to plantation labour on coffee farms in Rio and elsewhere. These contracts generally stated that the immigrant would pay for transport costs (trans-Atlantic and to the plantations) for which they were usually charged double the usual rate. Moreover, as stipulated by an engagement contract (*contrato de engajamento*) made in São Miguel Island (Azores) in 1836, the worker, himself, as well as his property and that of his heirs, was considered to be held as a pledge against the repayment of the original loan; 'workers could not leave the ship without the Captain's authorization.'[17] Upon arrival in Brazil, the contracted workers' labour was 'sold' to plantation owners by intermediaries. In 1843, Portuguese authorities investigating the labour conditions of their countrymen reported that most workers so contracted had to work for at least three years without pay in order to pay off their accumulated (chiefly 'transport') debts.[18] Thomas Davatz, a schoolmaster, emigrated with his family in 1855 from Switzerland to work as a contracted worker on a Ibicaba coffee plantation owned by Nicolau Vergueiro on the western frontier of São Paulo province. In 1847, Vergueiro had experimented with 'free' contract labour through establishing a sharecropping system (*parceria*) wherein workers would be remunerated according to their productivity and the variations of the coffee market. Davatz, who fled Brazil in 1857 after leading a tenant-farmers uprising in Ibicaba, wrote contrasting the contracts workers signed upon entering this 'model farm' with the often harsh ways in which they were subsequently treated.[19]

The São Paulo hinterland often suffered from unpredictable weather conditions such as cold temperatures and low rainfall, both of which had a deleterious impact upon coffee bushes. Hence plantation productivity, unlike production costs, could not be predicted. At the same time, coffee was hardly compatible with subsistence cultivation. Workers were thus almost always dependent for food – as they were for medical care and tools – on plantation managers who charged often exhorbitant prices and subtracted the costs from future wages, thus multiplying the chances of debt escalation and the perpetuation of bondage for workers and their families.

Comparisons between free workers and slaves were inevitable. Quoting a Swiss commissioner's report on working conditions in São Paulo plantations, Davatz narrates the story of a planter who had bought a farm along with all its tenant-farmers (*colonos*, as they were called) who 'reached the point of beating the *colonos* for refusing to sign a contract proposed by the same farmer, whom they did not want to be their employer'.[20] Even though physical violence towards the *colonos* was less common than his account might suggest, Davatz likened the punishments inflicted by private planters and their agents on nominally 'free' labourers to those suffered by slaves: Workers received severe monetary fines for hosting strangers, protesting against short-measure supplies, or complaining about mistreatment to local judges.[21] Such comparisons were not just rhetoric; legislators and planters openly admitted that the introduction of 'free' workers would not challenge their control – one informed by long experience of slave ownership – over labour.[22]

The tension caused by the different expectations of colonists and planters was partly responsible for the failure of the free labour experiment in new plantations – at least until the 1870s when, due to the imminence of abolition, the issue of labour supplies again seized parliament's attention parliament.[23]

Freedom, Debt and Contract before the Law

The early legislation restricting slave imports impacted on the management of all (free and slave) African labour in Brazil. The first concerned Africans on illegal slave ships captured by British and Brazilian authorities who were introduced into Brazil as '*africanos livres*' (lit. 'free Africans' but better defined as 'liberated') and, as Beatriz Mamigonian shows, subject to all the ambiguities of the concept of 'freedom'.[24] They were not slaves – they could not be sold, donated, pawned or manumitted. However, they were classified as non-citizen foreigners who were allowed neither to return to Africa, nor to live in the new continent as truly 'free' persons. Denied juridical personhood, they could be legally represented only by curators and legal guardians and thus had no right to enter into contracts. Rather, the state kept 'liberated Africans' as a reserve workforce, assigning their work at public auctions to private citizens as domestic servants, labourers, or *'ganhadores'* ('earners') who performed urban odd jobs (as carriers, masons, street-sellers, etc.). They received food, clothing and 'training', but any earnings received were retained by state authorities for a mandatory term of fourteen years after which the Africans received official papers granting them complete 'freedom' (and associated entitlements), and either their accumulated wages or a passage back to Africa.[25]

The unstable conditions that the law established for *africanos livres* not only increased the opportunities for their illegal enslavement[26] but also, more generally, made the conditions under which they lived virtually indistinguishable those of Brazil's enslaved population. Compulsory work, supervision and coercion were intrinsic parts of their 'free' status. The combination of tutelage and precarious freedom was by no means exclusive to the lives and labour arrangements of 'liberated Africans'; this particular population's experience only reveals especially sharply the ambiguities that many other workers of African descent would face in their many transitions from legal bondage to free labour.

What the simultaneous regulation of 'liberated Africans' and the whole set of laws concerned with the labour of European immigrants had in common was the fact that they were responsible for establishing a new horizon of possibilities for forms of free labour in Brazil. But this horizon was inseparable from the continuity of slavery in practice, and thus these emerging labour arrangements not only affected all free workers but also influenced the lives and expectations of those Brazilians who still were, or who had formerly been, enslaved.

Despite the 1831 law proscribing the slave trade, slave imports remained vigorous for almost two more decades. The new plantations growing coffee for export in the west of São Paulo province were overwhelmingly dependent on newly imported slaves from Central Africa. Not until September 1850, due to mounting British pressure, did Eusébio de Queirós Mattoso da Gama, Imperial Secretary of Justice, proclaim a law equating the slave trade with piracy and suppressing the custom of assigning illegally introduced slaves to private citizens. Unlike previous legislation, it included adequate measures effectively to suppress slave imports.[27] Within a fortnight, two further pieces of legislation were passed: the 'Land Law' and the regulation of the National Guard.[28] The first established that the only way to assert legal private propriety rights over vacant lands would be through purchase, severely restricting the access to land by the free Brazilian labouring poor, as well as immigrant workers. The second law reinforced the state's power of compulsory recruitment for the National Guard, thus strengthening one of its most important tools of labour coercion.

The combined impact of these different but associated pieces of legislation on the legal and practical conditions of the labour market – free and unfree – was widespread. The end of the Atlantic trade impacted first the Brazilian slave market by inflating prices, which, in addition to the strong and continuous demand for a labour force, led to a considerable increase in the internal slave trade. The uninterrupted arrival of immigrants affected the labour market in urban areas, depreciating wages even as the cost of living increased.

Promoting the transfer of slaves from the peripheral areas less involved in the export markets – and thus less dependent to captive labour – and increasing the costs of manumissions for the captives themselves, the abolition of the slave traffic had a paradoxically negative impact on the life conditions of many enslaved men and women. In urban areas, however, despite the new difficulties, there is no evidence that the practice of slave manumission had lost its importance, even if the terms of the negotiation between slaves and masters had changed.[29] Therefore, wherever the slave population decreased, former slaves became even more visible. Growing official concern with the 'idle' and the 'vagrant' poor – who were already the favourite targets for compulsory military recruitment – developed in tandem with a set of government policies broadly aimed at disciplining and controlling the labour force that paid special attention to the formerly enslaved.

The growing presence of poor immigrant workers competing with freedmen and rented slaves in the urban labour market after 1850 also contributed to the socioeconomic changes that made free wage labour more influential in defining the legal and practical content of labour relations in Brazil, for both employers' and (free and un-free) workers.

There was also increasing monetarization of both free and unfree labour relations. The common practice of renting out slaves expanded so that work for wages and slavery often intertwined. Alencastro cites two examples from advertisements in 1864 that appeared in *Jornal do Commercio*, an important Rio de Janeiro newspaper. In one, a plantation owner from a rural area near the city was looking to rent 200 slaves to be 'employed and directed as wage workers' growing cotton, and in the second, a slave owner offered 300 slaves for hire in Rio.[30] These examples show that employers were willing to pay wages to free and enslaved labourers alike – thus perpetuating the institution of slavery. At the same time, whereas before mid-century access to currency and cash rewards was a major incentive for slaves to buy their own freedom, increased slave access to paid work after 1850 undermined that motivation.[31] In the cities, paying for manumission was also connected to access to informal credit, usually at high interest rates, which often resulted in further indebtedness – usually paid off by working for long periods without payment.

The dynamics of social change connected to the expansion of free labour and the gradual disintegration of slavery is much better documented for urban areas. In cities, there exist detailed notarial records of formerly enslaved men and women who gained their freedom through arrangements involving some sort of indebtment. In January 1848, for example, in Desterro, capital of the southern province of Santa Catarina, a freed black woman named Maria Leocadia, accompanied by a Captain Fernando Antonio Cardoso, visited a notary to sign a 'Deed of Service Rental' (*Escritura de loucação de serviços*), an arrangement she appears to have made in order to pay a debt to Cardoso incurred in order to purchase her freedom. She promised to pay off the debt with ten years of her services, the work of her daughter (then just seven months old) for a term of twenty years, and committed herself to 'accompany the creditor anywhere he goes and obey him as if she were his captive'. In return, Cardoso pledged 'to feed her, to clothe her, and to treat her illnesses' and provide her daughter 'with proper education'.[32] Again, in 1869, in the parish of Nossa Senhora da Lapa, also in Desterro, the freed '*crioulo*' João Caetano rented his services for eight years to Manoel Carlos Viganigo from whom he received a loan of $300,000 *réis* to pay for his manumission. According to their contract, should the former slave decide to seek employment with someone else, he would be forced to repay the full amount of the debt, regardless of services rendered in the interim.[33]

These are samples of the many labour arrangements into which former slaves entered in order to obtain their legal manumission. They clearly reflect some Iberian world practices that date to medieval times – notably that manumission could be granted under the condition of service for long periods of time, which thus maintained relations of dependence that tied former slaves to their masters and patrons. On the other side, however, these arrangements must be understood primarily as products of the new ideologies of free contract and the language of free labour that had become increasingly important in defining civil relations in nineteenth-century Brazil, particularly from 1830s on. What highlights the contractual (yet voluntary) dimension of these arrangements is precisely the fact that they bound former slaves to new employers through indebtedness. Despite striking similarities between former captivity and new freedom – embedded in expectations of dependence and personal domination, and limitations on renegotiating contractual terms and conditions – these contracts were made between 'free' people defined as juridically equal before the law.

A significant number of contracts similar to those signed by Maria Leocadia and João Caetano exist in the Brazilian notarial 'Deeds of Debt and Obligation to Service' records from at least the 1840s. In many, terms such as 'debt', 'mortgage' and 'pawnship' were invoked in order to articulate the obligations that connected workers (debtors) to employers (creditors). That such relationships were common, reveals the complex balance between the new legal status of freed persons and the vulnerable circumstances in which they found themselves when the only collateral they possessed was that of their own bodies. The access to freedom through debt, and the articulation of debt bondage through contractual obligations was an intrinsic dimension of the labour arrangements made by former slaves in the process of giving meaning and content to the legal freedom they achieved, before and after Abolition.

From Contract to Freedom

Unsurprisingly, Brazilian legislators did not express anxieties, as other lawmakers did elsewhere in the Atlantic world, about the need to codify a definition of 'freedom', as sharply distinguished from what could be perceived as the continuity of slavery under another name. Quite the contrary, lawmakers in Brazil overwhelmingly concerned themselves with preserving the prerogatives of the master class through their power to define the terms of free labour.[34] To this end they manipulated the language of labour contracts to emphasize their 'voluntary' character. This is, for example, clearly reflected in Law 2040, passed on 28 September 1871 which, partially inspired by the processes of emancipation elsewhere in America, was designed to solve the problem of the so-called 'servile element' – a euphemism used for slaves and ex-slaves during the period of gradual abolition of slavery. Article 4 of the law foresaw the legal possibility of slave manumission through self-purchase.[35] It stipulated that slaves might contractually offer their future services to a third party for a period of no more than seven years in order to pay for their freedom. The law thereby effectively converted slave bondage into a debt to be paid by slaves to their own masters in order to redeem a prior debt that they had never incurred. The concept of 'freedom' as a form of 'redemption' of a pawn thus became a central part of the main legislation governing the labour of freed persons. Many slaves viewed this provision as an opportunity to flee slavery, although in embracing debt bondage to become free persons, they in effect replaced the legal, physical coercions of slavery with new economic constraints.

The 'gradualist' model for slave emancipation under the 1871 law, was a clear attempt simultaneously to satisfy the conflicting legal principles of 'freedom' and 'property'. The central idea behind it was that slaves should be responsible for the financial compensation of their former owners through the conversion of slavery into a debt to be redeemed with years of service. This became the legal model for the gradual emancipation of slaves in Brazil, which would powerfully condition both workers' and employers' expectations of free labour in the many decades to follow.

Laws abolishing the slave trade and emancipating the enslaved did not pass unopposed, and there arose significant conflicting interpretations of the meaning of new labour relations. Indeed, the new measure proved unsustainable over the long term and, under the Abolition Law of 1888, slavery was finally declared 'extinct', and no provision was made for the indemnification of former slaveholders. At the same time, however, no provisions or rights were granted to the almost 700,000 slaves freed by the law.[36] Former slaves were entirely at liberty to join the rest of the disenfranchised labouring poor, and voluntarily to become entangled in other, future debts.

9 INDIGENOUS DEBT AND THE SPIRIT OF COLONIAL CAPITALISM: DEBT, TAXES AND THE CASH-CROP ECONOMY IN THE ANGLO-EGYPTIAN SUDAN, 1898–1956

Steven Serels

In late December 1933, a group of twenty-three Ja'aliyyin tenants in the Gezira Scheme submitted a petition to the local government asking for financial assistance. The Gezira Scheme had been officially inaugurated in 1924 on 240,000 *faddans*[1] in the fertile Jazira plain between the two Niles south of Khartoum. The scheme, which focused on the commercial cultivation of cotton for export, was worked on a tenancy system and managed jointly by the Anglo-Egyptian government and the Sudan Plantation Syndicate (SPS), a private firm. C. G. Davies, the district commissioner of the Gezira, visited the petitioning tenants, who explained that the returns in the scheme were insufficient to meet their needs and that they feared that they would have to make the choice between paying for the labour necessary to work their plots and purchasing sufficient *dhurra* (sorghum, the staple grain) to feed their families.[2] Davies was sympathetic to the tenants' complaint. When he brought the petition to the attention of the SPS's local managers, they insisted that the tenants were exaggerating and that, as Anglo-Egyptian officials subsequently recounted, 'the general feeling in the Gezira still was that those inside the scheme were better than those outside'. Nonetheless, the SPS's management agreed to accompany Davies on an inspection tour.[3] W. P. Archdale, the SPS's representative, assured Davies that he could produce a group of tenants that 'would rebut the facts and figures' contained in the petition. On 30 December 1933, Davies met with Archdale's selected tenants. Far from contradicting the petition, these tenants stated that they were financially worse off than those cultivators who remained outside the scheme. They claimed that the returns from their tenancies were insufficient to cover the cost of cultivation and to maintain their families and, as a result, they supported themselves by selling land, animals and other privately owned assets.[4]

Tenants in the Gezira Scheme perceived themselves as 'unfree' and bound to the scheme by debt and poverty. From the mid-1920s to the mid-1930s, tenancies were unprofitable. The SPS, seeking to ensure continued cultivation, offered loans to tenants so that they could purchase agricultural inputs. Returns were insufficient to pay back these loans and tenants quickly fell into debt. In 1934, following seven years of poor harvests and low prices, the tenants collectively owed £E700,000.[5] Tenants began to refer ironically to the scheme as 'the free advice that impoverishes the people'.[6] Proverbs, songs and sayings deriding the scheme became popular. One such proverb described cultivators outside the scheme as 'free like a nomad' and those in the scheme as trapped like 'soldiers in a camp'.[7] The Gezira Scheme tenants recognized that debt and poverty limited their freedom and forced them to continue to work for the benefit of others. Debt bound tenants to the land and compelled them to continue to produce cash-crops for the benefit of others. This chapter shows that these tenants were not unique in this regard. In the first half of the twentieth century, cultivators in many regions of the Sudan were pushed into debt. This forced many cultivators to cultivate continuously land owned or managed by the Anglo-Egyptian state or a select group of local elites. Debt denied cultivators the resources necessary to establish themselves elsewhere, to take up other pursuits or otherwise to pursue other economic strategies that would maintain their independence.

The role of debt in compelling Sudanese participation in an export-oriented, cash-crop economy suggests a critique of conventional histories of the transformation of African economies under direct colonial rule. Historians, in keeping with a line of analysis developed by Marxist scholars and Dependency School theorists in the 1960s and 1970s, conventionally assume that the colonial requirement to pay taxes in money compelled African men to enter the wage labour economy or to produce cash-crops.[8] Recently historians have questioned some of the central assumptions of economically deterministic models of historical change, namely that Africans passively accepted the colonial interventions in the economy or that colonial administrators were always acting in the interest of foreign capital.[9] This chapter further problematizes the link between taxes and African participation in the colonial economy by showing that Sudanese cultivators were effectively able to resist the implementation of a rigid tax system. However, cultivators were unable to prevent themselves from falling into debt. As a result, debt, and not taxes, forced Sudanese cultivators to produce cash-crops continuously. Debt abrogated the freedom of Sudanese cultivators and bound them to the land and to the cash-crop economy.

The Evolution of Anglo-Egyptian Taxation Policy

The tax system implemented by the Anglo-Egyptian state at the beginning of the twentieth century was informed by a belief that a just tax policy that responded to local conditions would strengthen Sudanese support for Anglo-Egyptian rule. This belief first emerged amongst British intelligence officers in the Egyptian Army during the decade-and-a-half campaign to contain and, ultimately, defeat the Mahdist Rebellion. In 1882, the British army conquered Egypt, brought an end to the 'Urabi Revolt, restored the deposed Egyptian Khedieve and assumed command of the Egyptian army. British officers subsequently utilized the Egyptian army to address the rebellion in the Sudan that had begun shortly after Muhammad Ahmad ibn 'Abd Allah, a Sudanese religious leader, had proclaimed himself in June 1881 to be *al-Mahdi*, i.e. the prophesied Islamic eschatological leader who would herald the end of days. The following year al-Mahdi announced a *jihad* against the Turko-Egyptian rulers of the Sudan. Unable to defeat the Mahdist threat, British officials ordered Egypt to withdraw its Sudanese administration. As they struggled to prevent al-Mahdi's supporters from invading Egyptian territory,[10] the Egyptian army collected intelligence on the emerging Sudanese Mahdist state. Intelligence officers quickly concluded that the Mahdist Rebellion, though outwardly religious in nature, was, at its core, a tax revolt. Reginald Wingate, the Director of the Intelligence Department of the Egyptian army, asserted that the small-scale cultivators who had formed the bulk of al-Mahdi's early supporters had allied themselves with the movement as a way of protesting against Egyptian tax policy.[11] This assertion was confirmed by Rudolph von Slatin. Slatin had been the last Turko-Egyptian governor of Dar Fur and was a prisoner of the Mahdist state until 1895. Following his escape to Egypt, Slatin described the Turko-Egyptian government's tax system as having been 'unjust'. Widespread corruption 'resulted in the bulk of taxation falling on the poor landed proprietors'. The wealthy simply bribed the tax collectors so as to avoid paying taxes. These collectors 'mercilessly ground down' small-scale cultivators 'in order to make up the heavy deficit which resulted from this most nefarious system'. According to Slatin, this system was 'oppressive and tyrannical' and led to a deep 'discontent' and, in the end, formed the basis for al-Mahdi's popular appeal.[12]

The Anglo-Egyptian state's taxation policy was also informed by a belief that the payment of tribute was a locally recognized customary gesture indicating submission and public deference to authority. Following the Anglo-Egyptian conquest of the Sudan (1896–8), officials used this principle to regularize relationships with pastoralist communities indigenous to the Sudan.[13] Further, officials drew on this principle to establish working relations with Ali Dinar, who proclaimed himself the Sultan of Dar Fur following the collapse of Mahdist power in Western Sudan at the end of the nineteenth century. In June 1901,

Wingate, acting as the second governor-general of the Sudan, wrote to Dinar stating 'as this would tend to show your submission and obedience to its orders, as well as your connection with it, I am therefore pleased to impose upon you the payment of a sum of 100 purses (500*l.*) to the Treasury of the Government'.[14]

In the formative years of the Anglo-Egyptian state, the payment of tribute became central to a system of indirect rule rooted in public displays of deference to authority. In an 1898 memorandum sent to provincial governors, Herbert Kitchener, the first governor-general of the Anglo-Egyptian Sudan, outlined his programme for establishing effective, long-term political control in the Sudan. Kitchener stated that the government's central task was 'to acquire the confidence of the people, to develop their resources, and to raise them to a higher level'. To effect this end, officials had to become acquainted with 'the better class of native, through whom we may hope gradually to influence the whole population'. Kitchener insisted that the best way to develop these relationships was to demonstrate that 'our object is to increase their prosperity. Once it is thoroughly realized that our officers have at heart, not only the progress of the country generally, but also the prosperity of each individual with whom they come into contact, their exhortations to industry and improvement will gain force'.[15] Kitchener's programme for establishing this system of indirect rule required the government to facilitate an immediate and sustainable expansion of indigenous elites' privately-held wealth and to create a public mechanism whereby non-elite Sudanese would materially and symbolically show deference to indigenous elites, who, in turn, would show deference to the Anglo-Egyptian state.

At the beginning of the twentieth century, Anglo-Egyptian officials tried to use the tax system as a means of integrating agriculturalist communities into a symbolic universe based in tribute and public displays of deference. *The Land Tax and Date Tax Ordinance* and *The Title of Lands Ordinance*, both of which were promulgated in May 1899, created the mechanisms for establishing a tribute system for agriculturalist communities. As I have discussed elsewhere, *The Title of Lands Ordinance* effectively recognized both communally- and privately-held land as the exclusive property of indigenous elites.[16] This ordinance set up land registration commissions, comprising three Egyptian army officers and two local *shaykhs*, charged with registering land ownership. These commissions were only permitted to recognize individual, alienable land tenure and were barred from recognizing communal, partial or unalienable claims to land. *The Title of Lands Ordinance* recognized the receipt of a tithe as a stronger claim to ownership then simply the cultivation of the land.[17] In so doing, this ordinance created a legal mechanism for tithe-receiving *shaykhs* to expand their land holdings and to re-cast tithe-paying cultivators as the dependents of these *shaykhs*. Under this ordinance, tithe-paying cultivators were not considered landowners and, therefore, were exempt from the land tax outlined in *The Land Tax and Date Tax Ordinance*. As a result, the land tax was only to be levied on tithe-receiving *shaykhs*.

Resistance from Sudanese cultivators to these measures prevented the system of indirect rule through public deference from being fully implemented. Cultivators routinely subverted the land registration process by refusing to bring claims before the commissions,[18] failing to demarcate their land,[19] putting forth claims to land that they did not own[20] and by ignoring land commissions' rulings.[21] In August 1905, officials repealed *The Title of Lands Ordinance* and replaced it with *The Lands Settlement Ordinance*, which allowed land claims to be evaluated by settlement officers, rather than by a land commission.[22] Nonetheless, cultivators continued to resist registering the title of their land. In 1908, land owners in the Jazira violently rebelled against the land commission, requiring the government to send police escorts with all settlement and surveying parties.[23] Elsewhere, Sudanese cultivators regularly lied to settlement officers[24] and refused to register land transfers. As a result, official land registries quickly fell out of date,[25] and officials feared that requiring the mandatory registration of land ownership would lead to widespread social unrest and, eventually, stopped enforcing this requirement.[26]

Local conditions similarly made officials abandon the fixed land tax outlined in *The Land Tax and Date Tax Ordinance* and adopt a more flexible tax on agricultural produce. *The Land Tax and Date Tax Ordinance* categorized land by its source of irrigation (for example, Nile flooding, pump irrigation, wells, etc.) and assigned a fixed tax rate to each category. Officials had originally planned to defer levying taxes until after land was registered. However, as part of an effort to address an ongoing famine, officials began to collect the land tax in the spring of 1900. The Anglo-Egyptian conquest had disrupted the Sudanese grain market and prevented grain from reaching key administrative centres.[27] Following their conquest of Umm Durman, the Mahdist capital, in September 1898, Anglo-Egyptian officials continued to have trouble securing grain supplies for their newly captured territory. To increase the amount of grain at their disposal during the 1899–1900 cultivation year, officials levied a land tax, to be collected in grain, in Dongola Province, Wadi Halfa District in Halfa Province and the Districts of Robatab and Berber in Berber Province.[28] Grain collected in these regions, which officials knew were not the most fertile regions in the Sudan,[29] could easily be moved to administrative centres because these regions were along the recently constructed government railway. However, Sudanese cultivators resisted this new tax. At the end of the 1899–1900 cultivation year, Herbert Jackson, the governor of Dongola Province, observed that 'the collection of taxes was attended with great difficulties, the people doing their best to avoid or defer payment'.[30] Officials in Berber Province were only able to collect half of the assessed land tax.[31] Officials encountered similar resistance the following year and were forced to abandon plans to levy the land tax in Khartoum and Kassala Provinces.[32]

In 1901, the governor-general increased the provincial governors' discretion in the levying and collection of taxes. Provincial governors were no longer required to use the official schedule for land tax assessment and were permitted to assess tax rates using whichever criteria they saw appropriate.[33] Provincial governors were also given the option of levying *ushar*, i.e. a 10 per cent tithe on agricultural produce, instead of the land tax.[34] Over the next decade, Provincial governors annually increased the area subject to taxation. However, they overwhelmingly elected to levy the *ushar* rather than extend the land tax. For example, in 1907, an additional 1,000,000 *faddans* became subject to the *ushar*, but only 89,000 *faddans* became subject to the fixed land tax.[35]

The *ushar* and land tax comprised a steadily decreasing relative contribution to the Anglo-Egyptian budget. In 1904, the total revenue collected from the land tax and the *ushar* combined was approximately £E77,000, accounting for approximately 13 per cent of the state's revenue.[36] In 1911, the total revenue from these two taxes was approximately £E141,900, accounting for approximately 8.5 per cent of the government's revenue.[37] By comparison, receipts collected by the government-owned railroad network totalled approximately £E175,000 in 1905 (16.5 per cent of the state's total revenue)[38] and approximately £E442,000 in 1911 (26.5 per cent of the state's total revenue).[39] The government railroad network was built between 1896 and 1924, and was comprised of a main line that ran from Wadi Halfa on the Egyptian–Sudanese frontier through Khartoum and the Jazira to Kurdufan, and branch lines that ran to Dongola Province, the Red Sea and the Eritrean frontier.[40] By 1924, direct taxes accounted for less than 11 per cent of state revenue, but receipts from government investment in commercial ventures, including the railroad and commercial agriculture schemes, accounted for more than half.[41]

Debt as the Driver of Economic Development

The construction of the government railroad network facilitated the trade in imported goods, including such in demand products as refined sugar and foreign textiles. Both of these goods had been prohibitively expensive for most Sudanese households prior to the twentieth century and, therefore, had been reserved for elite consumption. In the nineteenth century, the consumption of sugar was limited. For example, in 1880, approximately 110,000 kg of sugar were imported into the Sudan.[42] At the beginning of the twentieth century, the quantity of sugar imported into the Sudan rose rapidly as prices decreased and drinking heavily-sugared tea became a widespread custom. The amount of sugar imported into the Sudan increased from approximately 2,000,000 kg in 1903[43] to approximately 13,000,000 kg in 1913.[44] The opening of the railway also fuelled an increase in the demand for imported cloth. During the nineteenth century, wearing foreign textiles had been a sign of social prestige and elite economic status.[45] Though most Sudanese men and women continued to wear locally-woven cloth throughout the first half of the twentieth century,[46] increasing numbers incorporated foreign textiles into their dress. As a result, the quantity of textiles imported into the Sudan increased dramatically. In the years immediately preceding the Mahdist Rebellion, 1,400,000 kg of textiles were imported annually into the Sudan.[47] By contrast, in 1913 the total weight of imported textiles was 3,500,000 kg.[48]

The increased demand for sugar and imported textiles transformed Sudanese society and contributed to increasing levels of indigenous indebtedness. Greek and Syrian merchants controlled the trade in sugar and foreign textiles. These merchants purchased goods in Egypt, often in very small quantities, and then travelled between rural Sudanese settlements to sell their wares. Successful merchants were able to reinvest their profits in their trade and open small shops in Sudanese villages and market centres.[49] Sudanese customers did not, at all times of the year, have the cash necessary to purchase goods. Most Sudanese incomes were cyclical because they were derived from the cultivation of crops for market, the harvesting of forest produce or the exploitation of pastoral herds. To overcome this impediment to trade, Greek and Syrian merchants offered forms of credit. Some merchants offered direct loans at high rates of interest, a practice known locally as *shayl*. Rates on these loans could be as high as 200 per cent.[50] In addition, merchants routinely purchased crop futures at extremely low rates.[51] In 1914, Anglo-Egyptian officials estimated that merchants frequently earned profits up to 250 per cent from purchasing crop futures.[52] Though officials sought to curtail this practice by issuing a proclamation in 1914 fixing the maximum profit on crop futures at 25 per cent,[53] this measure was not enforced and the practice continued unchecked.[54] Since no alternative money lending institutions were established, merchants continued to act as moneylenders into the post-independence period.[55]

The implementation of large-scale commercial agriculture development programmes further indebted Sudanese cultivators. The first of these programmes to be implemented was the Gezira Scheme, which converted 1,000,000 *faddans* in the Jazira plain into a cotton plantation managed through a partnership between the Anglo-Egyptian state and the SPS. This plantation was worked on a tenancy system, under which tenants, most of whom were Sudanese, worked plots of approximately 30 *faddans* each and received 40 per cent of the profits from the sale of their cotton yields. The Gezira Scheme impoverished the tenants because it tied their fortunes to varying cotton yields and fluctuating international raw cotton prices. During the boom years, which lasted until 1927, tenants prospered. For example, following the 1925–6 cultivation year, tenants received a profit payment from the SPS of, on average, £E117.[56] However, these boom times did not last because both cotton yields and cotton prices declined. Between 1927 and 1931, yields in the scheme dropped progressively from 4.7 to 1.4 *qintars* per *faddan*,[57] as a result of blackarm, a bacterial infection that affects cotton plants. The negative financial effects of declining yields were compounded in 1929 by the global collapse of commodity prices. In the years that followed, the SPS was unable to sell most of the Gezira Scheme's cotton yield, and the cotton that was sold fetched as little as half of pre-collapse prices.[58] To ensure that tenants had sufficient capital to cover agricultural inputs, the SPS offered advances on future profits. These advances allowed tenants to fall rapidly into debt and, by the end of 1934, the tenants collectively owed the scheme nearly £E700,000.[59] Though officials were alarmed by this debt, they did not implement measures to increase tenants' profits. Rather, Anglo-Egyptian officials and the SPS's senior management agreed, in 1935, to establish a Tenants' Reserve Fund, financed from levies on the tenants' share of the profits, which would be responsible for repayment of the tenants' debt. Though cotton yields subsequently improved, tenants did not immediately recover their lost wealth and, in 1940, they still collectively owed approximately £E240,000.[60] Though the Gezira Scheme pushed many tenants into debt, it became the model for the development of commercial agriculture after the Second World War.

Cultivators in Northern Nilotic Sudan, who were negatively affected by changes in the colonial economy, developed an alternative model for economic development. This model was born out of necessity. Increasing levels of indebtedness contributed to the devastating 1914 famine in Dongola Province, during which cultivators, many of whom had sold futures to itinerant merchants, lacked access to the cash necessary to purchase their sustenance.[61] Indebtedness prevented these cultivators from recovering financially after the acute crisis had subsided. In 1915, H. C. Jackson, the provincial governor, noted that these once prosperous cultivators were living 'in a state of abject poverty'.[62] Three years later, senior Anglo-Egyptian officials reported that the population continued to suffer from persistent food insecurity.[63] Impoverished cultivators were unable to maintain the slaves that worked their fields, and thousands of slaves absconded. Though officials had previously assisted masters in retrieving their self-manumitted slaves,[64] the Anglo-Egyptian state adopted a series of measures in the late 1920s and early 1930s, as a result of international pressure, designed to hasten the decline of agricultural slavery in the Sudan. Without the government's assistance, slave owners were unable to prevent their slaves from absconding, and large numbers self-manumitted.[65] The loss of slave labour led to a decline in the extent of cultivation in Northern Nilotic Sudan. Irrigation in this region was extremely labour intensive because it was dependent on *saqiyas* (water wheels).[66] To address this labour shortage, cultivators sought out labour saving technologies, such as irrigation pumps. Unfortunately, debt and poverty prevented them from purchasing these technologies on their own. As a result, some indigenous cultivators pooled their limited resources and established a number of agricultural co-operatives, including the Koya Cooperative Society, the Urbi Cooperative and the Sali Cooperative Scheme.[67] However, officials blocked these efforts. Believing that the decline in international cotton prices rendered these initiatives unprofitable, officials decided in the 1930s as a rule to deny requests from co-operatives to erect mechanical pumps.[68]

International commodity prices recovered after the Second World War and, as a result, there was renewed interest in implementing new commercial agriculture development programmes. Indigenous elites promoted the Gezira Scheme as a model for development, despite its history of pushing tenants into debt. The end of the war was followed by a boom in international cotton prices, and annual profit payments to tenants in the Gezira Scheme rose from a wartime average of approximately £E24 to £E96 in 1947, £E204 in 1948, £E221 in 1949 and £E281 in 1950.[69] The tenants' increased purchasing power drove up the price of staple goods, including grain, throughout the Sudan. The increased prices caused hardship elsewhere in the Sudan and prevented cultivators from repaying their debt and raising the capital necessary to invest in commercial agriculture.[70] Seeking to profit from current conditions, indigenous elites, many of whom were closely connected to the Anglo-Egyptian state, established pump-irrigation projects on underworked, fallow or recently abandoned land.[71] The number of these schemes jumped from 140 in 1945 to 1,166 in 1955, and on the eve of independence these schemes were watering over 740,000 *faddans*, or one-third of all irrigated land in the Sudan.[72] The owners of these projects modelled them off of the Gezira Scheme, and the projects were worked on a profit- or produce-sharing tenancy system based on the commercial cultivation of cash-crops.[73] Sudan's independence in 1956 accelerated the process that turned independent cultivators into the tenants of politically-connected elites. Between 1956 and 1963, wealthy elites, with capital derived, primarily, from cotton, opened 1,117 privately owned pump irrigation schemes, bringing the total amount of land under pump irrigation to approximately 1,300,000 *faddans*.[74]

The transformation of the rural Sudanese economy during the first half of the twentieth century was driven by debt. Debt opened new markets for foreign produce, contributed to the decline in agricultural slavery and converted many independent cultivators into the dependent tenants of a small group of wealthy elites. In many ways, indigenous debt created the system of indirect rule that Anglo-Egyptian officials had attempted to establish in the wake of the conquest of the Sudan. At the start of the twentieth century, officials sought to develop state structures that capitalized on indigenous cultural systems. Officials believed that these structures were inherently based in relations of dependence in which the payment of tribute compelled dependent populations to show deference symbolically and materially to authority. Officials attempted to transform customary payments of agricultural tithes into a formal system of dependence in which a small group of elites owned the land, received tribute from cultivators and showed obedience to the state through the payment of an annual land tax. However, local resistance forced officials to abandon these efforts. Nonetheless, over the course of the first half of the twentieth century, increasing levels of indebtedness prevented Sudanese cultivators from adapting to changing economic conditions. As a result, these cultivators were compelled to give up their land and to enter into new relations of dependence with the state or with a small group of state-connected indigenous elites. Formerly independent cultivators moved onto state- or elite-owned agricultural estates, where they were required to cultivate cash crops for the benefit of others. Debt bound these cultivators to the land and prevented them from regaining their lost independence.

NOTES

Stanziani and Campbell, 'Introduction'

1. Among the others are: D. B. Davis, *The Problem of Slavery in the Western Culture* (Ithaca, NY: Cornell University Press, 1966); M. Finley, *Ancient Slavery and Modern Ideology* (London and New York: Penguin Books, 1983); D. Eltis (ed.), *Slavery in the Development of the Americas* (Cambridge: Cambridge University Press, 2006); O. Patterson, *Slavery and Social Death: A Comparative Study* (Cambridge: Cambridge University Press, 1982).

2. A. Testart, *L'esclave, la dette et le pouvoir* (Paris: Editions errance, 2001); C. Meillassoux, *Anthropologie de l'esclavage* (Paris: PUF, 1986); Finley, *Ancient Slavery and Modern Ideology*; S. Miers and I. Kopytoff (eds), *Slavery in Africa: Historical and Anthropological Perspectives* (Madison, WI: University of Wisconsin Press, 1977); E. Williams, *Capitalism and Slavery* (Chapel Hill, NC: University Of North Carolina Press, 1944); M. Bush (ed.), *Serfdom and Slavery* (New York and London: Longman, 1996); S. Engerman (ed.), *Terms of Labor. Slavery, Freedom and Free Labor* (Stanford, CA: Stanford University Press, 1999); M. Klein, *Breaking the Chains. Slavery, Bondage and Emancipation in Modern Africa and Asia* (Madison, WI: University of Wisconsin Press, 1993); Patterson, *Slavery and Social Death*; P. Lovejoy, *Transformations in Slavery: A History of Slavery in Africa* (Cambridge: Cambridge University Press, 1983).

3. International Labour Organization (ILO), 89th Session of the International Labour Conference, 5–21 June 2001, papers and proceedings; International Programme on the Elimination of Child Labour (IPEC), *Every Child Counts: New Global Estimates on Child Labour* (Geneva: BIT Press, 2002); H. Cunningham and P. Viazzo, *Child Labour in Historical Perspective, 1800–1985. Historical Studies from Europe, Japan, Colombia* (Florence: Unicef, 1996); Bureau international du travail (BIT), *La fin du travail des enfants: un objectif à notre portée, rapport du directeur général* (Geneva: Bureau international du travail, 2006); S. Miers, 'Contemporary Forms of Slavery', in R. Roberts and P. Zachuernuk (eds), *Canadian Journal of African Studies* (special issue on slavery and Islam in African history: A tribute to Martin Klein), 34:3 (2000), pp. 714–47.

4. G. Campbell, S. Miers and J. Miller (eds), *Children in Slavery through the Ages* (Athens, OH: Ohio University Press, 2009).

5. On this, see S. Engerman, *Terms of Labor. Slavery, Freedom and Free Labor* (Stanford, CA: Stanford University Press, 1999); A. Stanziani (ed.), *Le travail contraint en Asie et en Europe* (Paris: MSH éditions, 2010); A. Stanziani (ed.), *Labour, Coercion, and Economic Growth in Eurasia, 17th–20th centuries* (Leiden: Brill, 2012).

6.   Some example in E. Domar, 'The Causes of Slavery and Serfdom: An Hypothesis', *Journal of Economic History*, 300 (1970), pp. 18–32; M. Bush (ed.), *Serfdom and Slavery: Studies in Legal Bondage* (Manchester: Manchester University Press, 1996).

7.   M. Mauss, *Sociologie et anthropologie* (Paris: PUF, 2010), in particular, 'Essai sur le don'. For a recent review of the wide literature developed ever since, see G. Peebles, 'The Anthropology of Credit and Debt', *Annual Review of Anthropology*, 39 (2010), pp. 225–40; J. Carrier, *Gifts and Commodities: Exchange and Western Capitalism Since 1700* (London: Routledge, 1995); M. Godelier, *The Enigma of the Gift* (Chicago, IL: University Chicago Press, 1999).

8.   C. Lévi-Strauss, *Anthropologie structurale* (Paris: Plon, 1958); Testart, *L'esclave, la dette et le pouvoir*.

9.   A. Testart, 'The Extent and Significance of Debt Slavery', *Revue Française de Sociologie*, 43, supplement (2002), pp. 173–204.

10. Patterson, *Slavery and Social Death*, p. 124.

11. K. Polanyi, C. M. Arensberg and H. W. Pearson (eds), *Trade and Market in the Early Empires: Economies in History and Theory* (Glencoe, IL: Free Press and Falcon's Wing Press, 1957); K. Polanyi in collaboration with A. Rotstein, *Dahomey and the Slave Trade: An Analysis of an Archaic Economy* (Seattle, WA: University of Washington Press, 1966).

12. For example, C. Coquery-Vidrovitch, Compte rendu de Karl Polanyi', *Journal of African History*, 2 (1966), pp. 197–214.

13. A. Sen, *Poverty and Famines: An Essay on Entitlements and Deprivation* (Oxford: Clarendon Press, 1982).

14. P. K. Bardhan (ed.), 'Interlocking Factor Markets and Agrarian Development. A Review of Issues', *Oxford Economic Papers*, 32:1 (1980), pp. 82–98.

15. G. Austin, 'Markets With, Without and in Spite of States: West Africa in Pre-Colonial Nineteenth Century Western Africa', *LSE Working Papers*, 3:4 (2004); G. Austin, 'Reciprocal Comparison and African History: Tackling Conceptual Eurocentrism in the Study of Africa's Economic Past', *African Studies Review*, 50:3 (2007), pp. 1–28; G. Austin, 'Indigenous Credit Institutions in West Africa, c. 1750– c. 1960', in G. Austin and K. Sugihara (eds), *Local Suppliers of Credit in the Third World, 1750–1980* (London: Palgrave MacMillan, 1993), pp. 117–30.

16. C. Tilly, *Coercion, Capital and European States, AD 990–1992* (London: Wiley Blackwell, 1992).

17. On this, see A. Stanziani, *Bâtisseurs d'Empire. Russie, Chine et Inde à la croisée des mondes* (Paris: Raison d'agir, 2012).

18. J. Burbank and F. Cooper, *Empires* (Princeton, NJ: *Princeton University Press*, 2011).

19. M. Klein, 'The Slave Trade and Decentralized Societies', *Journal of African History*, 42:1 (2001), pp. 49–65.

20. For ancient Rome, see P. Temin, *The Roman Market Economy* (Princeton, NJ: Princeton University Press, 2012). For Africa, see R. Austin, *African Economic History* (London: James Currey, 1987).

21. M. I. Finley, *The Ancient Economy* (Berkeley, CA: University of California Press, 1973); F. Tannenbaum, *Slave and Citizen* (New York: Alfred Knopf, 1946).

22. J. L Watson, 'Slavery as an Institution, Open and Closed Systems', in J. L. Watson (ed.), *Asian and African Systems of Slavery* (Berkeley and Los Angeles, CA: University of California Press, 1980), pp. 1–15.

23. Finley, *Ancient Slavery and Modern Ideology*.

24. A. Schiavone, *The End of the Past: Ancient Rome and the Modern World* (Cambridge, MA: Harvard University Press, 2000).

25. See, for example, Schiavone, *The End of the Past*.

26. On this, see N. McKeown, 'Greek and Roman Slavery', in G. Heuman and T. Burnard (eds), *The Routledge History of Slavery* (London: Routledge, 2011), pp. 19–34.

27. P. Temin, 'The Labour Market of the Early Roman Empire', *Journal of Interdisciplinary History*, 34:4 (2004), pp. 513–38.

28. W. Scheidel, 'Quantifying the Source of Slaves in the Early Roman Empire', *Journal of Roman Studies*, 87 (1997), pp. 157–69; S. Joshel, *Slavery in the Roman World* (Cambridge: Cambridge University Press, 2010).

29. J. Andreau and R. Descat, *Esclave en Grèce et à Rome* (Paris: Hachette, 2006).

30. W. Davies, 'On Servile Status in the Early Middle Ages', in M. Bush (ed.), *Serfdom and Slavery* (London and New York: Longman, 1996), pp. 225–46.

31. H. Berman, *Law and Revolution. The Formation of the Western Legal Tradition* (Cambridge, MA: Harvard University Press, 1983).

32. Verlinden, *L'esclavage dans l'Europe médiévale*.

33. J. Heers, *Esclaves et domestiques au Moyen Age dans le monde méditerranéen* (Paris: Hachette, 1996), p. 67; C. Verlinden, 'L'origine de sclavus-esclave', *Bulletin du Cange*, 17 (1942), pp. 97–128; C. Verlinden, 'L'esclavage du sud-est et de l'est européen en Europe orientale à la fin du moyen-âge', *Revue historique du sud-est européen*, 19 (1942), pp. 18–29; Verlinden, *L'esclavage dans l'Europe médiévale*; S. Epstein, *Speaking of Slavery* (Ithaca, NY and London: Cornell University Press, 2001).

34. D. Romano, *Housecrafts and Statecrafts: Domestic Service in Renaissance Venice, 1400–1600* (Baltimore, MD: Johns Hopkins University Press, 1996).

35. Epstein, *Speaking of Slavery*, pp. 66–7.

36. Y. Rotman, *Byzantine Slavery and the Mediterranean World* (Boston, MA: Harvard University Press, 2009), p. 83.

37. Epstein, *Speaking of Slavery*, p. 96.

38. Rotman, *Byzantine Slavery and the Mediterranean World*; H. Van der Wee, 'Structural Changes in European Long-Distance Trade, and Particularly in the Re-export Trade from South to the North, 1350–1750', in J. Tracy (ed.), *The Rise of Merchant Empires. Long-Distance Trade in the Early Modern World, 1350–1750* (Cambridge: Cambridge University Press, 1990), pp. 14–33.

39. R. S. Lopez, *The Commercial Revolution of the Middle Ages, 950–1350* (New York: Cambridge University Press, 1972), p. 92.

40. D. Deletant, 'Genoese, Tatars and Rumanians at the Mouth of the Danube in the Fourteenth Century', *Slavonic and East European Review*, 62:4 (1984), pp. 511–30.

41. Epstein, *Speaking of Slavery*; D. Giuffré, *Il mercato degli schiavi a Genova nel secolo XV* (Genova: Fratelli Bozzi, 1971); R. Delort, 'Quelques précisions sur le commerce des esclaves à Gênes vers la fin du XIVe siècle', *Mélanges d'archéologie et d'histoire*, 78:1 (1966), pp. 215–50.

42. M. Balard, 'Esclavage en Crimée et sources fiscales génoises au XVe siècle', *Byzantinische Forschungen*, 22 (1996), pp. 9–17, reprinted in H. Bresc (ed.), *Figures de l'esclave au Moyen-Age et dans le monde moderne. Actes de la table ronde organisée les 27 et 28 octobre 1992 par le Centre d'Histoire sociale et culturelle de l'Occident de l'Université de Paris-X Nanterre* (Paris: Université Paris X, 1996), pp. 77–87.

43. Heers, *Esclaves et domestiques au Moyen Age*; C. Verlinden, 'La traite des esclaves. Un grand commerce international au Xe siècle', in *Études de civilisation médiévale (IXe–XIIe*

siècles). *Mélanges offerts à Edmond-René Labande* (Poitiers: C.É.S.C.M, 1974), pp. 721–30; Gioffré, *Il mercato degli schiavi a Genova*; F. Panero, *Schiavi, servi e villani nell'Italia medievale* (Torino: Paravia, 1999).

44. Gioffré, *Il mercato degli schiavi a Genova*.

45. M. V. Kirilov, 'Slave Trade in Early Modern Crimea from the Perspective of Christian, Muslim and Jewish Sources', *Journal of Early Modern History*, 11:1 (2007), pp. 1–32.

46. S. McKee, 'Domestic Slavery in Renaissance Italy', *Slavery and Abolition*, 29:3 (2008), pp. 305–26.

47. G. V. Scammell, *The World Encompassed. The First European Maritime Empires, c. 800–1650* (Berkeley, CA: University of California Press, 1981).

48. Rotman, *Byzantine Slavery and the Mediterranean World*; R. Hellie, *Slavery in Russia*, (Chicago, IL: Chicago University Press, 1982).

49. A. Zysberg, *Les galériens. Vies et destins de 60000 forçats sur les galères de France, 1680–1748* (Paris: Seuil, 1987).

50. M. Aymard, 'Chiourmes et galères dans la méditerranée du XVIe siècle', in *Mélanges en l'honneur de Fernand Braudel* (Toulouse: Privat, 1973), pp. 49–64.

51. G. Weiss, *Captives and Corsairs. France and Slavery in the Early Mediterranean World* (Stanford, CA: Stanford University Press, 2011); R. Davis, *Christian Slaves, Muslim Masters. White Slavery in the Mediterranean, the Barbary Coast, and Italy, 1500–1800* (Basingstoke: MacMillan, 2003).

52. M. Aymard, 'De la traite aux chiourmes. La fin de l'esclavage dans la Sicile moderne ', *Bulletin de l'Institut historique belge de Rome*, 44 (1974), pp. 1–21; A. Stella, *Histoires des esclaves dans la Peninsula iberique* (Paris: EHESS, 2000). F. Braudel, *La Méditerranée et le monde méditerranéen à l'époque de Philippe II*, 2nd edn, 2 vols (Paris: Colin, 1966), vol. 2, pp. 190–212; R. Blackburn, *The Making of the New World Slavery. From the Baroque to the Modern, 1482–1800* (London: Verso, 1998).

53. R. Davis, 'Counting European Slaves on the Barbary Coast', *Past and Present*, 172 (2001), pp. 87–124; S. Bono, *Schiavi musulmani nell'Italia moderna: galeotti, vu'cumpra', domestici* (Napoli: Edizioni scientifiche italiane, 1999).

54. R. Austen, *African Economic History, Internal Development and External Dependency* (London: James Currey, 1987).

55. P. Lovejoy, *Transformations of Slavery* (Cambridge: Cambridge University Press, 2000).

56. H. Inalcik, *An Economic and Social History of the Ottoman Empire, vol. 1, 1300–1600* (Cambridge: Cambridge University Press, 1997), p. 285; Y. H. Erdem, *Slavery in the Ottoman Empire and its Demise, 1800–1909* (London: Macmillan, 1996). W. G. Clarence-Smith, *Islam and the Abolition of Slavery* (Oxford: Oxford University Press, 2006).

57. R. Brunschvig, 'Abd', in H. A. R. Gibb, *Encyclopedia of Islam*, 10 vols (Leiden: Brill, 1960), vol. 1, pp. 24–40.

58. N. G. Kodjo, 'Contribution à l'étude des tribus dites serviles du Songai', *Bulletin de l'IFAN*, 38:4 (1976), pp. 790–812.

59. J. Vogt, *The Portuguese Rule on the Gold Coast, 1469–1682* (Athens, GA: University of Georgia Press, *1979*).

60. Lovejoy, *Transformations in Slavery*, p. 37

61. Ibid., p. 41

62. D. Northrup, *Indentured Labour in the Age of Imperialism. 1834–1922* (Cambridge: Cambridge University Press, 1995), pp. 129–32.

63. T. W. Allen, *The Invention of the White Race*, 3 vols (New York: Verso, 1994); A. S. Parent, Jr, *Foul Means: The Formation of a Slave Society in Virginia* (Chapel Hill, NC: North Carolina University Press, 2003).

64. D. Eltis and D. Richardson, *Extending the Frontiers: Essays on the New Trans-Atlantic Slave Trade Database* (New Haven, CT: Yale University Press, 2008); D. Eltis, D. Richardson, S. Behrendt and H. Klein, *The Atlantic Slave Trade: A Database* (Cambridge: Cambridge University Press, 1999), online at http://www.slavevoyages.org/tast/index.faces.

65. Lovejoy, *Transformations in Slavery*, p. 71.

66. Ibid., p. 133.

67. Eltis and Richardson, *Extending the Frontiers*.

68. D. Eltis, *Economic Growth and the Ending of Trans-Atlantic Slave Trade* (Oxford: Oxford University Press, 1989), p. 59

69. Lovejoy, *The Abolition*, p. 137.

70. C. Meillassoux, *Anthropologie de l'esclavage* (Paris: PUF, 1986).

71. S. Meyer and I. Kopytoff (eds), *Slavery in Africa: Historical and Anthropological Perspectives* (Madison, WI: University of Wisconsin Press, 1977).

72. G. Austin, 'Human Pawning in Asante, 1820–1950: Markets and Coercion, Gender and Cocoa', in P. Lovejoy and T. Falola (eds), *Pawnship, Slavery, and Colonialism in Africa* (Asmara: Africa World Press, 2003), pp. 187–220.

73. Lovejoy and Falola, *Pawnship, Slavery, and Colonialism in Africa*, p. 4.

74. P. Lovejoy and D. Richardson, 'Pawns will Live when Slaves is Apt to Dye: Credit, Risk and Trust at Old Calabar in the Era of Slave Trade', in Lovejoy and Falola (eds), *Pawnship, Slavery, and Colonialism in Africa*, pp. 71–96.

75. For discussions on this, see Lovejoy and Falola (eds), *Pawnship, Slavery, and Colonialism in Africa*; F. Cooper, *Colonialism in Question. Theory, Knowledge, History* (Berkeley and Los Angeles, CA: University of California Press, 2005).

76. G. Austin and K. Sugihara (eds), *Local Suppliers of Credit in the Third World, 1750–1980* (London: MacMillan, 1993).

77. T. Falola, 'Slavery and Pawnship in the Yoruba Economy of the Nineteenth Century', in Lovejoy and Falola (eds), *Pawnship, Slavery, and Colonialism in Africa*, pp. 109–36.

78. House of Commons, Papers in explanation of the condition of the slave population, 5 November 1831, *British Parliamentary Papers*, 230:16.1 (1830–1), pp. 59–88.

79. J. R. Ward, *British West India Slavery, 1750–1834: the Process of Amelioration* (Oxford: Oxford University Press, 1988).

80. M. Turner, 'The British Caribbean, 1823–1838. The Transition from Slave to Free Legal Status', in D. Hay and P. Craven (eds), *Masters, Servants and Magistrates in Britain and the Empire, 1562–1955* (Chapel Hill, NC and London: University of North Carolina Press, 2004), pp. 303–22.

81. T. Holt, *The Problem of Freedom: Race, Labour and Politics in Jamaica and Britain, 1832–1938* (Baltimore, MD and London: Johns Hopkins University Press, 1992).

82. R. Conrad, *The Destruction of Brazilian Slavery, 1850–1888* (Berkeley, CA: University of California Press, 1972).

83. For discussions on these points, see E. Toledano, *Slavery and Abolition in the Ottoman Middle East* (Seattle, WA and London: University of Washington Press, 1998); Clarence-Smith, *Islam and the Abolition of Slavery*; Y. H. Erdem, *Slavery in the Ottoman Empire and its Demise, 1800–1909* (London and New York: MacMillan, 1996);

E. Toledano, *The Ottoman Slave Trade and its Suppression, 1840–1890* (Princeton, NJ: Princeton University Press, 1982).

84.   Toledano, *Slavery and Abolition in the Ottoman Middle East*, p. 15.
85.   E. Toledano, *As if Silent and Absent: Bond of Enslavement in the Islamic Middle East* (New Haven, CT: Yale University Press, 2007), p. 257.

1 Kleijwegt, 'Debt Bondage and Chattel Slavery in Early Rome'

1.   M. I. Finley, *Ancient Slavery and Modern Ideology* (London: Chatto & Windus, 1980), pp. 67–93, esp. pp. 82–5. Finley never addressed the question of the abolition of *nexum* and its consequences directly. According to him (pp. 86–7), the change in exploitation from an internal to an external supply of labour occurred in Athens as well as Rome, but because he felt that the evidence for Rome was unsatisfactory he decided to concentrate on Athens. For a critical reading of Finley's argument for Athens, cf. T. Rihll, 'The Origin and Establishment of Ancient Greek Slavery', in M. Bush (ed.), *Serfdom and Slavery: Studies in Legal Bondage* (New York: Longman Press, 1996), pp. 89–111; E. M. Harris, 'Did Solon Abolish Debt-Bondage?', *Classical Quarterly*, 52 (2002), pp. 415–30; also in E. M. Harris, *Democracy and the Rule of Law in Classical Athens: Essays on Law, Society, and Politics* (Cambridge and New York: Cambridge University Press, 2006), pp. 249–71. Harris distinguishes between enslavement for debt and debt bondage (pp. 415–6). In enslavement for debt the debtor becomes the slave of his creditor, while in debt bondage the debtor is given the opportunity to work off his debt. Unlike enslavement for debt, debt bondage is not a permanent condition; the debt bondsman is only in his condition until he has worked off his debt. Harris argues in his study that Solon only abolished enslavement for debt.
2.   The criticism was expressed in E. Gabba, 'Il nuovo libro di M. Finley sulla schiavitù antica', *Athenaeum*, 60 (1982), pp. 276–81; H. W. Pleket, 'Slavernij in de Oudheid: voer voor oudhistorici en comparatisten', *Tijdschrift voor Geschiedenis*, 94 (1982), pp. 1–30.
3.   Cf. S. P. Oakley, *A Commentary on Livy Books VI to X, vol. 2: Books VII and VIII* (New York and Oxford: Clarendon Press, 1998), pp. 690; J. Bodel, 'Slave Labour and Roman Society', in K. Bradley and P. Cartledge (eds), *The Cambridge World History of Slavery, volume 1: The Ancient Mediterranean World* (Cambridge: Cambridge University Press, 2011), pp. 311–37.
4.   To start with the most obvious problem, it is uncertain in which year *nexum* was abolished. Livy discusses it among the events taking place in 326 BC, but in the narrative of Dionysius of Halicarnassus it is discussed after Rome's humiliating defeat at the hands of the Samnites in 321 BC. Varro (*On the Latin Language*, 7.105) states that Gaius Poetelius Libo Visulus who abolished *nexum* acted in his capacity as dictator, an office which he held in 313, but not in 326 BC.
5.   For the problems raised by the passage, cf. M. Salvatore, 'Varrone in tema di *nexum*', *Annali di Facoltà di Lettere e Filosofia di Bari*, 31 (1988), pp. 115–33. For the other view, endorsed by Manilius, cf. M. Bretone, 'Manilio e il *nexum*', *Iura*, 32 (1981), pp. 143–6; S. Tondo, 'Il *nexum* e Manilio', *Iura*, 32 (1982), pp. 116–21. I have followed the argument of A. Watson, *Rome of the XII Tables: Persons and Property* (Princeton, NJ: Princeton University Press, 1975), pp. 111–4.
6.   D. B. Hollander, *Money in the Late Roman Republic* (Leiden: Brill Academic Publishers, 2007), pp. 73–4 suggests that *obaeratus* was used to identify a debt-slave in early Rome, cf. Cicero, *On the Republic*, 2.38, who claims that the *obaerati* were freed by Servius Tullius,

a legendary king of the sixth century BC, who was believed to have been a slave himself. In the first century BC the term *obaeratus* is used without the connotation of enslavement.

7. Livy uses both *addictus* and *iudicatus* to describe ordinary members of the plebs and their leaders who were in debt during the crisis preceding the introduction of the Licinian-Sextian laws (6.34.2; 377 BC), while *iudicatus pecuniae* is reserved for the centurion at 6.14.3 (dated to 385 BC). Livy uses those terms before his discussion of the abolition of *nexum* (3.56.8: *in servitutem addixisset*).

8. Quintilian, the writer of a handbook on public speaking in the late first century AD, states that there is a difference between being a slave and being in servitude (5.10.60: *ut aliud est servum esse, aliud servire*). When a slave is manumitted he becomes a freedman, while an *addictus* does not, meaning that the latter would recover his citizenship rights. I am inclined to believe that Quintilian has mixed up the position of the *addictus* with that of the *nexus*.

9. T. J. Cornell, 'The Recovery of Rome', in F. W. Walbank, A. E. Astin, M. W. Frederiksen and R. M. Ogilvie (eds), *The Cambridge Ancient History, vol. VII, part 2: The Rise of Rome to 220 B.C.* (Cambridge: Cambridge University Press, 1989), pp. 309–51, on p. 330.

10. These marks of dishonor provide a striking contrast with the scars of the injuries on his chest incurred during his military career, cf. 2.23.4–5.

11. It is of course true that some of the people running out into the street were, literally, chained, for they displayed their chains to the other members of the public (2.23.10). The second group consists of former *nexi*: cf. Livy's reference to *nexi soluti* in his discussion of the abolition of *nexum* in 8.28.8.

12. For the similarities and the differences between this episode and the one involving the anonymous veteran, cf. C. S. Kraus (ed.), *Livy: ab urbe condita, book VI* (Cambridge and New York: Cambridge University Press, 1994), 171.

13. Kraus, *Ab urbe condita, book VI*, p. 270 argues that debt bondage had become automatic.

14. S. P. Oakley (ed.), *A Commentary on Livy, Books VI–X, volume 1: Introduction and Book VI* (Oxford and New York: Oxford University Press, 1997), pp. 500–1 argues that bankruptcy could lead to loss of esteem. For the play on *fides* as credit and trust, cf. Kraus, *Ab urbe condita, book VI*, p. 270.

15. Livy introduces the story as follows: 'In that year the liberty of the Roman people had as it were a new beginning.' This is a clear reference to the freedom which the Roman people had been enjoying since the establishment of the Republic in 509 BC. Livy's introduction suggests that the events which he is about to describe are of an epoch-making magnitude in an ongoing struggle for freedom.

16. Valerius Maximus (*Memorable Deeds and Sayings*, 6.1.9), a compiler of historical anecdotes who lived in the first part of the first century AD, and Dionysius of Halicarnassus (*Roman Antiquities*, 16.5.1–3), a Greek historian who lived and worked in Rome in the final decades of the first century BC, have the same story-line, but the names of the individuals involved are different. Cicero (*On the Republic*, 2.59) has a story about a young man and a money-lender, but both remain anonymous and the general context suggests that Cicero had very little understanding of the events.

17. Livy does not indicate what happened to Lucius Papirius. In Dionysius's version of the story the creditor is named Caius Laetorius Mergus and he is indicted, condemned, and put to death.

18. The same conclusion is drawn by J.-U. Krause, *Gefängnisse im Römischen Reich* (Stuttgart: Steiner, 1996), p. 153.

19. P. Garnsey, 'Non-Slave Labour in the Roman World', in P. Garnsey (ed.), *Non-Slave Labour in the Greco-Roman World* (Cambridge: Cambridge University Press, 1980), p. 36 stresses that chattel slavery and debt bondage co-existed. For the *obaerarii*, cf. E. L. Cascio, '*Obaerarii (obaerati)*. La nozione della dipendenza in Varrone', *Index*, 11 (1982), pp. 265–84.

20. Finley, *Ancient Slavery and Modern Ideology*, p. 83. By observing that the figure of 40,000 may have been incomplete, Finley is suggesting that the actual total numbers may have been even higher. He calls the number 'maybe not accurate', because ancient writers are notoriously unreliable when they supply numbers.

21. H. Volkmann, *Die Massenversklavungen der Einwohner eroberter Städte in der hellenistisch-römischen Zeit*, ed. G. Horsmann, 2nd edn (Wiesbaden: Akademie der Wissenschaften und der Literatur, 1990), pp. 113–4. Volkmann's figure of 40,000 is the number of soldiers taken captive in sieges. If all the captives of war are added up, the figure is just under 70,000, while more than 100,000 Samnites were killed.

22. E. L. Cascio, 'Recruitment and the Size of the Roman Population from the Third to the First Century BCE', in W. Scheidel (ed.), *Debating Roman Demography* (Leiden: Brill Academic Publishers, 2001), pp. 111–37. W. Scheidel, 'Roman Population Size: the Logic of the Debate', in L. de Ligt and S. Northwood (eds), *People, Land, and Politics: Demographic Developments and the Transformation of Roman Italy, 300 BC–AD 14* (Leiden: Brill Academic Publishers, 2008), pp. 17–70, on p. 38.

23. The tax was named the *vicesima libertatis* and it was levied at 5 per cent of the value of the slave; value was established on the basis of the original purchase price, cf. K. R. Bradley, *Slaves and Masters in the Roman Empire: A Study in Social Control* (Brussels: Revue d'Études Latines, 1984), pp. 149–50. K. Bradley, 'Slavery in the Roman Republic', in K. Bradley and P. Cartledge (eds), *The Cambridge World History of Slavery, volume 1: The Ancient Mediterranean World* (Cambridge: Cambridge University Press, 2011), p. 245: 'The establishment of the manumission tax recognised the structural presence of slavery in Roman society'. Finley is aware of the manumission tax, but appears to misunderstand the implications of its introduction in 357 BC for his own argument (*Ancient Slavery and Modern Ideology*, p. 83).

2 Stanziani, 'Slavery, Debt and Bondage: The Mediterranean and the Eurasia Connection from the Fifteenth to the Eighteenth Century'

1. Some references from a huge bibliography include: C. Meillassoux, *Anthropologie de l'esclavage* (Paris: PUF, 1986); M. Finley, *Esclavage moderne et idéologie antique* (Paris: Editions de minuit, 1981); S. Meier and I. Kopytoff (eds), *Slavery in Africa: Historical and Anthropological Perspectives* (Madison, WI: University of Wisconsin Press, 1977); E. Williams, *Capitalism and Slavery* (Chapel Hill, NC: University Of North Carolina Press), p. 1944; M. Bush (ed.), *Serfdom and Slavery* (Longman: New York and London, 1996); S. Engerman (ed.), *Terms of Labour. Slavery, Freedom and Free Labour* (Stanford, CA: University Of California Press, 1999); O. Patterson, *Slavery and Social Death: a Comparative Study* (Cambridge: Cambridge University Press, 1982); P. Lovejoy, *Transformations in Slavery: A History of Slavery in Africa* (Cambridge: Cambridge University Press, 1983). On the translation of Islamic institutions with slavery: E. Toledano, *Slavery and Abolition in the Ottoman Middle East* (Seattle, WA and London: University of

Washington Press, 1998). M. Klein, *Breaking the Chains. Slavery, Bondage and Emancipation in Modern Africa and Asia* (Madison, WI: University of Wisconsin Press, 1993).

2. J. Heers, *Esclaves et domestiques au Moyen Age dans le monde méditerranéen* (Paris: Hachette, 1996), p. 67; C. Verlinden, 'L'origine de sclavus=esclave', *Bulletin du Cange*, 17 (1942), pp. 97–128; C. Verlinden, 'L'esclavage du sud-est et de l'est européen en Europe orientale à la fin du moyen-âge', *Revue historique du sud-est européen*, 19 (1942), pp. 18–29; C. Verlinden, *L'esclavage dans l'Europe médiévale* (Bruges: De Tempel, 1955); S. Epstein, *Speaking of Slavery* (Ithaca, NY; London: Cornell University Press, 2001).

3. R. Hellie, *Slavery in Russia, 1450–1725* (Chicago, IL: Chicago University Press, 1982).

4. H. Inalcik, *Sources and Studies on the Ottoman Black Sea. The Custom Register of Caffa, 1487–1990* (Cambridge: Cambridge University Press, 1996).

5. P. Perdue, *China Marches West. The Qing Conquest of Central Eurasia* (Harvard, MA: Belknap Press, 2005); M. Khodarkovsky, *Russia's Steppe Frontier. The Making of a Colonial Empire, 1500–1800* (Bloomington, IN: Indiana University Press, 2002); T. J. Barfield, *The Nomadic Alternative* (Englewood Cliffs, NJ: Prentice-Hall, 1993); N. di Cosmo, 'Ancient Inner Asian Nomads: Their Economic Basis and its Significance in Chinese History', *Journal of Asian Studies*, 53 (1993), pp. 1092–126, and 'State Formation and Periodization in Inner Asian History', *Journal of World History*, 10 (1999), pp. 1–40; D. Christian, *A History of Russia, Central Asia and Mongolia* (London: Blackwell, 1998); S. A. M. Adshead, *Central Asia in World History* (New York: St Martin's Press, 1993); A. G. Frank, *The Centrality of Central Asia* (Amsterdam: VU University Press, 1992); G. Seaman and D. Marks (eds), *Rulers from the Steppe: State Formation on the Eurasian Periphery* (Los Angeles, CA: Ethnographics Press, 1991).

6. At the same time, as we will see, even in Perdue's case, the problem is that the exclusive accent put on Russian and Chinese sources leads to the underestimation of the importance of the Safavid and Persian power in the area. This constitutes a major distortion of current historiography, mostly due, on the one hand, to the over-attention devoted to China and, on the other hand, to the quasi-disappearance of specialists of ancient Safavides and Persian powers (and languages).

7. Inalcik, *The Custom Register of Caffa*.

8. Massaria Caffae, 1374, ASG, fol. 1–354. See G. Bratianu, *Actes des notaires genois de Pira et de Caffa de la fin du XIIIe siècle (1281–1290)* (Bucharest: Académie Roumaine, 1927); M. Balard, *Gênes et L'Outre-Mer*, I: *Les Actes de Caffa du notaire Lamberto di Sambuceto 1289– 1290* (Paris; The Hague: Mouton, 1973). For later testimony see G. Balbi, 'Atti rogati a Caffa da Nicolo Beltrame (1343–44)', in G. Balbi and S. Raiteri, *Notai genovesi in Oltremare: Atti rogati a Caffa e a Licostomo (sec. XIV)* (Genova: Istituto internazionale di studi liguri, 1973), and M. Maowist, *Kaffa-Kolonia genuerska na Krymie i problem wschodi w latach 1453–1475* (Warsaw: Prache Instytutu istorycznego Uniwersytetu Warszawskiego, 1947).

9. G. Pistarino, *Notai genovesi in Oltremare: Atti rogati a Chilia da Antonio di Ponzo (1362–69)* (Genova: Istituto internazionale di studi liguri, 1971).

10. J. Heers, *Esclaves et domestiques au Moyen Age*, p. 67; Verlinden, 'L'origine de sclavus=esclave', pp. 97–128; Verlinden, 'L'esclavage du sud-est et de l'est européen en Europe orientale', pp. 18–29; Verlinden, *L'esclavage dans l'Europe médiévale*; Epstein, *Speaking of Slavery*.

11. H. Van der Wee, 'Structural Changes in European Long-distance Trade, and Particularly in the Re-export Trade from South to the North, 1350–1750', in J. Tracy (ed.), *The*

Rise of Merchant Empires. Long-distance Trade in the Early Modern World, 1350–1750 (Cambridge: Cambridge University Press, 1990), pp. 14–33.

12. R. S. Lopez, *The Commercial Revolution of the Middle Ages, 950–1350* (New York: Cambridge University Press, 1972), p. 92.

13. D. Deletant, 'Genoese, Tatars and Rumanians at the Mouth of the Danube in the Fourteenth Century', *Slavonic and East European Review*, 62:4 (1984), pp. 511–30.

14. Epstein, *Speaking of Slavery*; D. Gioffré, *Il mercato degli schiavi a Genova nel secolo XV* (Genova: Fratelli Bozzi 1971); R. Delort, "Quelques précisions sur le commerce des esclaves à Gênes vers la fin du XIVe siècle', *Mélanges d'archéologie et d'histoire*, 78:1 (1966), pp. 215–50.

15. M. Balard, 'Esclavage en Crimée et sources fiscales génoises au XVe siècle', *Byzantinische Forschungen*, 22 (1996), pp. 9–17, reprinted in H. Bresc (ed.), *Figures de l'esclave au Moyen-Age et dans le monde moderne. Actes de la table ronde organisée les 27 et 28 octobre 1992 par le Centre d'Histoire sociale et culturelle de l'Occident de l'Université de Paris-X Nanterre* (Paris: Université Paris X 1996), pp. 77–87.

16. Heers, *Esclaves et domestiques au Moyen Age*; C. Verlinden, 'La traite des esclaves. Un grand commerce international au Xᵉ siècle', in *Études de civilisation médiévale (IXᵉ–XIIᵉ siècles) Mélanges offerts à Edmond-René Labande* (Poitiers: C.É.S.C.M, 1974), pp. 721–30; Gioffré, *Il mercato degli schiavi a Genova nel secolo XV*; F. Panero, *Schiavi, servi e villani nell'Italia medievale* (Torino: Paravia, 1999).

17. Gioffré, *Il mercato degli schiavi a Genova nel secolo XV.*

18. M. V. Kirilov, 'Slave Trade in Early Modern Crimea from the Perspective of Christian, Muslim and Jewish Sources', *Journal of Early Modern History*, 11:1 (2007), pp. 1–32.

19. G. V. Scammell, *The World Encompassed. The First European Maritime Empires, c. 800–1650* (Berkeley, CA: University of California Press, 1981).

20. Some classical references: F. Braudel, *Civilisation matérielle, économie et capitalism*, 3 vols (Paris: Colin, 1977–79); I. Wallerstein, *The Modern World System*, 2 vols (New York and London: Academic Press, 1974–80).

21. Khodarkovsky, *Russia's Steppe Frontier*, pp. 102–3.

22. Perdue, *China Marches West*, p. 39.

23. Ibid. See also B. Davis, *State, Power and Community in Early Modern Russia: The Case of Kozlov, 1635–1649* (Basingstoke, NY: Palgrave, Macmillan, 2004).

24. E. N. Shipova, *Slovar' turkizmov v russkom iazyke* (Dictionary of Turkish into Russian language) (Alma–Ata: Nauka, 1976), p. 442.

25. A. Fisher, 'Muscovy and the Black Sea Trade', *Canadian-American Slavic Studies*, 6:4 (1972), pp. 582–93.

26. A. A. Novosel'skii, *Bor'ba Moskovskogo gosudarstva s Tatarami v pervoi polovine 17 veka* (The Fight of the Muscovite State against the Tatars during the First Half of the Seventeenth Century) (Moscow: Leningrad: Nauka, 1948).

27. SIRIO, 41 (1885), n. 72, p. 360; N. Davies, *God's Playground: a History of Poland*, 2 vols (New York: Columbia University press, 1982), vol. 1, pp. 139–41; Khodarkovsky, *Russia's Steppe Frontier*, pp. 21–2.

28. *Materialy po istorii Uzbeksoi, Tadzhiskoi i Turkmenskoi SSR*, 2 vols (Leningrad; Moscow: Nauka, 1932), vol. 1, pp. 386–97, quoted in Hellie, *Slavery in Russia*, p. 25, n. 43.

29. *Materialy po istorii Uzbeksoi, Tadzhiskoi i Turkmenskoi SSR*, pp. 386–97.

30. W. G. Clarence-Smith, *Islam and the Abolition of Slavery* (Oxford: Oxford University Press, 2006), pp. 118–19.

31. R. Hellie (ed.), *The Muscovite Law Code (Ulozhenie) of 1649, Part I* (Irvine, CA: Charles Schlacks, 1988), pp. 17–18.

32. Rossiiskaia Akademiia nauk. Arkhiv, A.A. Novosel'skii, fonds 1714, opis 1, delo 66, l. 123; RGADA, fonds 123, opis 3, delo 13.

33. RGADA, fonds 123, Krymskie dela 13, l. 53; *Materialy po istorii Uzbeksoi, Tadzhiskoi i Turkmenskoi SSR*, pp. 386–7

34. RGADA, fonds 109, opis'1, 1643; Khodarkovsky, *Russia's Steppe Frontier*, pp. 24–25.

35. Hellie, *Slavery in Russia*, pp. 68–9.

36. Paul of Aleppo, *The Travels of Macarius; Extracts From the Diary of the Travels of Macarius, Patriarch of Antioch*, ed. Lady L. Ridding (London: Oxford University Press, 1936), pp. 28, 76.

37. A. L. Khoroshkevich, *Russkoe gosudarstvo v sisteme mezhdunarodnykh otnoshenii kontsa XV–nachala XVI v.* (The Russian State in the System of International Relations towards the End of the Fifteenth and Beginning of the Sixteenth Century) (Moscow: Nauka, 1980), pp. 30–2.

38. Khodarkovsky, *Russia's Steppe Frontier*, p. 24.

39. RGADA, fonds 89, Turetskie dela, delo 3.

40. Christian, *A History of Russia, Central Asia and Mongolia*.

41. *Kazakhsko-russkie otnosheniia v 16–18 vekakh, Sbornik dokumentov i materialov* (The Russian-Kazakh relations during the Sixteenth to Eighteenth Century. Collected Documents and Materials) (Alma-Ata: Akademia nauk Kazakhskoi SSSR, 1961 and 1964), n. 88: p. 209, n. 33: p. 64, n. 76: pp. 181, 184. Also see *Mezhdunarodnye otnosheniia v Tsentral'noi Azii: 17–18vv. Dokumenty I materialy*, 2 vols (International relations in Central Asia: Seventeenth to Eighteenth Century) (Moscow: Nauka, 1989).

42. After the disbanding of what the Russians called 'the Golden Horde', Mongol power fractured into several khanates in Inner and Central Asia. The Small, Middle and Great Hordes were ruled each by a khan, and their members called themselves Kazakhs who were descended from Mongol and Turkic clans. They spoke Turkic and were Sunni Muslims (M. Brill-Olcott, *The Kazhaks* (Stanford, CA: Hoover Institutions Press, 1987).

43. Clarence-Smith, *Islam and the Abolition of Slavery*, p. 13.

44. A. Fisher, 'The Ottoman Crimea in the 16th Century', *Harvard Ukrainian studies*, 2 (1981), pp. 141–2.

45. H. Inalcik, 'Servile Labour in Ottoman Empire', in A. Ascher, T. Halasi-Kun and B. Kiraly (eds), *The Mutual Effects of the Islamic and Judeo-Christian Worlds: The East European Patterns* (New York and Brooklyn: College Press, 1979), pp. 39–40; Y. Seng, 'Fugitives and Factotums: Slaves in Early 16th-Century Istanbul', *Journal of the Economic and Social History of the Orient*, 39:2 (1996), pp. 136–69.

46. Fisher, 'Muscovy and the Black Sea Trade'.

47. Inalcik, *The Custom Register of Caffa*, pp. 93, 145–6.

48. *Sbornik Imperatorskogo Russkogo Istoricheskogo Obshchestvo* (Collected Works of the Imperial Russian Historical Society) (Saint Petersburg, 1884), vol. 41, pp. 42–3, 52–3, 104–7, 115–21, 146–57.

49. Toledano, *Slavery and Abolition in the Ottoman Middle East*, p. 8.

50. T. Barrett, 'Lines of Uncertainty: The Frontier of the North Caucasus', *Slavic Review*, 54:3 (1995), pp. 578–601; Clarence-Smith, *Islam and the Abolition of Slavery*, pp. 13–14.

51. Toledano, *Slavery and Abolition in the Ottoman Middle East*, p. 81; Ö. L. Barkan, 'Le Servage existait-il en Turquie?', in *Annales: economies, societes, civilisations*, 11 (1956), pp. 54–60.

52. D. B. Davis, *Slavery and Human Progress* (New York: Oxford University Press, 1984); R. Crummey, *The Formation of Muscovy, 1304–1614* (London: Longman, 1987).

3 Ferguson, 'Clientship, Social Indebtedness and State-Controlled Emancipation of Africans in the Late Ottoman Empire'

1. D. Quataert, *The Ottoman Empire 1700–1922* (Cambridge: Cambridge University Press, 2005), p. 63.

2. Ibid., p. xii.

3. For a discussion and examples of the *mukātaba* contract from the early Ottoman period, see H. Inalcik, 'Servile Labor in the Ottoman Empire', in A. Ascher, T. Halasi-Kun and B. K. Király (eds), *The Mutual Effects of the Islamic and Judeo-Christian Worlds: The East European Pattern* (Brooklyn, NY: Brooklyn College Press, 1979), pp. 27–9.

4. R. Brunschvig, ''Abd', in P. Bearman, T. Bianquis, C. E. Bosworth, E. van Donzel and W. P. Heinricks (eds), *Encyclopaedia of Islam*, 2nd edn (2012), at http://referenceworks. brillonline.com/browse/encyclopaedia-of-islam-2 [accessed 20 November 2008].

5. G. Campbell, 'Introduction: Abolition and its aftermath in the Indian Ocean World', in G. Campbell (ed.), *Abolition and its Aftermath in Indian Ocean Africa and Asia* (New York: Routledge, 2005), pp. 15–17.

6. For a detailed discussion of routes, see E. Toledano, *The Ottoman Slave Trade and its Suppression, 1840–1890* (Princeton, NJ: Princeton University Press, 1982).

7. K. Karpat, 'The Transformation of the Ottoman State, 1789–1908', *International Journal of Middle East Studies*, 3 (1972), pp. 256–61.

8. Toledano, *The Ottoman Slave Trade and its Suppression*, pp. 43–8; G. Campbell, 'Introduction: Abolition and its Aftermath in the Indian Ocean World', pp. 4–5.

9. For a full discussion, see Erdem, *Slavery in the Ottoman Empire and its Demise*, pp. 152–60; Brunschvig, ''Abd'.

10. Despite this theoretical equality, A. Fisher has found that, the status of being an emancipated slave was often recorded in legal documents; see A. Fisher, 'Studies in Ottoman Slavery and Slave Trade, II: Manumission', *Journal of Turkish Studies*, 4 (1980), p. 54.

11. Brunschvig, ''Abd'.

12. Ibid.; H. Wehr, *A Dictionary of Modern Written Arabic* (Urbana, IL: Spoken Language Services, Inc., 1994), pp. 1288, 1290.

13. Brunschvig, ''Abd'.

14. Ibid.

15. J. Hathaway and K. K. Barbir, *The Arab Lands Under Ottoman Rule, 1516–1800* (Harlow: Pearson-Longman, 2008), p. 13.

16. Ibid.

17. Toledano, *Slavery and Abolition in the Ottoman Middle East*, p. 4.

18. Hathaway with Babir, *Arab Lands Under Ottoman Rule*, p. 204.

19. C. Melchert, 'Maintenance and Upkeep', in J. D. McAuliffe (ed.), *Encyclopaedia of the Qurān* (2009), at http://www.brillonline.nl/subscriber/entry?entry=q3_SIM-00271 [accessed 31 March 2009].

20. R. Levy, *The Social Structure of Islam: Being the Second Edition of the Sociology of Islam* (Cambridge: Cambridge University Press, 1957), p. 81; also see J. Hathaway, *The Politics of Households in Ottoman Egypt: The Rise of the Qazdaglis* (New York: Cambridge University Press, 1997).

21. E. Toledano, *As if Silent and Absent: Bonds of Enslavement in the Islamic Middle East* (New Haven, CT: Yale University Press, 2002), p. 257.

22. Toledano, *Slavery and Abolition in the Ottoman Middle East*, p. 67. For an example of the risks faced when a patron–client relationship broke down, see E. Toledano, 'Slave Dealers, Women, Pregnancy and Abortion: The Story of a Circassian Slave Girl in Mid-Nineteenth Century Cairo', *Slavery and Abolition*, 2:1 (1981), pp. 53–68.

23. The literature on this topic is vast. For example, see B. Lewis, *The Emergence of Modern Turkey* (Oxford: Oxford University Press, 2001); S. J. Shaw and E. K. Shaw, *History of the Ottoman Empire and Modern Turkey*, 2 vols (Cambridge; New York: Cambridge University Press, 1976–7); H. Inalcik and D. Quataert (eds), *An Economic and Social History of the Ottoman Empire*, 2 vols (Cambridge: Cambridge University Press, 1994); E. Zürcher, *Turkey: A Modern History* (New York: I. B. Tauris, 1998).

24. D. Quataert, 'Part IV: The Age of Reforms: 1812–1914', in H. Inalcik and D. Quataert (eds), *An Economic and Social History of the Ottoman Empire*, 2 vols (Cambridge: Cambridge University Press, 1994), vol. 2, p. 762.

25. D. C. Blaisdell, *European Financial Control in the Ottoman Empire: A Study of the Establishment, Activities, and Significance of the Administration of the Ottoman Public Debt* (New York: Columbia University Press, 1929).

26. *Great Britain, House of Commons Command Paper, Class B, Correspondence with British Ministers and Agents in Foreign Countries, and with Foreign Ministers in England, relating to the Slave Trade. From April 1, 1856, to March 31, 1857* (London; Harrison & Sons, 1857) [C.2282], pp. 492–4, no. 626; Toledano, *The Ottoman Slave Trade and its Suppression*, pp. 135–8.

27. Toledano, *As if Silent and Absent*, pp. 118–24.

28. Ibid.

29. For example, see Toledano, *The Ottoman Slave Trade and its Suppression*, pp. 200, 203–4.

30. Erdem, *Slavery in the Ottoman Empire and its Demise*, p. 184.

31. Toledano, *As if Silent and Absent*, p. 115.

32. Erdem, *Slavery in the Ottoman Empire and its Demise*, pp. 173–6; M. Ferguson, 'Enslaved and Emancipated Africans on Crete', in T. Walz and K. M. Cuno (eds), *Race and Slavery in the Middle East: Histories of Trans-Saharan Africans in Nineteenth-Century Egypt, Sudan, and the Ottoman Mediterranean* (Cairo and New York: American University in Cairo Press, 2010), pp. 171–95; G. Güneş, 'Kölelikten Özgürlüğe: İzmir'de Zenciler ve Zenci Folkloru', *Topulumsal Tarih*, 11:62 (1999), pp. 4–10; Toledano, *As if Silent and Absent*, pp. 203–54.

33. Erdem, *Slavery in the Ottoman Empire and its Demise*, pp. 160–76; Toledano, *As if Silent and Absent*.

34. Toledano, *The Ottoman Slave Trade and its Suppression*, p. 137.

35. Ibid., pp. 246–7.

36. *Great Britain, House of Commons Command Paper, Convention between H.M. and the Sultan of Turkey for the Suppression of the African Slave Trade, Constantinople, January 1880. Slave Trade. No. 2, 1881.* (London: Her Stationery Office, 1881) [C.3060]), p. 2.

37. Erdem, *Slavery in the Ottoman Empire and its Demise*, pp. 158–9.

38. Ibid., p. 159.

39. Ibid., p. 157.
40. For a complete discussion of how this process unfolded elsewhere in the Muslim world, see T. Mitchell, *Colonising Egypt* (Cambridge; New York: Cambridge University Press, 1988).
41. E. J. Zürcher, *Arming the State: Military Conscription in the Middle East and Central Asia, 1775–1925* (New York: I. B. Tauris, 1999), p. 80.
42. A. Bein, 'Politics, Military Conscription and Religious Education in the Late Ottoman Empire', *International Journal of Middle East Studies*, 38 (2006), p. 288.
43. Bein, 'Politics, Military Conscription and Religious Education', p. 295.
44. Zürcher, *Arming the State*, pp. 85, 90.
45. Ibid., p. 86.
46. Bein, 'Politics, Military Conscription and Religious Education', p. 286.
47. S. Deringil, 'Legitimacy Structures in the Ottoman State: The Reign of Abdülhamid II (1876–1909)', *International Journal of Middle East Studies*, 23:3 (1991), p. 347; R. Kasaba, *A Moveable Empire: Ottoman Nomads, Migrants and Refugees* (Seattle, WA: University of Washington Press, 2009).
48. N. Özbek, 'Philanthropic Activity, Ottoman Patriotism, and the Hamidian Regime, 1876–1909', *International Journal of Middle East Studies*, 37 (2005), p. 66.
49. Quataert, 'Part IV: The Age of Reforms: 1812–1914', p. 812.
50. Ibid., p. 809; Deringil, 'Legitimacy Structures in the Ottoman State', p. 352.
51. Deringil, 'Legitimacy Structures in the Ottoman State', p. 347.
52. Özbek, 'Philanthropic Activity, Ottoman Patriotism, and the Hamidian Regime', p. 69.
53. Ibid.
54. M. Dean, *Governmentality: Power and Rule in Modern Society* (London: Sage Publications, 1999), pp. 99–100.
55. C. Bilsel, 'Vers une métropole modern de la méditerranée', in M.-C. Smyrnelis (ed.), *Smyrne, la ville oubliée? 1830–1930: mémoires d'un grand port Ottoman* (Paris: Edition Autremont, 2006), pp. 122–37.
56. A. Temizsoy, 'Cultural and Architectural Significance of Planned Refugee Houses in Izmir (Turkey) from the Point of Conservation', in *1st International CIB Endorsed METU Postgraduate Conference Built Environment & Information Technologies* (Ankara, 2006), pp. 741–56.
57. N. Özbek, 'Policing the Countryside: Gendarmes of the Late 19th-Century Ottoman Empire (1876–1908)', *International Journal of Middle East Studies*, 40 (2008), pp. 47–67.
58. D. Quataert, *Miners and the State in the Ottoman Empire: The Zonguldak Coalfied 1822–1900* (New York: Berghan Books, 2006), p. 4.
59. A. Martal, 'Afrika'dan İzmir'e: Izmir'de Bir Köle Misafirhanesi', *Kebikeç*, 10 (2000), pp. 174–5.
60. Toledano, *As if Silent and Absent*, p. 111.
61. Ibid., pp. 111, 139; Erdem, *Slavery in the Ottoman Empire and its Demise*, p. 177.
62. Great Britain, House of Commons Command Paper. *Correspondence with British Representatives and Agents Abroad and Reports from Naval Officers and the Treasury Relative to the Slave Trade. Africa. No. 1, 1881* (London: Her Stationery Office, 1881) [C.3052]), pp. 251–5, no.199. This petition is also discussed in Toledano, *As if Silent and Absent*, pp. 149–50; Erdem, *Slavery in the Ottoman Empire and its Demise*, p. 173.
63. Toledano, *The Ottoman Slave Trade and its Suppression*, p. 247.

64. Great Britain, House of Commons Command Paper. *Africa. No. 1, 1881*, pp. 251–5, no. 199.

65. Great Britain, House of Commons Command Paper. *Africa. No. 1, 1881*, pp. 251–5, no. 199.

66. Toledano, *As if Silent and Absent*, p. 142.

67. Erdem, *Slavery in the Ottoman Empire and its Demise*, p. 177.

68. At this time, a number of factors combined which made Benghazi, not much more than an Ottoman outpost on the shores of the southern Mediterranean, the Ottoman North African slaving port *par excellence*. Toledano, *The Ottoman Slave Trade and its Suppression*, p. 238. For a full discussion of this trade route, see J. Wright, 'The Wadai – Benghazi Slave Route', in E. Savage (ed.), *The Human Commodity: Perspectives on the Trans-Saharan Slave Trade* (New York: Routledge, 1992), pp. 174–84.

69. Erdem, *Slavery in the Ottoman Empire and its Demise*, p. 178.

70. Ibid.

71. Great Britain, House of Commons Command Paper. *Correspondence with British Representatives and Agents Abroad and Reports from Naval Officers and the Treasury Relative to the Slave Trade. Africa. No. 1, 1885*. (London: Her Stationery Office, 1884–5) [C.4523]), p. 32, no. 53.

72. For a description of Africans and the African quarter in Chania, see Ferguson, 'Enslaved and Emancipated Africans on Crete', pp. 171–95.

73. Great Britain, House of Commons Command Paper. *Correspondence with British Representatives and Agents Abroad and Reports from Naval Officers and the Treasury Relative to the Slave Trade. Africa. No. 1, 1886* (London: Her Stationery Office, 1886) [C.4476]), p. 76, no.74.

74. Great Britain, House of Commons Command Paper. *Africa. No. 1, 1886*, pp. 82–5, no. 87.

75. Great Britain, House of Commons Command Paper. *Africa. No. 1, 1886*, pp. 68–9, no. 59.

76. Great Britain, House of Commons Command Paper, *Paper Relating to Slave Trade in Benghazi. Africa. No. 10, 1893* (London: Her Stationery Office, 1893) [C.7158], p. 2, no.3. Emancipated Africans were adherents of a religio-belief system called *Zar* or *Bori*, in which music was a crucial part of religious ceremonies. Furthermore, Sufism, of which many male slaves were also practitioners, had a central place for music in their ceremonies as well. For Zar, see A. Al-Safi, I. M. Lewis and S. Hurreiz (eds), *Women's Medicine: The Zar-Bori Cult in Africa and Beyond* (Edinburgh: Edinburgh University Press, 1991); J. Boddy, *Wombs and Alien Spirits: Women, Men, and the Zar Cult in Northern Sudan* (Madison, WI: University of Wisconsin Press, 1989). For music and Sufism, see L. Lewisohn, 'The Sacred Music of Islam: Samā' in the Persian Sufi Tradition', *British Journal of Ethnomusicology*, 6 (1997), pp. 1–33.

77. Great Britain, House of Commons Command Paper, *Africa. No. 10, 1893*, p. 4, no. 6.

78. For information on the Ottomans in North Africa in the late nineteenth century see A. A. Ahmida, *The Making of Modern Libya: State Formation, Colonization, and Resistance, 1830–1932* (Albany, NY: State University of New York Press, 1994).

79. Erdem, *Slavery in the Ottoman Empire and its Demise*, p. 179.

80. For a full discussion of Izmir's rise to prominence in the nineteenth century, see R. Kasaba, *The Ottoman Empire and the World Economy: The Nineteenth Century* (Albany, NY: State University of New York Press, 1988).

81. Erdem, *Slavery in the Ottoman Empire and its Demise*, p. 179; G. Güneş, 'İzmir'de Zenciler Vs Zenci Folkloru', p. 5; Martal, 'Afrika'dan Izmir'e: Izmir'de Bir Kole Misafirhanesi', p. 176.
82. 'Mithatpaşa Teknik ve Endüstri Meslek Lisesi – Tanıtım', at http://www.mithatpasa.k12.tr/tanitim [accessed 29 January 2011].
83. Erdem, *Slavery in the Ottoman Empire and its Demise*, p. 180.
84. Ibid.
85. Ibid., p. 181.
86. Ibid.
87. Ibid.
88. Kasaba, *The Ottoman Empire and the World Economy*, pp. 67–9.
89. E. Eldem, D. Goffman and B. Masters, *The Ottoman City between East and West: Aleppo, Izmir, and Istanbul* (Cambridge: Cambridge University Press, 1999), pp. 86–7; Kasaba, *The Ottoman Empire and the World Economy*, p. 61.
90. Kasaba, *The Ottoman Empire and the World Economy*, p. 73.
91. Ş. Pamuk, *The Ottoman Empire and European Capitalism, 1820–1913: Trade, Investment and Production* (Cambridge: Cambridge University Press, 1997), p. 88.
92. Erdem, *Slavery in the Ottoman Empire and its Demise*, p. 181.
93. Martal, 'Afrika'dan İzmir'e: Izmir'de Bir Köle Misafirhanesi', pp. 177–8.
94. *Aydın Vilayet Salnamesi* (Aydın: Provincial Press, 1307/1308[1890/1]), p. 273.
95. Kasaba, *The Ottoman Empire and the World Economy*, pp. 99–100.
96. For a similar argument, see B. Silverstein, 'Sufism and Governmentality in the Late Ottoman Empire', *Comparative Studies of South Asia, Africa and the Middle East*, 29:2 (2009), p. 173.
97. For an example of how this contest unfolded elsewhere, see K. Butler, *Freedoms Given, Freedoms Won: Afro-Brazillians in Post-Abolition São Paulo and Salvador* (New Brunswick: Rutgers University Press, 2000).

4 Lovejoy, 'Pawnship and Seizure for Debt in the Process of Enslavement in West Africa'

1. T. Falola and P. E. Lovejoy, 'Pawnship in Historical Perspective', in P. E. Lovejoy and T. Falola (eds), *Pawnship, Slavery and Colonialism in Africa* (Trenton, NJ: Africa World Press, 2003), pp. 1–26.
2. A. N. Klein, 'Inequality in Asante: A Study of the Forms and Meaning of Slavery and Social Servitude in Pre- and Early Colonial Akan-Asante Society and Culture' (PhD dissertation, University of Michigan, 1980); and G. Austin, 'Indigenous Credit Institutions in West Africa, c. 1750–c. 1960', in G. Austin and K. Sugihara (eds), *Local Suppliers of Credit in the Third World, 1750–1980* (Basingstoke: Macmillan, 1993), pp. 117–30. There is scattered discussion of pawning in many of the studies on slavery in Africa, particularly in such collections as those by Meillassoux, Miers and Kopytoff, Miers and Roberts, and others. For references, also see L. Sundstrom, *The Trade of Guinea* (Upsala: Akademisk avhandling, 1965), pp. 36–45.
3. In addition to my collaboration with Falola, and hence the papers of our edited publication, the pioneering work of E. A. Oroge and A. N. Klein should be mentioned, and specifically Oroge, 'The Institution of Slavery in Yorubaland with Particular Reference to the Nineteenth Century' (PhD dissertation, University of Birmingham, 1971);

and Oroge, '*Iwofa*: An Historical Survey of the Yoruba Institution of Indenture', *African Economic History*, 14 (1985), pp. 75–106, and reprinted in P. E. Lovejoy and T. Falola (eds), *Pawnship, Slavery and Colonialism in Africa* (Trenton, NJ: Africa World Press, 2003), pp. 325–56. Also see Klein, 'Inequality in Asante' and the discussion in Lovejoy and Falola, 'Pawnship in Historical Perspective', pp. 1–26. Also see T. Falola, 'Slavery and Pawnship in the Yoruba Economy of the Nineteenth Century', in P. E. Lovejoy and N. Rogers (eds), *Unfree Labor in the Development of the Atlantic World* (London: Frank Cass, Ltd, 1994), pp. 221–45. Surprisingly, there is only brief mention of pawning, despite the focus on colonial south-western Nigeria, in J. L. Guyer, *Money Matters: Instability, Values and Social Payments in the Modern History of West African Communities* (Portsmouth, NH: Heinemann, 1995), pp. 175–77.

4.   On panyarring, see R. Kea, *Settlements, Trade and Polities in the Seventeenth-Century Gold Coast* (Baltimore, MD: Johns Hopkins University Press, 1982); R. Law, 'On Pawning and Enslavement for Debt in the Precolonial Slave Coast', in Lovejoy and Falola, *Pawnship, Slavery and Colonialism in Africa*, pp. 62–5; and O. Ojo, '*Ẹ̀mú* (*Àmúyá*): The Yoruba Institution of Panyarring or Seizure for Debt', *African Economic History*, 35 (2007), pp. 31–58.

5.   Oroge, 'The Institution of Slavery in Yorubaland'; and Oroge, '*Iwofa*: An Historical Survey of the Yoruba Institution of Indenture'.

6.   P. E. Lovejoy, '*Murgu*: The Wages of Slavery in the Sokoto Caliphate', *Slavery and Abolition*, 24:1 (1992), pp. 168–85.

7.   R. H. Stone, *In Africa's Forest and Jungle or Six Years among the Yorubans* (New York: Fleming H. Revell, 1899), pp. 42–5. In the mid-1850s, W. H. Clarke put the average daily wage at 1,600–3,200 cowries but he did not specify the location. See Clarke, *Travels and Exploration in Yorubaland, 1854–1858*, ed. J. A. Atanda (Ibadan: Ibadan University Press, 1972), p. 268. D. J. May, 'Journey in the Yoruba and Nupe Countries in 1858', *Journal of Royal Geographical Society*, 30 (1860), pp. 223, 229; and W. Baikie to Foreign Office, April 24 1860, National Archives of the United Kingdom, Kew, Surrey, #24, FO 97/433; Charles Phillips, diary, January 4 and 9, June 25–26, September 7 and 21 and November 23 1896, Nigerian National Archives, Ibadan, Phillips 3/8; and Moses Lijadu, diary, November 2 1899, Nigerian National Archives, Ibadan, Lijadu Family papers (LFP) 2/1/5.

8.   J. Lofkrantz, 'Ransoming of Captives and Slavery in the Sokoto Caliphate in the Nineteenth Century', in B. Mirzai, I. M. Montana and P. E. Lovejoy (eds), *Slavery, Islam and Diaspora* (Trenton, NJ: Africa World Press, 2009), pp. 125–37; and J. Lofkrantz, 'Ransoming in the Western and Central Bilād al-Sūdān c. 1800–1910' (PhD dissertation, York University, 2008); and J. Lofkrantz, 'Protecting Freeborn Muslims: The Sokoto Caliphate's Attempts to Prevent Illegal Enslavement and its Acceptance of the Strategy of Ransoming', *Slavery and Abolition*, 32:1 (2011), pp. 109–27.

9.   Also see O. Ojo, 'Warfare, Slavery and the Transformation of Eastern Yorubaland c.1820–1900' (PhD dissertation, York University, 2003), pp. 243–61, 347–8.

10. See Ojo, 'Business of "Trust" and Enslavement of Yoruba Women and Children for Debt', included in this collection, pp. 77–91.

11. Samuel Crowther to Thomas Hutchinson, September 10 1856, Church Missionary Society Archives, University of Birmingham, CA2/031/78. I wish to thank Olatunji Ojo for this reference.

12. P. E. Lovejoy, 'Transformation of the *Ẹ̀kpẹ̀* Masquerade in the African Diaspora', in C. Innes, A. Rutherford and B. Bogar (eds), *Carnival: Theory and Practice* (Trenton, NJ:

Africa World Press, 2013), pp. 125–50; and U. Röschenthaler, *Purchasing Culture in the Cross River Region of Cameroon and Nigeria* (Trenton, NJ: Africa World Press, 2011).

13. M. Douglas, 'Matriliny and Pawnship in Central Africa', *Africa*, 34:4 (1964), pp. 301–13. Also see Falola and Lovejoy, 'Pawnship in Historical Perspective', pp. 1–26.

14. See the several co-authored publications with D. Richardson on pawnship and the slave trade, including 'Trust, Pawnship and Atlantic History: The Institutional Foundations of the Old Calabar Slave Trade', *American Historical Review*, 104:2 (1999), pp. 332–55; 'The Business of Slaving: Pawnship in Western Africa, c. 1600–1810', *Journal of African History*, 42:1 (2001), pp. 67–89; '"This Horrid Hole": Royal Authority, Commerce and Credit at Bonny, 1690–1840', *Journal of African History*, 45:3 (2004), pp. 363–92; 'Letters of the Old Calabar Slave Trade, 1760–89', in V. Carretta and P. Gould (eds), *Genius in Bondage: Literatures of the Early Black Atlantic* (Louisville, KY: University of Kentucky Press, 2001), pp. 89–115; 'Anglo-Efik Relations and Protection against Illegal Enslavement at Old Calabar 1740–1807', in S. Diouf (ed.), *Fighting the Slave Trade: West African Strategies* (Bloomington, IN: Indiana University Press, 2003), pp. 101–20; 'Slaves to Palm Oil: Afro-European Commercial Relations in the Bight of Biafra, 1741–1841', in D. Killingray, M. Lincoln and N. Rigby (eds), *Maritime Empires* (London: Boydell & Brewer), pp. 13–29; and 'The Slave Ports of the Bight of Biafra in the Eighteenth Century', in C. Brown and P. E. Lovejoy (eds), *Repercussions of the Atlantic Slave Trade: The Interior of the Bight of Biafra and the African Diaspora* (Trenton, NJ: Africa World Press, 2010). Also see Lovejoy, 'Transformation of the *Ékpè* Masquerade in the African Diaspora', pp. 125–50; and Röschenthaler, *Purchasing Culture in the Cross River Region of Cameroon and Nigeria*.

15. See the discussion of pawnship in the 1780s at Old Calabar in the entries in the diary of Antera Duke in S. D. Behrendt, A. J. H. Latham and D. Northrup (eds), *The Diary of Antera Duke: An Eighteenth-Century African Slave Trader* (Oxford: Oxford University Press, 2010), pp. 24, 72, 79, 90, 92, 112, 156–7, 159, 179, 203, 207.

16. For *Bada'i* ' in the classical book on *hanafi* jurisprudence, which was the school of the Ottomans, see A. B. b. Masūd Kāsānī, *Badā'i ' al--anā'i ' fi tartīb al-sharā'i* ', 10 vols (Beirut: Dar al-Fikr, 1996), vol. 6, pp. 205, 221. For *Sharh*, see the 17 volumes on Ibadi jurisprudence by M. b. Yūsuf Atfiyash (died 1914), *Sharh kitāb al-Nīl wa shifā' al-'alīl* (Jaddah: Maktabat al-Irshad, 1972–1973), vol. 11, pp. 162, 224–25, 250, 251. I wish to thank Y. Daddi Addoun for these references.

17. A. B. Tuwat, 'Kitab Zima-mun Duyun', 1245 AH (AD 1829), Nigerian National Archives, Kaduna, KATPROF, G/AR3/1. For an in-depth discussion of Balghīth, see A. B. Sani, 'A Biographical Note on the Life and Adventures of Ahmad Abu al-Ghaith', paper presented at the conference 'Slavery, Memory and Citizenship', The Harriet Tubman Institute for Research on the Global Migrations of African Peoples, York University, August 2011; Y. Daddi Addoun and P. E. Lovejoy, 'Commerce and Credit in Katsina in the Nineteenth Century', in E. Brownell and T. Falola (eds), *Africa, Empire and Globalization: Essays In Honor of A.G. Hopkins* (Durham, NC: Carolina Academic Press, 2011), pp. 111–24; and J. Lofkrantz and P. E. Lovejoy, 'Crossing Network Boundaries: Islamic Law and Commerce from Sahara to Guinea Shores', forthcoming.

18. P. E. Lovejoy and J. S. Hogendorn, *Slow Death for Slavery. The Course of Abolition in Northern Nigeria, 1897–1936* (Cambridge: Cambridge University Press, 1993), pp. 259–280; and various studies in Lovejoy and Falola, *Pawnship, Slavery and Colonialism in Africa*.

19. Douglas, 'Matriliny and Pawnship in Central Africa', pp. 301–13.

5 Ojo, 'The Business of "Trust" and the Enslavement of Yoruba Women and Children for Debt'

1. J. Johnson, 'Tour of Inspection by the Rev. James Johnson', *Church Missionary Intelligencer and Record*, new series (3 February 1878), p. 91.

2. James Thomas, 16 April 1864, Church Missionary Society Archives (CMS), Gbebe journal, CA3/038.

3. *Lagos Annual Report* (1899), pp. 91–2; S. Johnson, *The History of the Yorubas from the Earliest to the Beginning of the British Protectorate* (1921; Lagos: CSS Books, 1976), p. 325 and A. K. Ajisafe-Moore, *The Laws and Customs of the Yoruba People* (Abeokuta: Fola Bookshops, 1924), pp. 54–5.

4. P. C. Lloyd, 'Osifekunde of Ijebu', in P. D. Curtin (ed.), *Africa Remembered: Narratives by West African from the Era of the Slave Trade* (Madison, WI: University of Wisconsin Press, 1967), pp. 270–1.

5. *Appendix to Iwe Irohin*, 24 December 1861, p. 1.

6. Ibid.

7. John Clemison (for Caboceer of Lagos) to Richard Miles, 27 January 1777. Cf. T. Hodgkin (ed.), *Nigerian Perspectives: An Historical Anthology* (London: Oxford University Press, 1975), pp. 225–6.

8. J. Adams, *Remarks on the Country Extending from Cape Palmas to the River Congo* (1823; London: Frank Cass, 1966), pp. 245–8. Also see L. J. Herbert to James Macdonald, 15 August 1808, NAUK, Chancery Master's Exhibits, C114/157. Cf. E. W. Evans and D. Richardson, 'Hunting for Rents: The Economics of Slaving in Pre-Colonial Africa', *Economic History Review*, 48 (1995), p. 665.

9. R. Smith (ed.), *Memoirs of Giambattista Scala: Consul of His Italian Majesty in Lagos in Guinea, 1862*, trans. B. Packman (Oxford: Clarendon Press, 2000).

10. See Kosoko Letters, #1, Manoel Joaquim d'Almeida to Kosoko, 17 April 1848; #3, Domingos Maria em Sorion to Kosoko, 20 March 1849; #6, Je. De Santos Ferra to Kosoko, 21 May 1849; #27, Gantois and Marbak, 15 October 1849; and #35, Franco. J. Godinho to Kosoko, 13 July 1850.

11. *African Times (London)*, 23 April 1862, pp. 4–5.

12. Campbell to Clarendon, 5 December 1854, NAUK, FO 84/950.

13. Isaac H. Willoughby to John Glover, 7 February 1873, Royal Commonwealth Society Library, London, John Glover Papers, and K. Mann, *Slavery and the Birth of an African City: Lagos, 1760–1900* (Bloomington, IN: Indiana University Press, 2007), p. 145. On J. P. L. Davies, see J. H. Kopytoff, *A Preface to Modern Nigeria: The 'Sierra Leonians' in Yoruba, 1830–1890* (Madison, WI: University of Wisconsin Press, 1965), pp. 286–7.

14. William McCoskry to Benjamin Campbell, 19 August 1855, in Benjamin Campbell to Clarendon, 30 August 1855, NAUK, FO 84/976; Benjamin Campbell to Alake, 4 April 1856, NAI, CSO 8/1/1; and E. F. Lodder to James Harris, Third Earl of Malmesbury, 30 May 1859, NAUK, FO 2/28.

15. Mann, *Slavery and the Birth of an African City*, pp. 145–7.

16. R. Lander and J. Lander, *Journal of an Expedition to Explore the Course and Termination of the Niger* (New York: J. & J. Harper, 1832), vol. 1, p. 124 and P. E. Lovejoy and D. Richardson, 'British Abolition and its Impact on Slave Prices at the Atlantic Coast of Africa, 1783–1850', *Journal of Economic History*, 55 (1995), pp. 98–119.

17. Kosoko to Francisco Godinho, 27 April 1849, Kosoko Letters, #5. The slave voyages database shows that in the few months preceding the latter at least three vessels loaded

with slaves from Lagos were seized by the British naval patrol. These are the *Miquelina*; the brig *Pensamento* (#3683), owned by Godinho, which left Lagos on 14 June 1848 under Capt J. P. A. Vianna with 538 slaves and was seized on 28 June; and a schooner, *Quantro Andorinha* (#3760), which left Lagos under Capt M. V. da Cunha with 388 slaves on 5 November 1848 and was captured on 28 November.

18. R. Lander, *Records of Captain Clapperton's Last Expedition to Africa*, 2 vols (London: Henry Colburn and Richard Bentley, 1830), vol. 2, p. 242; Henry Townsend to Captain Trotter, 10 December 1850 and Charles Gollmer to Arthur Fanshawe, 26 March 1851, in 'Papers on the Destruction of Lagos', *British Parliamentary Papers*, 64 (1852), p. 221; and Evans and Richardson, 'Hunting for Rents', pp. 665–6.

19. Samuel Ajayi Crowther, journal, 25 December 1850, CMS, CA2/031; Anna Hinderer to H. Venn, 26 October 1855, CMS, CA2/049b; and M. R. Delaney and R. Campbell, *Search for a Place: Black Separatism and Africa* (1861; Ann Arbor, MI: University of Michigan Press, 1969), p. 191.

20. R. Law (ed.), *From Slave Trade to 'Legitimate' Commerce: The Commercial Transition in Nineteenth Century West Africa* (Cambridge: Cambridge University Press, 1995).

21. Bello to Kosoko, 11 September and 15 October 1849, Kosoko Letters, #12 and 15.

22. Cando. Fz. Lima to Acheron, 30 April 1850, and Bello to Kosoko, 28 October and 21 November 1850, Kosoko Letters, #31, 45 and 47. Acheron is probably a poor rendition of Asogbon of Lagos.

23. Johnson, *History of the Yorubas*, pp. 357, 452, 459–60, 490–93 and J. F. A. Ajayi and R. S. Smith, *Yoruba Warfare in the Nineteenth Century* (Cambridge: Cambridge University Press, 1964), p. 20.

24. Samuel Rowe, Governor of Gold Coast Colony, to Earl of Derby, 15 February 1883, PP, C4957.

25. Journal, 4 November 1886 in despatch #8, Henry Higgins and Oliver Smith to Colonial Office, Second Part of Report to the Interior of Lagos, 20 June 1887, PP. vol. 60, C5144.

26. See 'Trade Report', in *Appendix to Iwe Irohin* (English Edition), 7 January 1861, pp. 2–3 and *African Times (London)*, 23 April 1862, pp. 4–5.

27. Samuel Rowe to Earl of Derby, 18 May 1883, PP, encl. 1 no. 8, C4957.

28. Anna Hinderer, journal, October 1860, cf. C. A. Hone and D. Hone, *Seventeen Years in the Yoruba Country: Memorials of Anna Hinderer Gathered from Her Journals and Letters* (London: Religious Tract Society, 1872), p. 229 and A.G. Hopkins, 'The Currency Revolution in Southwest Nigeria in the Late Nineteenth Century', *Journal of the Historical Society of Nigeria*, 3 (1966), pp. 476–83.

29. Delaney and Campbell, *Search for a Place*, p. 191.

30. Anna Hinderer, journal, 20 June and 7 August 1860, cf. Hone and Hone, *Seventeen Years in the Yoruba Country*, pp. 226, 229–30. Also see *Appendix to Iwe Irohin* (English Edition), 7 January 1861, pp. 1–2 and A. Mann in C. H. Gollmer, *Charles Andrew Gollmer: His Life and Missionary Labours in West Africa* (London: Hodder and Stoughton, 1889), p. 168.

31. M. A. S. Barber, *Oshielle or Village Life in the Yoruba Country from the Journals and Letters of a Catechist* (London: James Nisbet, 1857), p. 116.

32. Samuel Crowther to Thomas Hutchinson, 10 September 1856, CMS, CA2/031and T. Hutchinson, *Impressions of Western Africa* (London: Longman, Brown, Green, Longmans & Roberts, 1858), pp. 276–8.

33. 'Manumission of Slaves', NAI, CMS (Y) 2/2/3, and *Lagos Colony Annual Report, 1901–02* (London: HMSO, 1903), p. 200.
34. Anna Hinderer, journal, 21 February 1854, cf. Hone and Hone, *Seventeen Years in the Yoruba Country*, p. 92. My italics.
35. Daniel Olubi to C. C. Fenn, Annual letter, 26 February 1876, CMS, CA2/075.
36. Anna Hinderer, journal, 21 February 1854, cf. Hone and Hone, *Seventeen Years in the Yoruba Country*, p. 92.
37. Andrew Wilhelm, Oyo Station Report, 1866, CMS, CA2/011/31.
38. D. Hinderer to H. Venn, 27 February 1856, CMS, C/A2/O49/26.
39. S. A. Crowther, journal, 21 August 1846, CMS, CA2/031 and M. Tucker, *Abbeokuta or Sunrise within the Tropics* (London: James Nisbet, 1853), pp. 116–20.
40. S. A. Crowther to Hutchinson, 10 September 1856, CMS, CA2/031.
41. David Williams and James A. Maser to CMS Secretary, 24 November 1879, in 'Manumission of Slaves, March 1880', NAI, CMS (Y) 2/2/3.
42. R. Law, 'On Pawning and Enslavement for Debt in the Pre-Colonial Slave Coast', in Lovejoy and Falola (eds), *Pawnship, Slavery, and Colonialism in Africa*, pp. 60–6; P. E. Lovejoy and D. Richardson, '"This Horrid Hole": Royal Authority, Commerce and Credit at Bonny, 1690–1840', *Journal of African History*, 45:3 (2004), pp. 363–92; P. E. Lovejoy and D. Richardson, 'The Business of Slaving: Pawnship in Western Africa, c. 1600–1810', *Journal of African History*, 42:1 (2001), pp. 67–89; P. E. Lovejoy and D. Richardson, 'Trust, Pawnship, and Atlantic History: The Institutional Foundations of the Old Calabar Slave Trade', *American Historical Review*, 104 (1999), pp. 333–55; and P. E. Lovejoy, 'Pawnship, Debt and Slavery', paper presented at the workshop on 'Debt and Slavery: the History of a Process of Enslavement', Indian Ocean World Centre, McGill University, Montreal, Canada, 7–9 May 2009.
43. Joaquim Manoel D'Almeida to Kosoko, 17 April 1848, Kosoko Letters, #1.
44. Martinez (Porto Novo) to Kosoko, 19 September 1849, Kosoko Letters, #14.
45. R. F. Burton, *Abeokuta and the Camaroons Mountains: An Exploration* (London: Tinsley Brothers, 1863), vol. 1, p. 301.
46. E. Roper, 'What I Saw in Africa: Sketches of Missionary Life in the Yoruba Country, Part II', *Church Missionary Gleaner*, 3:27 (1876), pp. 34–6.
47. See R. Law, 'Legal and Illegal Enslavement in West Africa in the Context of the Trans-Atlantic Slave Trade', in T. Falola (ed.), *Ghana in Africa and the World: Essays in Honor of Adu Boahen* (Trenton, NJ: African World Press, 2003), p. 518.
48. Roper, 'What I Saw in Africa', p. 35.
49. E. A. Oroge, 'Iwofa: An Historical Study of the Yoruba Institution of Indenture', *African Economic History*, 14 (1985), pp. 76–81; P. E. Lovejoy and T. Falola (eds), *Pawnship, Slavery and Colonialism* (Trenton, NJ: Africa World Press, 2003), pp. 137–63, 357–408; J. D. Y. Peel, *Religious Encounter and the Making of the Yoruba* (Bloomington, IN: Indiana University Press, 2000), pp. 59–63; F. Shields, 'Palm Oil and Power: Women in an Era of Economic and Social Transition in Nineteenth Century Yorubaland (South-Western Nigeria)' (PhD dissertation, University of Stirling, 1997), pp. 106–8, 153–62; and O. Ojo, 'Warfare, Slavery and the Transformation of Eastern Yorubaland c. 1820–1900' (PhD dissertation, York University, 2003), pp. 234–50.
50. See M. Douglas, 'Matriliny and Pawnship in Central Africa', *Africa*, 34 (1964), pp. 301–13; M. Wright, *Strategies of Slaves & Women: Life Stories from East/Central Africa* (London: James Currey, 1993); E. A. Alpers, 'The Story of Swema: Female Vulnerability in 19th Century East Africa', in C. Robertson and M. Klein (eds), *Women and Slavery*

in Africa (Portsmouth: Heinemann, 1997), pp. 185–219; E. A. Alpers, 'Debt, Pawnship and Slavery in Nineteenth-Century East Africa', paper presented at the workshop on 'Debt and Slavery: the History of a Process of Enslavement', Indian Ocean World Centre, McGill University, Montreal Canada, 7–9 May 2009; F. Morton, 'Pawning and Slavery on the Kenya Coast: The Miji Kenda Case', in Lovejoy and Falola (eds), *Pawnship, Slavery, and Colonialism*, pp. 239–54; and J. Giblin, 'Pawning, Politics and Matriliny in Northeastern Tanzania', in Lovejoy and Falola (eds), *Pawnship, Slavery and Colonialism*, pp. 255–66.

51. Roper, 'What I Saw in Africa', p. 35.
52. On the enslavement of pawns, see Wood to Venn, 6 September 1861, CMS, CA2/096 and Mann to Venn, 19 September 1869, CMS, CA2/066.
53. Fraser to Malmesbury, 20 February 1853, dispatch #1, encl. 1–6 and #15 Campbell to Clarendon, 23 July 1853, PP, vol. 63, Class B.
54. Fraser to Malmesbury, 20 February 1853, dispatch #1, encl. 1–6, PP, vol. 63, Class B.
55. Campbell to Clarendon, 23 July 1853, PP, vol. 63, Class B.
56. George Meakin, Oyo station, journals, 14–20 June 1858 and 8 August 1859, CMS, CA2/069/10.
57. Johnson, *History of the Yorubas*, pp. 324–5.
58. Ibid., pp. 443–4 and Oroge, 'Iwofa'.
59. Johnson, *History of the Yorubas*, pp. 131, 443–4 and Bello Iyanda, Olomi, Ibadan, interview, 14–15 July 1999.
60. 'Report of the Ijaye Relief Committee', 1 October 1861, CMS, CA/011; R. H. Stone, *In Africa's Forest and Jungle or Six Years Among the Yorubans* (New York: Fleming H. Revell Company, 1899), pp. 184–6 and Johnson, *History of the Yorubas*, p. 209.
61. James White, Report for Half-year to 25 September 1862, CMS, CA2/087.
62. Evidence of William George and Kemta Abeokuta at the CMS Conference on slavery, NAI, CMS (Y) 2/2/3.
63. Adolphus C. Mann, 6 July 1856, CMS, CA2/066 and George Meakin, journal, Oyo, 14–20 June 1858 and 8 August 1859, CMS, CA2/069/10.
64. Stone, *In Africa's Forest and Jungle*, pp. 123–4 and 248.
65. A. B. Ellis, *The Yoruba-Speaking Peoples of the Slave Coast of West Africa* (London: Chapman & Hall, 1894), p. 190; Johnson, *History of the Yorubas*, p. 612; Ajisafe-Moore, *The Laws and Customs of the Yoruba People*, p. 62; A. Folarin, *The Laws and Customs of Egbaland* (Abeokuta: E.N.A. Printing Press, 1939), pp. 60–1; A. G. Hopkins, 'A Report on the Yoruba, 1910', *Journal of the Historical Society of Nigeria*, 5 (1969), pp. 76, 91; Shields, 'Palm Oil and Power', pp. 158–9; and O. Ojo, 'Èmú (Àmúyá): The Yoruba Institution of Panyarring or Seizure for Debt', *African Economic History*, 35 (2007), pp. 31–58.
66. Shields, 'Palm Oil and Power', pp. 154–6.
67. Daniel Olubi, diary, 8–9 July and 17 August 1884, Kenneth Dike Library, University of Ibadan, Isaac B. Akinyele Papers, box 1.
68. Johnson, *History of the Yorubas*, pp. 459, 490–2, 612.
69. Johnson to Evans, 23 January 1887 in Evans to Stanhope, 3 February 1887, PP, C5144.
70. Charles Phillips, diary, 4 and 11 February 1888, NAI, Bishop S. C. Phillips Papers 3/3.
71. Enc. 8 in Alfred Moloney to Knutsford, 24 June 1890, NAUK, CO 879/33; *Lagos Annual Report* (1899) and Johnson, *History of the Yorubas*, pp. 492–3.
72. Olubi to James Maser, November 1879, NAI, CMS (Y) 2/2/3.
73. Gerald Ambrose, journal, June 2 1898, NAI, Ondo Div 8/1.

74. See O. Ojo, 'Slavery and Human Sacrifice in Yorubaland: Ondo c. 1870–1894', *Journal of African History*, 46:3 (2005), pp. 379–404.
75. Phillips, diary, 21–22, 27 February 1882, NAI, Phillips 3/4.
76. See Ake 'A' Civil Suit 163/17.
77. Ajisafe-Moore, *The Laws and Customs of the Yoruba People*, p. 84.
78. Testimony by Richard Miles and John Fountain, in *Abridgement of the Minutes of the Evidence, Taken Before a Committee of the Whole House on The Slave Trade Part 1* (London: House of Common, 1789), vol. 1, pp. 10, 15, 19, 43 and 44.
79. Testimony of James Frazier, in *Abridgement of the Minutes of the Evidence, Taken Before a Committee of the Whole House on The Slave Trade* (London: House of Common, 1790), vol. 2, p. 3.
80. See Lovejoy and Richardson, 'The Business of Slaving'; R. Law (ed.), The *English in West Africa: The Local Correspondence of the Royal African Company of England, 1681–1699*, 3 vols (Oxford: Oxford University Press, 1997–2007); and S. D. Behrendt, A. J. H. Latham and D. Northrup, *The Diary of Antera Duke, An Eighteenth-Century African Slave Trader* (Oxford: Oxford University Press, 2010).
81. Barber, *Oshielle or Village*, pp. xviii–xx; Thomas Birch Freeman, Wesleyan Methodist Missionary Society Archives, Box 597, 5, Fiche 260 and James Johnson, Annual Report for 1879, CMS, CA2/056/55.

6 Menard, 'The Africanization of the Workforce in English America'

1. Unless otherwise noted, all population figures in this essay are drawn from the tables in J. J. McCusker and R. R. Menard, *The Economy of British America, 1607–1789* (Chapel Hill, NC: University of North Carolina Press, 1985), pp. 54, 136, 153.
2. The question and quotation are from E. S. Morgan, *American Slavery, American Freedom. The Ordeal of Colonial Virginia* (New York: Norton, 1975), p. 397.
3. The earlier debate is reviewed in A. T. Vaughan, 'The Origins Debate: Slavery and Racism in Seventeenth-Century Virginia', *Virginia Magazine of History and Biography*, 97 (1989), pp. 311–54.
4. Records of Rappahannock, 1664–73, p. 21. Virginia State Library, Richmond, quoted in P. A. Bruce, *Economic History of Virginia in the Seventeenth Century* (New York: Mac-Millan, 1895), p. 11.
5. D. W. Galenson, *White Servitude in Colonial America: An Economic Analysis* (New York: Cambridge University Press, 1986), pp. 6–8. A. Kussmaul, *Servants in Husbandry in Early Modern England* (Cambridge: Cambridge University Press, 1981) is the best analysis of this form of service in England.
6. Galenson, *White Servitude in Colonial America*, p. 7.
7. Thomas Best, a servant in Virginia in 1623, as quoted in Morgan, *American Slavery, American Freedom*, p. 128.
8. Galenson, *White Servitude in Colonial America*, p. 8.
9. On differences between customary and contract servants, see L. S. Walsh, 'Servitude and Opportunity in Charles County, Maryland, 1658–1705', in A. C. Land, L. G. Carr, E C. Papenfuse and M. L. Radoff (eds), *Law, Society, and Politics in Early Maryland* (Baltimore, MD: Johns Hopkins University Press, 1977), pp. 111–15; and R. R. Menard, 'British Migration to the Chesapeake Colonies in the Seventeenth Century', in L. G. Carr, P. D. Morgan and J. B. Russo (eds), *Colonial Chesapeake Society* (Chapel Hill, NC: University of North Carolina Press, 1988), pp. 126–7.

10. Recent studies of the redemptioner system include F. Grubb, 'Immigrant Servants in the Colony and Commonwealth of Pennsylvania: A Quantitative and Economic Analysis' (PhD dissertation, University of Chicago, 1984) and M. S. Wockeck, *The Trade in Strangers: The Beginnings of Mass Migration to North America* (University Park, PA: Pennsylvania State University Press, 1999). On convicts, see A. R. Ekrich, *Bound for America: The Transportation of British Convicts to the Colonies, 1718–1775* (New York: Oxford University Press, USA, 1987).
11. Menard, 'British Migration to the Chesapeake Colonies', p. 121.
12. G. Nash, *Urban Crucible: Social Change, Political Consciousness, and the Origins of the American Revolution* (Cambridge, MA: Harvard University Press, 1979), p. 111.
13. J. Horn, 'Servant Emigration to the Chesapeake Colonies in the Seventeenth Century', in T. W. Tate and D. Ammerman (eds), *The Chesapeake in the Seventeenth Century* (Chapel Hill, NC: University of North Carolina Press, 1979), p. 92.
14. On conditions servants faced in Barbados, see R. R. Menard, *Sweet Negotiations: Sugar, Slavery, and Plantation Agriculture in Early Barbados* (Charlottesville, VA: University of Virginia Press, 2006). For conditions elsewhere, see McCusker and Menard, *Economy of British America, 1607–1789* and the literature cited therein.
15. Galenson, *White Servitude in Colonial America*, pp. 102–13.
16. For details on these tests, see Menard, 'British Migration to the Chesapeake Colonies', pp. 108, 118–19.
17. Galenson, *White Servitude in Colonial America*; G. L. Main, *Tobacco Colony: Life in Early Maryland, 1650–1720* (Princeton, NJ: Princeton University Press, 1982); P. G. E. Clemons, *The Atlantic Economy and Colonial Maryland's Eastern Shore, From Tobacco to Grain* (Ithaca, NY: Cornell University Press, 1980); A. Klikoff, *Tobacco and Slaves: The Development of Southern Cultures in the Chesapeake, 1680–1800* (Chapel Hill, NC: University of North Carolina Press, 1986). My contributions to the debate are collected in R. R. Menard, *Migrants, Servants and Slaves: Unfree Labor in Colonial British America* (London: Ashgate, 2001).
18. The difference between an elite and a popular slave society is developed in R. R. Menard, 'Building a Popular Slave Society in the Chesapeake Colonies: Some Evidence from St. Mary's County, Maryland', *Journal of Interdisciplinary History* (forthcoming, 2013).
19. Morgan, *American Slavery, American Freedom*; K. M. Brown, *Good Wives, Nasty Wenches, and Anxious Patriarchs: Gender, Race, and Power in Colonial Virginia* (Chapel Hill, NC: University of North Carolina Press, 1996); T. W. Allen, *The Invention of the White Race*, 3 vols (New York: Verso, 1994); A. S. Parent, Jr, *Foul Means: The Formation of a Slave Society in Virginia* (Chapel Hill, NC: University of North Carolina Press, 2003); T. H. Breen, 'A Changing Labor Force and Race Relations Virginia', *Journal of Social History*, 7 (1973), pp. 3–25.
20. The Atlanticist approach to the rise of African slavery in Virginia is developed in A. L. Hatfield, *Atlantic Virginia: Intercolonial Relations in the Seventeenth Century* (Philadelphia, PA: University of Pennsylvania, 2004). For a broader perspective on the notion of an Atlantic World, see J. P. Greene and P. D. Morgan (eds), *Atlantic History: A Critical Appraisal* (New York: Oxford University Press, USA, 2009).
21. E. Williams, *Capitalism and Slavery* (Chapel Hill, NC: University of North Carolina Press, 1944), chapter 1; Parent, *Foul Means*.
22. The phrase is from W. D. Jordan, *White Over Black: American Attitudes Toward the Negro, 1550–1812* (Chapel Hill, NC: University of North Carolina Press, 1968), p. 44.

23. J. C. Coombs, 'The Phases of Conversion: A New Chronology for the Rise of Slavery in Early Virginia', *William and Mary Quarterly*, 3rd series, 68 (2011), pp. 332–60, on p. 334.

24. This description of the changing fortunes of the two schools rests on my memory of conversations with scholars active in the field. Recognizing that at my age, 'memory is nothing if not eccentric' (C. Boujallian, *The Double Bind* (New York: Vintage, 2007), p. 27), I checked those recollections against early American textbooks and surveys of slavery and servitude in English America.

25. J. C. Coombs, 'Building the Machine: The Development of Slavery and Slave Society in Early Colonial Virginia' (PhD dissertation, College of William and Mary, 2002); L. S. Walsh, *Motives of Honor, Pleasure & Profit: Plantation Management in the Colonial Chesapeake, 1607–1763* (Chapel Hill, NC: University of North Carolina Press, 2010). L. S. Walsh, 'Summing the Parts: Implications for Estimating Chesapeake Output and Income Subregionally', *William and Mary Quarterly*, 3rd series, 46 (1999), pp. 53–69.

26. Coombs, 'The Phases of Conversion', p. 160.

27. Menard, 'Building a Popular Slave Society in the Chesapeake Colonies'.

28. For a review of the literature on the sugar revolution, see B. W. Higman, 'The Sugar Revolution', *Economic History Review*, 53 (2000), pp. 213–36.

29. A critique of the idea of a sugar revolution is a central theme of my *Sweet Negotiations*. See also J. J. McCusker and R. R. Menard, 'The Sugar Industry in the Seventeenth Century: A New Perspective on the Barbadian Sugar Revolution', in S. B. Schwartz (ed.), *Tropical Babylons: The Sugar Industry before the Seventeenth Century* (Chapel Hill, NC: University of North Carolina Press, 2004), pp. 289–320.

30. Or more detail on the migration and a guide to the literature see Menard, *Sweet Negotiations*, ch. 6.

31. For innovators and early adopters see D. E. O'Leary, 'The Impact of Gartner's Maturity Curve, on Information Systems Research, with Applications to Artificial Intelligence, ERRP, BPM, and RFID', *Journal of Emerging Technologies in Accounting*, 6 (2009), pp. 45–66.

32. On the slave trade between the islands and the main, see G. E. O'Malley, 'Beyond the Middle Passage: Slave Migration from the Caribbean to North America, 1610–1810', *William and Mary Quarterly*, 3rd series, 66 (2009), pp. 125–72.

33. The Barbados code is reprinted in part in S. Engerman, S. Dresher and R. Paquette (eds), *Slavery* (New York: Oxford University Press, USA, 2001), pp. 105–18. The original is in National Archives of the United Kingdom, Colonial Office, 30/2, ff. 16–25. For more on the code see B. Gaspar, 'With a Rod of Iron: Barbados Slave Laws a Model for Jamaica, South Carolina, and Antigua', in D. C. Hine and J. McLeod (eds), *Crossing Boundaries: Black People in Diaspora* (Bloomington, IN: Indiana University Press, 1999).

34. J. M. Price, 'Credit in the Slave Trade and Plantation Economies', in B. Solow (ed.), *Slavery and the Rise of the Atlantic System* (New York: Cambridge University Press, USA, 1991), pp. 293–340.

35. G. Wright, *Slavery and American Economic Development* (Baton Rouge, LA: Louisiana State University Press, 2006), p. 20.

36. The argument here is obviously speculative and included in the hope of provoking some research into the issues. I have started the process in R. R. Menard, 'Law, Credit, the Supply of Labour and the Organization of Sugar Production in the Colonial Greater Caribbean, a Comparison of Brazil and Barbados in the Seventeenth Century', in J.

J. McCusker and K. Morgan (eds), *The Early Modern Atlantic Economy* (Cambridge: Cambridge University Press, 2000), pp. 154–62.

37. For evidence of the importance of Barbadians in bringing slavery to the Chesapeake, see Hatfield, *Atlantic Virginia*; and D. D. Debe and R. R. Menard, 'The Transition to African Slavery in Maryland: A Note on the Barbados Connection', *Slavery and Abolition*, 32 (2011), pp. 129–41.

38. The quotation is from F. Tannenbaum, *Slave and Citizen* (Boston, MA: Beacon Press, 1992), p. 117.

7 Miller, 'Credit, Captives, Collateral and Currencies: Debt, Slavery and the Financing of the Atlantic World'

1. The present text represents an abbreviated version of a considerably more nuanced essay, with background establishing parallels and contrasts with four millennia of previous commercialization in Eurasia. The full discussion awaits a suitable venue for publication.

2. For readers unacquainted with the 'Avignon' tradition: 'Migration and Countries of the South/Migration et les pays du Sud', international conference, Université d'Avignon, Avignon, France, 18–21 March 1999; 'Slave Systems in Asia and the Indian Ocean: Their Structure and Change in the 19th and 20th Centuries', workshop, Université d'Avignon, Avignon, France, 18–20 May 2000; 'L'esclavage, la main-d'oeuvre forcée et la révolte en Asie et dans les pays riverains de l'Océan indien/Slavery, Unfree Labour and Revolt in Asia and the Indian Ocean Region', international conference, Université d'Avignon, Avignon, France, 4–6 October 2001; 'La Femme et l'esclavage: Colloque avignonnais sur l'Esclavage et la Main-d'œuvre forcé/ Women in Slavery: Avignon Conference on Slavery and Forced Labour, en l'honneur de/In Honour of Suzanne Miers', international conference, Université d'Avignon, Avignon, France, 16–18 October 2002; 'L'Enfant dans l'esclavage: Colloque avignonnais sur l'Esclavage et la Main-d'œuvre forcée', Université d'Avignon, Avignon, France, 20–22 May 2004. 'Sex, Power and Slavery: The Dynamics of Carnal Relations under Enslavement', Indian Ocean World Centre, McGill University, Montreal, Canada, 19–21 April 2007.

   The preceding published volumes that have emerged from this series include G. Campbell (ed.), *The Structure of Slavery in Indian Ocean Africa and Asia* (London: Routledge, 2003); G. Campbell (ed.), *Abolition and its Aftermath in the Indian Ocean Africa and Asia* (London: Routledge, 2005); G. Campbell, E. A. Alpers and M. Salman (eds), *Resisting Bondage in Indian Ocean Africa and Asia* (London: Routledge, 2006); G. Campbell, E. Alpers and M. Salman (eds), *Slavery, Forced Labour and Resistance in Indian Ocean Africa and Asia* (London: Routledge, 2005); G. Campbell, S. Miers and J. C. Miller (eds), *Women in Slavery. Vol. 1: Africa, the Indian Ocean World, and the Medieval North Atlantic* (Athens, OH: Ohio University Press, 2007), and *Vol. 2: The Modern Atlantic* (Athens, OH: Ohio University Press, 2008); G. Campbell, S. Miers and J. C. Miller (eds), *Children in Slavery Through the Ages* (Athens, OH: Ohio University Press, 2009); and G. Campbell, S. Miers and J. C. Miller, *Child Slaves in the Modern World* (Athens OH: Ohio University Press, 2011). We may anticipate further publications in this series, beyond the present one.

3. J. C. Miller, 'O Atlântico escravista: açúcar, escravos, e engenhos', *Afro-Ásia*, 19–20 (1997), pp. 9–36.

4.   And also the Indian Ocean World, though not considered here. See C. Bayly, *Imperial Meridian: The British Empire and the World, 1780–1830* (New York: Longman, 1989). For the Native Americas, for example, L. Matthew and M. R. Oudijk (eds), *Indian Conquistadors: Indigenous Allies in the Conquest of Mesoamerica* (Norman, OK: University of Oklahoma Press, 2007).

5.   Elaborated elsewhere, most recently in J. Miller, *The Problem of Slavery as History* (New Haven, CT: Yale University Press, 2012).

6.   From which derive the names Madeira (Portuguese for generic wood) and Sal (in the Cape Verde archipelago, or 'salt'); Brazil in the Americas was named similarly for its prime extracted commodity, a tropical red dye wood, as were the 'Ivory' and 'Gold' coasts of Africa. The later 'Slave Coast' referred to the human beings obtained by no-less-extractive violence.

7.   B. L. Solow, 'Capitalism and Slavery in the Exceedingly Long Run', *Journal of Interdisciplinary History*, 17:4 (1987), pp. 711–37, and B. L. Solow, 'Slavery and Colonization', in B. L. Solow (ed.), *Slavery and the Rise of the Atlantic System* (Cambridge, MA: W. E. B. Du Bois Institute for Afro-American Research; New York: Cambridge University Press, 1991), pp. 21–42.

8.   L. Benton, 'Legal Spaces of Empire: Piracy and the Origins of Ocean Regionalism', *Comparative Studies in Society and History*, 47:4 (2005), pp. 700–24; L. Benton, *A Search for Sovereignty: Law and Geography in European Empires, 1400–1900* (New York: Cambridge University Press, 2010).

9.   All general references to volumes and directions of the Atlantic trade in enslaved Africans are based on the 'Voyages' online database, http://www.slavevoyages.org/tast/index.faces [accessed 9 August 2012], compiled by David Eltis and collaborators.

10. For the evidence on climate, J. C. Miller 'The Significance of Drought, Disease, and Famine in the Agriculturally Marginal Zones of West-Central Africa', *Journal of African History*, 23:1 (1982), pp. 17–61.

11. D. B. Domingues da Silva and D. Eltis, 'The Transatlantic Slave Trade to Pernambuco, 1561–1851', in D. Eltis and D. Richardson (eds), *Extending the Frontiers: Essays on the New Transatlantic Slave Trade Database* (New Haven, CT: Yale University Press, 2008); T. Green, *Rise of the Trans-Atlantic Slave Trade* (New York: Cambridge University Press, 2012).

12. The Virginia Company, and then the settlers under crown control, in the Chesapeake followed the same halting course.

13. J. J. McCusker and R. R. Menard, 'The Sugar Industry in the Seventeenth Century: A New Perspective on the Barbadian "Sugar Revolution"', in S. B. Schwartz (ed.), *Tropical Babylons: Sugar and the Making of the Atlantic World, 1450–1680* (Chapel Hill, CT: University of North Carolina Press, 2004), pp. 289–330; R. R. Menard, *Sweet Negotiations: Sugar, Slavery, and Plantation Agriculture in Early Barbados* (Charlottesville, VA: University of Virginia Press, 2006).

14. The parallels with recent examples of lending to unqualified borrowers on corporate accounts, while skimming cash resources for the private gain of executives, seem obvious.

15. W. A. Pettigrew, *Freedom's Debt: Politics and the Escalation of American Slavery, 1688 – 1752* (Chapel Hill, NC: University of North Carolina Press, 2012).

16. E. Van Den Boogaart, 'The Trade between Western Africa and the Atlantic World, 1600–90: Estimates of Trends in Composition and Value', *Journal of African History*, 33:3 (1992), pp. 369–85; D. Eltis, 'The Relative Importance of Slaves and Commodities in the Atlantic Trade of Seventeenth-Century Africa', *Journal of African History*, 35:2 (1994), p. 237–49.

17. H. E. S. Fisher, *The Portugal Trade: A Study of Anglo-Portuguese Commerce, 1700–1770* (London: Methuen, 1971).

18. This sketch of a very complex series of strategies does not mention the accompanying development of insurance for other physical collateral.

19. Spain's royal contract to deliver captives to its American ports; like the Royal African Company, the slaving aspects of these contracts – awarded since the 1590s to the wealthiest merchant groups in the Atlantic – have been emphasized to the virtual exclusion of its financial value in the silver coin that it authorized its holders to receive in payment for the slaves they sold.

20. R. S. Dale, J. E. V. Johnson and Leilei Tang, 'Financial Markets Can Go Mad: Evidence of Irrational Behaviour during the South Sea Bubble', *Economic History Review*, 58:2 (2005), pp. 233–71; G. S. Shea, 'Understanding Financial Derivatives during the South Sea Bubble: The Case of the South Sea Subscription Shares', *Oxford Economic Papers*, 59, supplement 1 (2007), pp. 73–104. This company is another example of strategies misleadingly treated primarily in terms of their slaving activities; see, for example, C. A. Palmer, *Human Cargoes: The British Slave Trade to Spanish America, 1700–1739* (Urbana, IL: University of Illinois Press, 1981).

21. The *livranças* discussed in a preliminary way in J. C. Miller, *Way of Death: Merchant Capitalism and the Angolan Slave Trade, 1730–1830* (Madison, WI: University of Wisconsin Press, 1988).

22. P. Verger, *Trade Relations between the Bight of Benin and Bahia from the 17th to the 19th Century*, trans. E. Crawford (Ibadan: Ibadan University Press, 1976).

23. Merchants in the small New England outports of Rhode Island similarly used West Indian rum sent to Africa to buy captives to cover persisting trade deficits with England: J. A. Coughtry, *The Notorious Triangle: Rhode Island and the African Slave Trade, 1700–1807* (Philadelphia, PA: Temple University Press, 1981).

24. For similar negotiations in Luanda and Benguela, in Angola, see R. A. Ferreira, *Cross-Cultural Exchange in the Atlantic World* (New York: Cambridge University Press, 2012).

25. For this process, R. Shumway, *The Fante and the Transatlantic Slave Trade* (Rochester, NY: University of Rochester Press, 2011).

26. The story of refugee populations' defence and rebuilding has attracted historians' attention only recently. Among others, C. Piot, *Remotely Global: Village Modernity in West Africa* (Chicago: University of Chicago Press, 1999), R. M. Baum, *Shrines of the Slave Trade: Diola Religion and Society in Precolonial Senegambia* (New York; Oxford: Oxford University Press, 1999), and S. A. Diouf (ed.), *Fighting the Slave Trade: West African Strategies* (Athens, OH: Ohio University Press; Oxford: James Currey, 2003).

27. Not an issue raised by J. Thornton, *Warfare in Atlantic Africa, 1500–1800* (London: Routledge, 2000). R. J. Reid, *Warfare in African History* (New Approaches to African History) (New York: Cambridge University Press, 2012).

28. Miller, *Way of Death*.

29. The most recent contribution to an ample literature is G. U. Nwokeji, *The Slave Trade and Culture in the Bight of Biafra: An African Society in the Atlantic World* (New York: Cambridge University Press, 2010), and – in a fascinating study of the intricacies of the credit arrangements in force – N. Argenti, *The Intestines of the State: Youth, Violence, and Belated Histories in the Cameroon Grassfields* (Chicago, IL: University of Chicago Press, 2007).

30. For reasons behind Africans' slowness to make this move, see J. C. Miller, 'Creating Poverty – Investment Aspects of the Global Historical Dynamics of Commercialization',

paper presented at the conference 'Understanding African Poverty over the Longue Durée', the Weatherhead Center for International Affairs (WCFIA, Harvard University) in Partnership with the International Institute for the Advanced Study of Cultures, Institutions and Economic Enterprise (IIAS) in Ghana, 15–17 July 2010.

31. A. G. Hopkins, *An Economic History of West Africa* (New York: Columbia University Press, 1973).

32. For further details of the transition to commodity exports see R. Law (ed.), *From Slave Trade to 'Legitimate' Commerce: The Commercial Transition in Nineteenth-Century West Africa* (Cambridge: Cambridge University Press, 1995).

33. Selectively, R. A. Austen, 'The Slave Trade as History and Memory: Confrontations of Slaving Voyage Documents and Communal Traditions', *William and Mary Quarterly*, 58:1 (2001), pp. 229–44; E. A. Isichei, *Voices of the Poor in Africa* (Rochester, NY: University of Rochester Press, 2002); R. Shaw, *The Dangers of Temne Divination: Ritual Memories of the Slave Trade in West Africa* (Chicago, IL: University of Chicago Press, 2002); Argenti, *Intestines of the State*.

34. Interest in the financial aspects of slaving is growing among American historians; see C. Schermerhorn, *Money over Mastery, Family over Freedom: Slavery in the Antebellum Upper South* (Baltimore, MD: Johns Hopkins University Press, 2011). We may anticipate the work of B. M. Martin, following on 'Slavery's Invisible Engine: Mortgaging Human Property', *Journal of Southern History*, 76:1 (2010), pp. 1–50.

8 Espada Lima, 'Unpayable Debts: Reinventing Bonded Labour through Legal Freedom in Nineteenth-Century Brazil'

1. The definition of 'slavery' here is, obviously, connected to the current language used by many authorities (governments or others) that address contemporary forms of illegal (in terms of International Law) servitude which can be very different from the legal system of slavery that subsisted in places like Brazil until the late nineteenth century. Being a political term, its meaning is constantly disputed in many national and local contexts. On its current definition and international legal context, see D. Weissbrodt and Anti-Slavery International, 'Abolishing Slavery and its Contemporary Forms', *Office of the United Nations High Commissioner for Human Rights* (2002), online at http://www.ohchr.org/documents/publications/slaveryen.pdf [accessed 22 February 2012].

2. H. Théry, N. A. Mello-Théry, E. P. Girardi and J. HATO, 'Geografias do trabalho escravo contemporâneo no Brasil', *Revista NERA*, 13:17 (2010), pp. 7–28; P. Illes, G. L. S. Timoteo and E. S. Fiorucci, 'Tráfico de pessoas para fins de exploração do trabalho na cidade de São Paulo', *Cadernos Pagú*, 31 (2008), pp. 199–217.

3. 'Lei n. 2040, de 28 Setembro de 1871', in *Collecção das Imperio do Brasil de 1871. Tomo XXXI, Parte I* (Rio de Janeiro: Typographia Nacional, 1871), pp. 147–51. Also called 'Rio Branco' after the José Maria da Silva Paranhos (Viscount of Rio Branco), who was presiding over the Council of Ministers when the law was issued.

4. A. Gebara, *O Mercado de Trabalho Livre no Brasil* (São Paulo: Brasiliense, 1986).

5. About the 1831 law, see B. Mamigonian, 'O direito de ser africano livre: os escravos e as interpretações da lei de 1831', in S. H. Lara and J. Mendonça (eds), *Direitos e Justiças no Brasil* (Campinas: Ed. Unicamp/Cecult, 2006), pp. 129–60. See also the *dossier* organized by B. Mamigonian and K. Grinberg in '"Para inglês ver?": Revisitando a lei de 1831', *Revista Estudos Afro-Asiáticos*, 29:1–2–3 (2007), pp. 87–240 (introduction pp. 87–90).

6. With the British 'imposition in 1815 of a treaty to prohibit the participation of Portuguese subjects in slave trading on the African coast north of the equator', and the subsequent Additional Convention of 1817, which established a mixed commission to judge illegal traffickers in slaves. Cf. R. Conrad, 'Neither Slave nor Free: The *Emancipados* of Brazil, 1818–1868', *Hispanic American Historical Review*, 53:1 (1973), p. 51.

7. B. G. Mamigonian, 'To be a Liberated African in Brazil: Labour and Citizenship in the Nineteenth-Century' (PhD dissertation, University of Waterloo, 2002), p. 31. The 1831 law preventing the introduction of new slaves from the Atlantic trade was a direct consequence of the treaties between the United Kingdom after the Brazilian independence of 1822. The diplomatic recognition of the new country was 'conditioned on the establishment of a new convention on the Abolition of the Slave trade, signed in 1826, ratified in March, 13, 1827, and went into effect three years later'. Cf. Mamigonian and Grinberg, 'Apresentação' (Introduction to) "Para inglês ver?", pp. 87–8.

8. L. F. Alencastro, 'Proletários e escravos. Imigrantes portugueses e cativos africanos no Rio de Janeiro, 1850–1872', *Novos Estudos*, 21 (1988), pp. 32–3, footnote 8.

9. Ibid., p. 33.

10. The Brazilian Empire was established in 1822, after Independence from Portugal, conducted by Dom Pedro de Alcântara (then Royal Prince of the Portuguese Royal House of Bragança and regent of the Brazilian territory). Independence, declared by Pedro on 7 September, was followed by a brief and successful war against his father's kingdom and his further acclamation as Brazil's first emperor on 12 October, with the name of Pedro I. In 1831, Pedro abdicated and went back to Portugal in the context of struggle for the succession of Portugal's crown. His son was five years old in 1831, and the Empire was governed by different regents until 1840, when the young Pedro II was declared fit to become the new emperor, at the age of fifteen. The Constitution of 1824 was issued by Pedro I, after being discussed for a Constitutional Convention in the previous year; however, the final version of the Constitution was issued by the emperor without parliamentary approval. About the Constitutional Convention and the context of the Constitution, see J. H. Rodrigues, *A Assembléia Constituinte de 1823* (Petrópolis: Vozes, 1974).

11. See R. C. L. Xavier, 'Tratos e contratos de trabalho: debate em torno da sua normatização no século XIX', *História em Revista*, 10 (2004), online at http://www.ufpel.edu.br/ich/ndh/downloads/historia_em_revista_regina_xavier.pdf [accessed 22 February 2012], pp. 1–10.

12. 'Decreto de 13 de Setembro de 1830. Regula o contracto por escripto sobre prestação serviço feito por Brazileiro ou estrangeiro dentro e fora do Império', in *Collecção de leis do Império do Brazil de 1830. Parte I* (Rio de Janeiro: Typographia Nacional, 1876), pp. 32–3. According to Alencastro, 'Proletários e escravos', p. 37, Senator Vergueiro (1778–1859) was intensely involved with the trade of human beings, both slave and free: his firm, Vergueiro & Company, bought three American ships in 1843, two for the (illegal) slave trade, at the same time that it was introducing German and Portuguese immigrants to his plantations in São Paulo.

13. See H. E. Lima, 'Trabalho e lei para os libertos na Ilha de Santa Catarina no século XIX: arranjos e contratos entre a autonomia e a domesticidade', *Cadernos do AEL*, 26 (2009), pp. 145–7. For a detailed discussion of the 1830s law, see also J. M. N. Mendonça, 'Liberdade em tempos de escravidão', in C. M. G. Chaves and M. A. Silveira (eds), *Território, conflito e identidade* (Belo Horizonte: Argumentum, 2007), pp. 89–104; and J. M. N. Mendonça, 'Os juízes de paz e o mercado de trabalho – Brasil, século XIX', in G. S.

Ribeiro, E. A. Neves and M. d. F. C. M. Ferreira (eds), *Diálogos entre Direito e História: Cidadania e Justiça* (Niteróis: Editora da UFF, 2009), pp. 237–55.

14. 'Lei n. 108 de 11 de Outubro de 1837. Dando várias providencias sobre os Contractos de locação de serviços dos colonos', in *Collecção das leis do Império do Brasil de 1837. Parte I* (Rio de Janeiro: Typographia Nacional, 1861), pp. 76–80. See also H. E. Lima, 'Freedom, Precariousness, and the Law: Freed Persons Contracting out their Labour in Nineteenth-Century Brazil', *International Review of Social History*, 54 (2009), p. 401; and H. E. Lima, 'Trabalho e lei para os libertos', pp. 148–9. Here, the original expressions in Portuguese 'contrato de locação de seviço', 'locador' and 'locatário' are difficult to translate into English directly because the limits between 'rental' and 'leasing' regarding service are not clear in that language. I will use 'contract of service rental' for the first expression, and 'lessor' and 'lessee' for the following, considering that the worker leases/rents his services (his own property) for the employer/lessee.

15. 'Art 9. Lei n. 108 de 11 de Outubro de 1837', *Collecção das leis do Império do Brasil de 1837*, p. 78.

16. L. Alencastro, 'Proletários e escravos', p. 35. S. B. de Holanda, in his introduction to Davatz's book about his experience as a sharecropper in *Ibicaba*, also pointed out the similarities between Brazilian labour contracts and 'indentured servants': T. Davatz, *Memórias de um colono no Brasil*, trans. S. B. de Holanda (São Paulo: Livraria Martins, 1941), p. 18.

17. Alencastro, 'Proletários e escravos', p. 36.

18. Ibid.

19. Davatz, *Memórias de um colono no Brasil*. About Vergueiro's experiment, see also W. Dean, *Rio Claro: A Brazilian Plantation System, 1820–1920* (Stanford, CA: Stanford University Press, 1976), ch. 4. See also L. Lamounier, 'Between Slavery & Free Labour. Early Experiences with Free Labour & Patterns of Slave Emancipation in Brazil & Cuba', in M. Turner (ed.), *From Chattel Slaves to Wage Slaves. The Dynamics of Labour Bargaining in the Americas* (Bloomington, IN: Indiana University Press, 1995), pp. 185–200.

20. T. Davatz, *Memórias de um colono no Brasil*, p. 122

21. Ibid. In the second chapter of his book (pp. 71–139), Davatz described the treatment of colonists in detail. A copy of the contract model made by the Vergueiro company with colonists can be found on pp. 233–7.

22. According to Hall and Stolcke, the planters' 'experience with slaves made them acutely aware of the need for effective forms of labour control. Thus, the issue planters increasingly faced throughout the second half of the nineteenth century was not only of finding a new source of labour to replace their slaves, but also how to organize and control free labour efficiently', M. M. Hall and V. Stolcke, 'The Introduction of Free Labour on São Paulo Coffee Plantations', *Journal of Peasant Studies*, 10:2–3 (1983), p. 170.

23. In 1879, a new law strictly regarded to regulate free agricultural labour was issued. See Lamounier, 'Between Slavery & Free Labour', p. 196; and L. Lamounier, *Da escravidão ao trabalho livre: a lei de locação de serviços de 1879* (Campinas: Papirus, 1988).

24. Mamigonian, 'To be a Liberated African in Brazil'. This corroborates the argument from J. Mendonça, who showed that the definition of 'free labour' was still largely under construction in the 1830s (see Mendonça, 'Liberdade em tempos de escravidão', p. 102).

25. '6a. Que no ato da entrega ao arrematante o Juiz, por intérprete, fará conhecer aos Africanos, que são livres, e que vão servir em compensação do sustento, vestuário, tratamento, e mediante um módico salário, que será arrecadado anualmente pelo Curador, que se lhes nomear, depositado no Cofre do Juizo d'arrematação, e que servirá para ajudar de

sua reexportação, quando houver de se verificar': Aviso 29 de Outubro de 1834, com Instruções relativas à arrematação dos Africanos ilicitamente introduzidos no Império, 29 October 1834, AN (Arquivo Nacional do Rio de Janeiro), IJ6 469, in Mamigonian, 'To be a Liberated African', pp. 299–300. As Mamigonian points out, these forms of tutorship of the emancipated Africans were also inspired by previous forms of tutorship towards 'non-slaves', like the native (indian) workers in Colonial Brazil (after the abolition of indian slavery in the late eighteenth century and before Independence in 1822): cf. Mamigonian, 'To be a Liberated African', pp. 52–3.

26. The production of false ownership by ill-intentioned individuals could lead to illegal enslavement in some situations, and the risk of illegal enslavement was present not only for liberated Africans, but also for freed and free people of African origin who failed to prove their freedom through legal documents before state authorities. See S. Chalhoub, *A força da escravidão. Ilegalidade e costume no Brasil oitocentista* (São Paulo: Companhia das Letras, 2012).

27. 'Lei n. 581 de 4 de Setembro de 1850', in *Collecção de leis do Império do Brazil de 1850. Tomo XI, Parte I* (Rio de Janeiro: Typographia Nacional, 1850), pp. 267–70.

28. 'Lei n. 601 de 18 de Setembro de 1850', in *Collecção de leis do Império do Brazil de 1850*, pp. 307–313; 'Lei n. 602 de 18 de Setembro de 1850', in *Collecção de leis do Império do Brazil de 1850*, pp. 314–40.

29. Once the self-purchased manumissions 'gave way to more 'political' strategies, such as conditional manumissions and, especially, unpaid ones'. See M. Florentino, 'Sobre minas, crioulos e a liberdade costumeira no Rio de Janeiro', in M. Florentino (ed.), *Tráfico, Cativeiro e Liberdade, séculos XVII–XIX* (Rio de Janeiro: Civilização Brasileira, 2005), p. 344.

30. See Alencastro, 'Proletários e escravos', p. 40.

31. In Rio de Janeiro self-purchased manumissions were the most common way for slaves to attain their freedom. According to Florentino, however, that configuration changed from 1830 on, with the redefinition of what would be considered the 'fair price' for the manumission, directly connected with the growing monetization of labour relations. See Florentino, 'Sobre minas, crioulos e liberdade costumeira no Rio de Janeiro', p. 344. For a detailed discussion of the growing difficulties after 1850 which slaves seeking freedom through self-purchase and middling wealth-holders seeking access to wealth faced, see Z. Frank, *Dutra's World. Wealth and Family in Nineteenth-Century Rio de Janeiro* (Albuquerque, NM: University of New Mexico Press, 2004), especially pp. 96–121.

32. João Antonio Lopes Gondim (notary), Escriptura de loucação de serviços que faz a preta liberta Maria Leocadia ao Capitão Fernando Antonio Cardoso, 1847–1849, Livro 11 do 2o Oficio de Notas da Cidade do Desterro, fols 41, 41v and 42.

33. José Rodrigues Silva Junior (notary), Escriptura de loucação que faz o crioulo liberto João Caetano a Manoel Carlos Viganigo, Livro 6 do Cartório de Notas da Freguesia de Nossa Senhora da Lapa do Ribeirão, fols 2v–3v.

34. See, for instance, Mendonça, 'Liberdade em tempos de escravidão', pp. 93–101, which discusses the debate on the 1830 law in Parliament and Senate. See also Hall and Stolcke, 'The Introduction of Free Labour on São Paulo Coffee Plantations'.

35. 'Lei n. 2040 de 28 de Setembro de 1871', *Collecção das Imperio do Brasil de 1871*. On the legal discussions concerning the 1871 law, see E. S. Pena, *Pajens da Casa Imperial: jurisconsultos, escravidão e a lei de 1871* (Campinas: Edunicamp, 1999).

36. 'N. 3354. Agricultura. – A Lei de 13 de Maio de 1888 – Declara extincta a escravidão no Brazil', in *Collecção de Leis do Império do Brazil de 1888. Parte I. Tomo XXXV – Parte II, Tomo LI, Volume I* (Rio de Janeiro: Imprensa Nacional, 1889), p. 1.

9 Serels, 'Indigenous Debt and the Spirit of Colonial Capitalism: Debt, Taxes and the Cash-Crop Economy in the Anglo-Egyptian Sudan, 1898–1956'

1. One *faddan* equals 1.038 acres.
2. C. G. Davies, Note, late December 1933, National Records Office, Khartoum (hereafter NRO), CIVSEC2/12/53.
3. Clark to Gillan, 29 December 1933, NRO, CIVSEC2/12/53.
4. Clark to Gillan, 31 December 1933, NRO, CIVSEC2/12/53.
5. A. Gaitskell, *Gezira: A Story of Development in the Sudan* (London: Faber & Faber, 1959), p. 159.
6. Clark to Gillan, 31 December 1933, NRO, CIVSEC2/12/53. Author's translation.
7. From a local saying quoted in Gaitskell, *Gezira*, p. 156.
8. W. Rodney, *How Europe Underdeveloped Africa* (Washington, DC: Howard University Press, 1974), pp. 147–54.
9. F. Cooper, 'Africa and the World Economy', *African Studies Review*, 24:2/3 (June to September 1981), pp. 1–86; S. Berry, 'The Food Crisis and Agrarian Change in Africa: A Review Essay', *African Studies Review*, 27:2 (June 1984), pp. 59–112; B. Berman, 'Up From Structuralism', in B. Berman and J. Lonsdale (eds), *Unhappy Valley: Conflict in Kenya and Africa* (London: James Currey, 1992), pp. 179–202; A. A. Sikainga, *'City of Steel and Fire': A Social History of Atabara, Sudan's Railway Town, 1906–1984* (London: James Currey, 2002).
10. For an account of the early stages of the Mahdist Rebellion see P. M. Holt and M. W. Daly, *A History of the Sudan from the Coming of Islam to the Present Day*, 4th edn (London and New York: Longman, 1988), pp. 85–91.
11. R. Wingate, *Mahdiism and the Egyptian Sudan*, 2nd edn (London: Frank Cass & Co, 1968), pp. 7–11.
12. R. Slatin, *Fire and Sword in the Sudan: A Personal Narrative of Fighting and Serving the Dervishes, 1879–1895*, trans. R. Wingate (London: Edward Arnold, 1896), p. 4.
13. Intelligence Department, Egyptian Army, 9 December 1900 to 8 January 1901, *Sudan Intelligence Report*, No. 77, p. 2.
14. 'Letter from his Excellency the Governor General to Sultan Ali Dinar', reproduced in full in Intelligence Department, Egyptian Army, 1 to 30 June 1901, *Sudan Intelligence Report*, No. 83, p. 10.
15. Lord Kitchener, 'Memorandum to Mudirs', *Reports by His Majesty's Agent and Consul-General on the Finances, Administration and Condition of Egypt and the Soudan in 1899* (Cd. 95, 1900), pp. 55–6.
16. S. Serels, 'Political Landscaping: Land Registration, the Definition of Ownership and the Evolution of Colonial Objectives in the Anglo-Egyptian Sudan, 1899–1924', *African Economic History*, 35 (2007), pp. 59–67.
17. 'The Title of Lands Ordinance, 1899', *Sudan Gazette*, 2 (27 May 1899), pp. 4–6.
18. H. S. G. Peacock, *The Anglo-Egyptian Sudan: A Report of the Land Settlement of the Gezira* (London: Darling & Son, 1913), p. 21.
19. Peacock, *The Anglo-Egyptian Sudan*, p. 23.
20. E. B. Carter, 'Annual Report, Legal Secretary, 1904', in *Reports on the Finances, Administration and Conditions of the Sudan, 1904* (1904), vol. 3, p. 59, Sudan Archive, Durham University (hereafter SAD).

21. *Reports by His Majesty's Agent and Consul-General on the Finances, Administration and Condition of Egypt and the Sudan in 1900* (Cd. 441, 1901), p. 83.

22. 'The Land Settlement Ordinance, 1905', *Sudan Gazette*, 80 (24 August 1905), pp. 370–4.

23. Peacock, *The Anglo-Egyptian Sudan*, p. 24.

24. Ibid., p. 23.

25. E. B. Carter, 'Annual Report, Legal Department, 1910', in *Reports on the Finances, Administration and Conditions of the Sudan, 1910* (1910), p. 606, SAD.

26. Legal Department, Sudan Government. *Report of the Land Registration Committee* (1929) NRO, 4 REPORTS4/11/10.

27. B. Badri, *The Memoirs of Babikr Bedri*, trans. G. Scott (London: Oxford University Press, 1969), p. 240.

28. 'Notice, Land Tax and Date Tax Ordinance, 1899', *Sudan Gazette*, 6 (2 November 1899), p. 1.

29. W. Garstin, *Despatch from Her Majesty's Agent and Consul-General at Cairo: Inclosing a Report on the Soudan by William Garstin* (London: Harrison & Sons, 1899), p. 20.

30. Colonel Jackson, quoted in *Reports By His Majesty's Agent and Consul-General on the Finances, Administration and Condition of Egypt and the Sudan in 1905* (Cd. 2817, 1906), p. 148.

31. *Reports by His Majesty's Agent and Consul-General on the Finances, Administration and Condition of Egypt and the Soudan in 1899*, p. 47.

32. *Reports by His Majesty's Agent and Consul-General on the Finances, Administration and Condition of Egypt and the Soudan in 1900*, pp. 80–1.

33. 'Land Tax and Date Tax Ordinance, 1901', *Sudan Gazette*, 29 (1 November 1901), p. 16.

34. 'Payment of Usher', *Sudan Gazette*, 30 (1 December 1901), p. 3.

35. *Reports by His Majesty's Agent and Consul-General on the Finances, Administration and Condition of Egypt and the Sudan in 1907* (Cd. 3966, 1908), p. 51.

36. 'Detailed Statement showing the Receipts and Expenditure of the Sudan Government for the Year 1904 Under the Headings', *Sudan Gazette*, 76 (1 May 1905), p. 330.

37. *Reports by His Majesty's Agent and Consul-General on the Finances, Administration and Condition of Egypt and the Sudan in 1911* (Cd. 6149, 1912–13), pp. 53–4.

38. 'Detailed Statement showing the Receipts and Expenditure of the Sudan Government for the Year 1905 Under the Headings', *Sudan Gazette*, 95 (1 May 1906), p. 476.

39. *Reports by His Majesty's Agent and Consul-General on the Finances, Administration and Condition of Egypt and the Sudan in 1911*, pp. 53–4.

40. For a full account of the construction of the rail network see R. Hill, *Sudan Transport* (London: Oxford University Press, 1965).

41. M. Daly, *British Administration and the Northern Sudan, 1917–1924; The Governor-Generalship of Sir Lee Stack in the Sudan* (Istanbul: Nederlands Historisch-Archaeologisch Instituut, 1980), p. 198.

42. *Report on the Soudan by Lieutenant-Colonel Stewart* (Cd. 3670, 1883), p. 35.

43. G. B. Macauly, 'Annual Report, Railway Department, 1904', in *Reports on the Finances, Administration and Conditions of the Sudan, 1904*, 3 (1904), p. 120, SAD.

44. 'Annual Report, Sudan Customs, 1913', *Reports on the Finances, Administration and Conditions of the Sudan, 1913*, 2 (1913), pp. 198–9, SAD.

45. See H. G. Prout, *General Report on the Province of Kordofan Submitted to General C P Stone, Chief of the General Staff Egyptian Army* (Cairo: Printing Office of the General Staff, 1877), p. 22; Slatin, *Fire and Sword in the Sudan*, p. 559.

46. J. O'Brien, 'The Political Economy of Semi-Proletarianisation under Colonialism: Sudan 1925–1950', in B. Munslow and H. Finch (eds), *Proletarianisation in the Third World* (London and Sydney: Croom Helm, 1984), p. 133.

47. *Report on the Soudan by Lieutenant-Colonel Stewart* (Cd. 3670, 1883), p. 35.

48. *Annual Report of the Director, Commercial Intelligence Branch, Central Economic Board, 1925–1926* (1926), p. 104, SAD.

49. United States, Department of Commerce, Bureau of Foreign and Domestic Commerce, *Cotton Goods in Red Sea Markets, Special Agents Series No. 71* (Washington, DC, 1913), p. 57.

50. D. J. Shaw, 'The Effects of Moneylending (Sheil) on Agricultural Development in the Sudan', D. J. Shaw (ed.), *Agricultural Development in the Sudan*, 2 vols (Khartoum: Philosophical Society of the Sudan, 1965), pp. D56–D59.

51. 'Extracts from Reports on the State of the Crops, 1914', *Annual Report of the Director, Commercial Intelligence Branch, Central Economic Board, 1914* (1914), p. 97, SAD.

52. Jackson to Civil Secretary, 11 May 1914, NRO, CIVSEC2/1/2.

53. *Proclamation Published in the Sudan Government Gazette 265, 1 August 1914*, NRO, CIVSEC2/1/2.

54. Governor Halfa to the Arabic Secretary, 14 October 1915, NRO, CIVSEC1/40/101.

55. Shaw, 'The Effects of Moneylending (Sheil) on Agricultural Development in the Sudan', p. D58.

56. Gaitskell, *Gezira*, p. 106.

57. 1 *qintar* of ginned cotton equals 44.93 kg.

58. Gaitskell, *Gezira*, p. 144.

59. Ibid., p. 159.

60. Ibid., pp. 160–71.

61. Jackson to Civil Secretary, 11 May 1914, NRO, CIVSEC2/1/2.

62. Jackson to Wingate, 15 June 1915, SAD, 195/4/146.

63. *Reports by His Majesty's Agent and Consul-General on the Finances, Administration and Condition of Egypt and the Sudan, 1914–1919* (Cd. 957, 1920), p. 118.

64. *Sudan Government Circular Memorandum on Slavery*, 6 May 1925, British National Archives, London, FO 407/201.

65. See A. A. Sikainga *Slaves into Workers; Emancipation and Labor in Colonial Sudan* (Austin, TX: University of Texas Press, 1996), pp. 149–83. Owners of female slaves were better able to keep control of their slaves despite mounting international pressure on the Anglo-Egyptian government because officials were reluctant to interfere in what they believed to be domestic affairs; see A. A. Sikainga, 'Shari'a Courts and the Manumission of Female Slaves in the Sudan, 1898–1939', *International Journal of African Historical Studies*, 28:1 (1995), pp. 1–24.

66. A single *saqiya* required as many as eight labourers and eight cattle to turn the water wheel, lift the water and ensure its steady flow to the fields (*Reports on the Province of Dongola*, (Cd. 8427, 1897), p. 3).

67. *Extract from Minutes of 133th Meeting of the Board of Economics and Trade Held on 9th February 1938*, NRO, CIVSEC2/6/22.

68. *Minutes of the Sixth Meeting of the Pump Licensing Board Held in the Office of the Department of Agriculture on Saturday February 4th 1939*, NRO, CIVSEC2/6/22.

69. Gaitskell, *Gezira*, p. 270.

70. *Reports by His Majesty's Agent and Consul-General on the Finances, Administration and Condition of Sudan in 1947* (Cd. 7835, 1948–9), p. 47.

71. T. Niblock, *Class and Power in the Sudan: the Dynamics of Sudanese Politics, 1898–1985* (London: MacMillan Press, 1987), p. 36.
72. Department of Statistics, Government of the Sudan, *A Report on the Census of Pump Schemes, June-August 1963: A Coordinated Picture of Area Irrigated by Pump Schemes* (1967), p. 17.
73. Niblock, *Class and Power in the Sudan*, pp. 32–3.
74. Department of Statistics, Government of the Sudan, *A Report on the Census of Pump Schemes, June-August 1963: A Coordinated Picture of Area Irrigated by Pump Schemes*, p. 17.

INDEX

For Product Safety Concerns and Information please contact our EU
representative GPSR@taylorandfrancis.com
Taylor & Francis Verlag GmbH, Kaufingerstraße 24, 80331 München, Germany

www.ingramcontent.com/pod-product-compliance
Ingram Content Group UK Ltd.
Pitfield, Milton Keynes, MK11 3LW, UK
UKHW021611240425
457818UK00018B/499